3‾

John C. Chamberli
NAEA BOSTON

EXPLORING THE LEGENDS:
GUIDEPOSTS TO THE FUTURE

Sylvia K. Corwin, Editor

D1531049

NATIONAL ART EDUCATION ASSOCIATION

NATIONAL ART EDUCATION ASSOCIATION

The National Art Education Association is the nation's largest professional art education association and a leader in educational research, policy, and practice for art education. NAEA's mission is to advance art education through professional development, service, advancement of knowledge, and leadership.

Membership (approximately 40,000) includes elementary and secondary art teachers (and middle and senior high students in the National Art Honor Society programs), artists, administrators, museum educators, arts council staff, and university professors and college students from throughout the United States and several foreign countries. It also includes publishers, manufacturers and suppliers of art materials, parents, students, retired art educators, and others concerned about quality art education in our schools.

The Association publishes several journals, papers, and flyers on art education; holds an annual convention; conducts research; sponsors a teacher awards program; develops standards on student learning, school programs and teacher preparation; and cosponsors workshops, seminars and institutes on art education. For further information, contact our web site at www.naea-reston.org.

Location

The Association is located at 1916 Association Drive, Reston VA 20191-1590 (phone 703-860-8000; fax 703-860-2960; email naea@dgs.dgsys.com) about 25 miles outside of Washington, DC.

Beginnings

NAEA was founded in 1947 with the merger of four regional art education associations and the art department of the National Education Association. Celebrating its 50th anniversary in 1997, NAEA includes affiliation in fifty states plus the District of Columbia, most Canadian Provinces, U.S. military bases around the world, and numerous foreign countries.

NAEA's Mission

The Mission of the National Art Education Association is to promote art education through professional development, service, advancement of knowledge, and leadership.

To that end, the Association will: promote quality instruction in visual arts education conducted by certified teachers of art; encourage research in art education; hold public discussions; sponsor institutes, conferences, and programs; publish articles, reports, and surveys; and work with other related agencies in support of visual arts education.

ISBN 1-890160-04-0
© 2001 National Art Education Association

Table of Contents

Preface

Michael DeSiano

The University Council for Art Education (UCAE) was chartered in 1969 as a professional and social organization "to promote art education in the New York area." Our activities brought together art education faculty from more than 20 local colleges and universities. Although UCAE was formed during the apogee of art education, the last 30 years have been devoted to defining and preserving art education. UCAE's tenacity was unflinching as we contributed our energies to maintaining art education in New York City schools and universities. We believed that as New York art education went, so went the nation.

UCAE programs centered on revving up art education with new curricula, with resistance to the encroaching and potentially suffocating trends towards assessment, and behavioral objectives.

By the 1990s, art education stood strong, resuscitated by a powerful economy, the Discipline Based Art Education movement, and a renewed, nationwide interest in school reform. On a personal side, after serving 30 years in all positions on UCAE's executive board, I became UCAE President. Now, the organization represented nearly 50 colleges and universities in the tri-state region: New Jersey, Connecticut, and New York.

I remember an early meeting at Carl Hiller's apartment, on East 10th Street, in Greenwich Village. Gazing out the window on the side street that looked as it did 50 years ago, I felt an extremely pleasurable sense of aesthetic well-being. How many passersby know that these very buildings housed the study on Jackson Pollack and Wilhelm DeKooning? Abstract expressionism, one of the most influential forces in contemporary art, flourished here. Such historical reverie gripped Carl Hiller, too. He reminisced about his youth, working at the Museum of Modern Art with Victor D'Amico, Lois Lord, Muriel Silberstein-Storfer, and Prabha Sahasrabudhe spoke glowingly of their hero, D'Amico. Similarly, Peter London, Bob Saunders, and others who studied with Viktor Lowenfeld, fervently praised their teacher. The many UCAE-ers who completed their degrees at Teachers College, Elaine Foster, Phyllis Gold Gluck among them, lauded Edwin Ziegfeld. Of course, there was Sylvia Corwin who was mentored by Rudolf Arnheim and who developed a successful art and reading program based on Arnheim's theories. I thought, "Let's honor them. Let's ask those University Council members who knew and worked with the art education pioneers like Arnheim, D'Amico, Lowenfeld, and Ziegfeld to transmit what they remember of these four great men to art education undergraduate and graduate students." So, that's how it happened. A series of Saturday seminars, coordinated by UCAE colleagues, humanized the "legends" and brought history to life. After several years, and many memorable seminars, it became apparent to all of us that our old-fashioned oral history was worthy of a more permanent format. We sought to deliver the collective wisdom and insights about each giant to the art educators of the 21st century. Editor Sylvia Corwin, in her proposal to NAEA for the publication, said, "UCAE sees this as an opportunity to capture each author's knowledge of a legend, to humanize a myth, to clarify the enormous contribution each has made to the progress of our profession. The book represents a collaborative, refreshing look back in order to preserve a precious heritage before we become too feeble to put pen to paper."

Acknowledgments

Sylvia K. Corwin, Editor

Since 1995, numerous colleagues and organizations have worked to bring this volume to fruition. From the outset, University Council for Art Education was its steadfast sponsor, culminating in donor support for prepublication costs from Rikki Asher, Lucylee Chiles, Hilda Demsky, Michael DeSiano, Elaine Foster, Pearl Greenberg, Irving Hamilton, Jo Harris, Marilyn Honig, Nadine Gordon-Taylor, Helen Levin, Eva Pataki, Natalie Schifano, Dina Schutzer, Alice Wechsler, and Vivienne Thaul Wevhter. Simultaneously, the National Art Education Association, e.g., Dr. Thomas A. Hatfield, NAEA Executive Director, became collaborator and friend. Special gratitude is due Dr. Arthur Efland who, after writing his succinct overview of the 20th century, critiqued each chapter for historical accuracy and consistency. The genuine enthusiasm of the NAEA-ers who attended a Legends presentation at the 1999 NAEA Conference in Washington, DC, resulted in a wealth of information and illustrations. Noteworthy, here, is Dr. John Michael, who made available a treasure trove from the Miami Center for the Study of the History of Art Education, Miami University, Oxford, Ohio and Dr. Julia Lindsey, who facilitated the photographs. A wise companion on my literary expedition, husband Leonard Corwin, merits unqualified recognition. So, I thank myriad colleagues, both named and unnamed, whose advice and encouragement transformed so many collective memories into *Exploring the Legends: Guideposts to the Future*, which I hope will prove a useful resource for art educators in the 21st century.

University Council for Art Education

The University Council for Art Education is a nonprofit professional organization of college and university art educators principally in the New York, New Jersey, Connecticut area, but extending to other states and Canada. Its members also include museum educators, city and state art supervisors and administrators. The Council is an active forum for ideas and activities in art education and is dedicated to continuing the professional growth of its members and to serving the larger community. Its programs explore the relationship between theory and practice in the schools, in museum education, in the community and the media. It also sponsors art exhibitions for its members, as well as an annual series of public seminars and conferences. The Council works in conjunction with other art organizations and those concerned with the arts. Teachers College Columbia University Art & Art Education Program, Box 78, 525 West 120th Street, New York, NY 10027.

OVERVIEW OF THE 20TH CENTURY

Arthur D. Efland

When Georgio Vasari wrote his *Lives of the Artists* (1550), Leonardo and Raphael were dead and Michaelangelo was an old man whose life's work was done. Looking at the art of his lofty predecessors, Vasari must have felt that an age of greatness was passing. These were the giants of the golden age of Florentine art and their legacy was receding into history. In the history of U.S. art education, the era that followed World War II was also an age of heroes (Eisner, 1972), and it too, recedes into history.

Many of the writers of this volume came of age in this critical and eventful period. Many studied with the legendary individuals to be surveyed in this volume. My own experience is typical in that I began my undergraduate training in 1947, exactly the year that Viktor Lowenfeld published his reknowned *Creative and Mental Growth.* He and Victor D'Amico were then the formative influences as my notions of teaching art took shape in the late 1940s and 1950s. And when I pursued my doctoral studies in the early 1960s, it was Rudolf Arnheim's ideas about perceptual growth that formed one of the bases of my dissertation. My appreciation of Edwin Ziegfeld's contributions to art education did not come into focus until my interests turned to the history of the field. Then I began to realize the extent to which his ideas about art education and its role in daily living permeated the field.

Recalling the Postwar Era

World War II had ended and though it gave rise to the specter of a nuclear Armageddon, that awesome possibility had yet to take hold in our consciousness.[1] By 1946 the realization of the Cold War began with Winston Churchill's "Iron Curtain" speech in Fulton, Missouri in March 1946. The generation of returning GIs was occupied with the task of rebuilding their

lives, interrupted by years of military service. Yet unlike the generation that fought World War I, there was little desire to go "back to normalcy"[2] to things as they stood in the years before the war. The years preceding the war were years of economic hardship, despair and social unrest. I dwell on this to make the point that there was a readiness for change in many sectors of American life, and this included education.

In spite of growing cold war concerns, several factors made the first years following the war a time of hope and possibility. One was the economic prosperity of the time and the tremendous expansion in jobs and markets. A second was the shortage of new teachers to replace those rapidly approaching retirement age. A third was the G.I. Bill of Rights which underwrote the cost of a college education, providing the financial incentive that enabled many to seek training as teachers and artists. A fourth was the immigration of many Europeans to America, especially from the German speaking world. Not only did they bring new scholarship in such fields as the history of art, art education and psychology, there were artists and educators like Hans Hoffman, Wilhelm DeKooning, Josef Albers, and Lazlo Moholy-Nagy. A fifth was "the triumph of American painting," to use the phrase coined by Irving Sandler (1970). By 1952, Abstract Expressionism had become the dominant art style of the postwar era, and New York became the center of the art world.

In what follows I briefly describe these factors both to provide an overview of the time period and to indicate how the four individuals whose lives and work are celebrated in this volume responded to these events and gave shape to the art education emerging in the postwar era, for the new art education which they helped create bore little resemblance to what preceded it. I begin by recalling the Great Depression.

The Great Depression. By 1929 the idea of teaching art on a regular basis in public schools was on the threshold of gaining acceptance (Farnum, 1932). The stock market crash which initiated the Great Depression intervened to reverse that prospect. Programs in the arts were curtailed in many communities, managing to survive in the school, largely by becoming integrated into other studies like history, and the social studies. During this era the salaries of teachers were reduced and retiring teachers were not replaced. It was also during the depression era that the child labor laws were enforced by the Roosevelt Administration, and so many students remained in school rather than search for jobs which were scarce or non-existent.

The teacher shortage in the postwar era. Throughout the depression era and the war that followed, few people entered the teaching profession. Women in large numbers worked in factories dedicated to war production or entered the military rather than seek training as teachers. By the war's end a drastic shortage of teachers was in the offing. Teacher education programs in colleges and universities were suddenly called upon to prepare a new generation of teachers. A combination of postwar economic prosperity and the G.I. Bill of Rights made higher education affordable to large numbers of people.

When few teachers were needed in the depression years, state legislatures began raising professional standards. In 1930 teacher certification could be obtained in most states with a 2-year normal school certificate. By the postwar era, teaching certification had become a 4-year program. The degree usually included courses for elementary school teachers in art and music education, and the texts used in these courses were Lowenfeld's *Creative and Mental Growth* and D'Amico's *Creative Teaching of Art*. Certification of art and music specialists had also begun to make its appearance but at the war's end, art teachers at the elementary level were almost unknown, with the exception of private schools and a few wealthy suburbs of cities along the eastern seaboard.

The G.I. Bill of Rights and the expectation of change. In some ways the G.I. Bill of Rights was probably the most successful piece of social engineering ever attempted by a democratic society. It greatly expanded the size of America's middle class and resulted in one of the longest periods of economic prosperity in the history of the nation. As the G.I. generation entered the teaching profession, there was a growing expectation that old patterns of schooling would change. The generation that fought and won the war was not one readily disposed to going back to the traditions of the past. Older pedagogic traditions could now be set aside. Before the war professional educators were sharply divided into traditional or progressive camps. In the arts there were progressive art educators dedicated to the free expression of the child, and who stood in opposition to regimented step-by-step lessons commonly found in the schools (see Rugg & Shumaker, 1928).

After the war new forms of art teaching began to appear that were shaped by an entirely new aesthetic, namely the styles of modern art. Traditional lessons still continued to echo the stylistic influence of the arts and crafts movement from the end of the 19th century. Periodicals for art teachers like *School Arts Magazine* tended to favor these traditional styles, but as the consciousness of the postwar era took hold, they shifted to activities that can only be described as modernist in spirit. One can see evidence of this with the appearance of lessons inspired by the mobiles of Calder, and other lessons patterned after Bauhaus design. Somewhat later, abstract expressionism was in evidence.[3]

Immigration from the German speaking world. Many refugees fled to America to escape persecution by the Nazis. Not only did they bring new scholarship to America in such fields as the history of art, with individuals like Erwin Panofsky, it also included scholars in art education and psychology, such as Henry Schaeffer-Simmern, Viktor Lowenfeld, and Rudolf Arnheim. There were artists like Hans Hoffman, Wilhelm DeKooning, Josef Albers, Lazlo Moholy-Nagy, Mondrian, and Max Ernst. Many found employment in colleges and universities, and gradually their ideas from a variety of fields took root in American soil. Lowenfeld in particular was instrumental in setting the pattern for advanced degrees in art education with his program at Pennsylvania State University.

The triumph of American painting. The trauma of World War II, the atom bomb, and the Cold War began to take its toll upon the American psyche. The business world was optimistic and expanding but social critics like Paul Goodman (1960), David Reisman (1950), and William Whyte (1956) wrote volumes on the "beat generation," "the lonely crowd," and "the organization man," each trying to define the character of postwar consumer society. Artists also explored the troubled soul of America. Nowhere was the Cold War more apparent than in the work of artists like Adolph Gottlieb or Jasper Johns. Robert Hughes (1997, p. 514) suggests that the "submerged text" of John's target paintings was a response to the stresses of the Cold War with the whole nation feeling it was a target. The angst of the Cold War was also accompanied by the irrational fear of the Communist menace and the accompanying frenzy in the news media exploited by Senator Joseph McCarthy, who sooner or later managed to accuse everyone in government as being part of a vast international conspiracy. And modern artists were parties to the imagined assault upon American culture. In spite of these attacks, styles like abstract expressionism and pop art had succeeded in becoming the styles favored by the American cultural establishment.

Who Were These Legends?

Edwin Ziegfeld, apostle for art in daily living. It was during the depression era that a daring experiment was undertaken during the 1930s in Owatonna, Minnesota. Melvin Haggerty, Dean of the School of Education, with financial resources provided by the Carnegie Foundation, planned a 5-year experiment to see whether the arts could enhance the quality of life in a typical midwestern community which, heretofore, had no art education in its schools. Emphasis was placed upon art that serves individuals living a common life rather than upon art as the pursuit of beauty for its own sake, or art as an esoteric experience with timeless masterpieces. Art was also seen as a means of attaining community goals. Edwin Ziegfeld was a member of the project and, as a result of Haggerty's untimely death, came to direct it in its final year. In 1944, Ziegfeld voiced a theme that was to mark his work throughout his long career, namely that "if art is to become a useful medium of expression, it must be taught in relation to the fundamental areas of living" (Ziegfeld, 1944, p. 62). Art in daily living could well have been his motto.

Viktor Lowenfeld, apostle for freedom and psychological health. The distance between the old and the

new art education was not merely one that was waged over styles. It also entailed differences in ideology. World civilization had just been convulsed by the most disastrous war in the history of mankind, a war between totalitarianism and freedom, and so if art education were to have redeeming social value of lasting importance it would have to be identified with higher, social and moral purposes than the mere making of beautiful things. For years teachers who cultivated the creative expression of the child thought they were working to free the child from social repression, thus contributing to psychological development. Lowenfeld said that the goal of art education "is not the art itself, or the aesthetic product, or the aesthetic experience, but rather the child who grows up more creatively and sensitively and applies his experience in the arts to whatever life situations may be applicable" (Michael, J. A., 1982). Lowenfeld's great contribution was that he taught a generation of school teachers that the arts are more than pleasant diversions and that they can use the arts to achieve much larger social purposes. He helped art educators recognize that in working to counter the forces of social conformity, control and regimentation, they were also helping to build a free society and democracy itself. We see evidence for this in the preface to the second edition of *Creative and Mental Growth,* where he concludes that totalitarianism and the resulting war were the results of a rigidly conformist type of education in the German speaking world.

> Having experienced the devastating effect of rigid dogmatism and disrespect for individual differences, I know that force does not solve problems and that the basis for human relationships is created in homes and kindergartens. I feel strongly that without the imposed discipline common in German family lives and schools the acceptance of totalitarianism would have been impossible. Without it, this world might have been saved from the most devastating of wars (Lowenfeld, 1952, p. ix).

Victor D'Amico, apostle of modernism. The cultivation of the free expression of children in a certain sense reenacts the struggle of artists to free themselves from the academic conventions of the past. Both came to be identified with the production of artistic forms in the modernist canon. In the 1930s and 40s D'Amico clearly identified himself with the ideals of progressive education though he never supported the *laissez faire* approach to art teaching sometimes associated with that movement.[4] He was not one to leave things to chance and he was the master *par excellence* in organizing learning environments where children were sure to have a positive outcome. In the postwar era he was part of the effort put forth by the Museum of Modern Art to promote the position of modern art in American life. The newsletters of the National Committee on Art Education, an organization created by D'Amico's efforts, and sponsored by the Museum of Modern Art, was vigorous in its denouncements of attacks by politicians who thought that modern art was either a menace, or the butt of jokes. If there was to be radicalism in art education, it would be an aesthetic radicalism, a radicalism inspired by artist/teachers in pursuit of modern art education.

Rudolf Arnheim, apostle of cognition. Writing in the tradition of Gestalt psychology, Arnheim attempted to show how the various elements of the perceptual field presented by works of art are transformed into a unified whole in the percipient's experience. His book *Art and Visual Perception* appeared in 1954, but an even greater contribution was that he impressed upon the community of art educators something that they did not believe about themselves, namely that the arts are cognitive endeavors. *Art and Visual Perception* appeared when behaviorism was the dominant paradigm in education, and American education was held firmly in its grip. For example, Benjamin Bloom and his colleagues were developing their *Taxonomies of Educational Objectives* (1956) which all but placed the arts outside the realm of cognition, placing them instead in the affective domain, on the assumption that feeling was not a form of knowing.

Building The Art Education Platform of the Postwar Era

What made the individuals celebrated in this volume into the legends that they have become? Was it that they gave cohesion to a set of ideas that formed the basis for a new brand of art education? In certain ways there are pervasive themes that do unify their separate endeavors, but it is equally true that other differences kept them apart. I will identify four leading ideas or planks that in many respects formed the platform that characterized art education after the war. Then I will point to the differences in their perspectives which are still the source of rival positions within the field of art education, and that still continue to be a source of debate.

• **Ziegfeld's goal of promoting art in daily living.** This is the view that art is a part of the daily life of the individual, that art belongs to the common man, the man-in-the-street, that it is not the exclusive province of social or intellectual elites. He believed that art education should help shape a democratic art for a democratic society.

• **Lowenfeld's goal of cultivating the child's expressive impulses** through art education, thus to cultivate psychological health, freedom and democracy. Another is the belief that art education does not exist to create artists but well adjusted individuals. Art is less a body of subject matter than a developmental activity. In this regard Lowenfeld's instrumental use of art was compatible with Ziegfeld's.

• **D'Amico's goal of cultivating art within art education,** especially modern art. Modern art is desirable in art education not only because it values originality in expression but also because in encouraging creativeness it is a socially progressive influence in all aspects of society.

• **Arnheim's goal of cultivating the cognitive abilities** of individuals through the arts because they are principally cognitive endeavors. Art education is primarily concerned with understanding and thinking in the various media comprising the visual arts.

Differences in their positions. D'Amico's emphasis upon modern art was in some ways at variance with Ziegfeld's notion of art in daily living. Modern art was in many respects the product of an *avant garde*, a group of artists and critics that have intentionally isolated themselves from the social mainstream in order to challenge the status quo and its social conventions. Historically it was an art of an intellectual elite whereas Ziegfeld's pedagogical emphasis featured art's practical applications in areas such as home decoration, fashion design, architecture, and graphic design. He was less interested in the pursuit of modern art as pure formal expression though he promoted good design in the applied areas featured in his text *Art Today*, written with Ray Faulkner and Edward Lucie-Smith.

A more difficult schism was one that which erupted between Lowenfeld and D'Amico. In 1946 Lowenfeld accepted a position at Penn State where he created a new model of graduate study in art education. It was based upon research, and the models of research provided by experimental psychology. D'Amico objected to Lowenfeld's categories of creative types, such as the "visual" or "haptical minded" child in what he termed "the over-psychologizing of art education" (D'Amico, 1958). Moreover, he vehemently took exception to Lowenfeld's idea that elementary classroom teachers could teach art, and he was appalled at the decline in the quality of children's art that he saw being done in the schools by the cadres of Lowenfeld trained art teachers. Instead, he favored the artist/teacher, and sung the praises of gifted teachers like Jane Bland and Lois Lord as the models of excellence that the art education profession should strive to emulate. But gifted teachers like these are rare, and D'Amico's message lost ground. He had no legions of graduate students to spread his word, and his publisher felt that his book, *Creative Teaching of Art*, did not warrant a third edition. I believe that D'Amico's support for the artist/teacher philosophy was part and parcel of his support of modern art in general. The artist/teacher position advocated teaching art as an autonomous subject by qualified persons who were trained as artists as well as educators. This paralleled the modernist view of art as the product of vanguard artists whose detachment from mainstream popular culture made possible the creation of new aesthetic forms to effect cultural progress.

I can only speculate how Arnheim and D'Amico would have regarded each other. Both emphasized the role of media as a source of perceptual experience. Formalist writers often cite the Gestalt Principle that the whole is greater than the sum of its parts, but Arnheim's views on art and children's artistic development were also views that were grounded in psychology. My guess is that he would have been less open to Arnheim's views, even though Arnheim did not specify creative typologies as did Lowenfeld and Herbert Read in England. D'Amico trusted the intuition of the artist-teacher to establish the basis for pedagogy. Yet he would have been comfortable with Arnheim's tendency to characterize the perception of art as an autonomous and independent form of thought. But having met both of these individuals it is hard for me to imagine them having a conversation.

Their status as legends. Now we call them legends in the annals of art education, but what is a legend in the sense used here? Were they explorers discovering new territory or heroes in the sense that they did noble deeds? Were they missionaries introducing new values? Or was it the age in which they lived and worked that challenged them to innovate? Is it a combination of these two possibilities, namely that these were individuals who had special capabilities and who were also presented with an historical opportunity to do something extraordinary for the field, something that heretofore had not been done? My own view is that in spite of strong differences in their beliefs, they helped give shape to three aesthetic traditions in art education.

Giving Shape To New Aesthetic Traditions

Opposition to imitation. There have been four aesthetic traditions that have shaped the teaching of art in the twentieth century. The first is the mimetic tradition which holds that works of art are imitations of nature, while learning is by imitation. The psychology of learning associated with this view is behaviorism. And though behaviorism lives on in much American educational practice especially in the testing movement, it was universally opposed by the four individuals featured in this volume. Instead they offered three alternatives that came into prominence as models of learning that also were associated with modern art. These include the pragmatic stream, the expressive stream, and the stream which drew strength from formalism.

The pragmatic stream. In this tradition art is seen as a useful tool with which to solve personal and social problems. A viewer's experience is determined by the transaction between the object of perception and the viewer's disposition. Teaching in this tradition provides students with problem solving situations to give structure to their experience. In art education it is best exemplified by Edwin Ziegfeld's work in the Owatonna Project and by his text, *Art Today*.

Expressionism. The expressionist stream is the view that works of art are expressions of the artist's emotions. In many respects it is tied to the psychoanalytic view, that all behavior is expressive. Unconscious needs are elaborated and channeled into overt behavior.

Consequently art is not a product that is governed by rules but by inner needs. Learning involves social adaptation through what psychoanalysts called the sublimation of repressed desires, with teaching providing the therapeutic environment to permit this to happen in self-expression in art. The expressionist stream was exemplified by Viktor Lowenfeld.

Formalism. Art in the formalist stream describes the work of art as a self-sufficient autonomous whole accessible to the viewer directly in perception. The interpretation of the work proceeds directly with the perception of its form, with visual thinking, (and not with verbal explanations) a process which is a cognitive endeavor. In art education the formalist stream is represented by Arnheim.

These individuals helped to bring these traditions into the consciousness of art educators, and identified the purposes and goals of the field. They were not alone, but they had the magnetism, the charisma, the charm and the intellectual arguments to bring art education into the modern age.

When I was invited to prepare this overview, I was puzzled as to why no women were cited as legends, especially when persons like June King McFee had been influential to so many including this writer. I think also of the numerous women who kept art education alive in the schools during the lean years of the Great Depression. Of course they were professional heroes as well! My first impulse was to demand equity, but then it occurred to me to look at another question. After all, art education was largely a women's profession, like the teaching profession as a whole, but it was a struggling profession, a "lightsome vocation!" in the words of the social Darwinist David Snedden. It was all right for women but not a solid profession for men. But then these four male individuals appeared on the horizon and this fact has to count for something! And what it counts for is that they told the world that art education was educationally important, and they did *so as much by their presence in it as by their deeds.*

We are now passing through a time of reappraisal as the millennium nears, when the project of modernism is itself, undergoing reappraisal. Already modern art is seen and felt as a period style, not unlike the Baroque. I predict these individual legends will hold onto their place in the annals of art education, not only because of their ideas, but because the streams out of which their ideas emerged will continue to flow.

Endnotes

[1] The concern over nuclear weapons did not begin to arise until the Soviet Union exploded its first atom bomb in 1949 and with the onset of the Korean War in 1950. Then, the Cold War began to deepen.

[2] "Back to Normalcy" was President Warren Harding's slogan in his successful election campaign.

[3] Compare art lessons featured in *School Arts Magazine* in the 1930s with those that began to be seen in the 1950s.

[4] It should be noted that both Lowenfeld and D'Amico were opposed to *laissez faire* methods of art teaching. Yet it is part of the mythology of art education that they were proponents of these approaches.

References

Arnheim, R. (1954). *Art & visual perception.* Berkeley: University of California Press.

Bloom, B., Krathwohl, D. & others. (1956). *Taxonomy of educational objectives by a committee of college and university examiners.* New York: David McCay Publishers.

D'Amico, V. (1942). *Creative teaching in art.* Scranton, PA: International Textbook Co.

D'Amico, V. (1958). Coming events cast shadows: A reappraisal of art education. *School Arts*, Vol. 57 (Sept.), pp. 5-19.

Eisner, E. (1972). *Educating artistic vision.* NY: Macmillan Co.

Farnum, R.B. (1932). *Art education. Biennial survey of education: 1928-1930* Vol I, (pp. 297-322). Washington DC: U.S. Government Printing Office.

Faulkner, R., Ziegfeld, E. & Smith, E. (1941). *Art today.* NY: Holt Rinehart & Winston.

Goodman, P. (1960). *Growing up absurd.* NY: Random House.

Hughes, R. (1997). *American visions: The epic history of art in America.* NY: A. Knopf Publishers.

Lowenfeld, V. (1947). *Creative and mental growth.* NY: Macmillan Co.

Lowenfeld, V. (1952. *Creative and mental growth:* Second Edition. NY: Macmillan Co.

Michael, J.A. (1982). *The Lowenfeld lectures.* University Park: Pennsylvania State University Press.

Rugg, H. & Shumaker, A. (1928). The child centered school. NY: World Book Co.

Reisman, D. (1950). *The lonely crowd.* New Haven: Yale University Press.

Sandler, I. (1970). *The triumph of American painting: A history of abstract expressionism.* NY: Harper & Row Publishers.

Whyte, W. (1956). *The organization man.* NY: Simon & Schuster.

Ziegfeld, E. (1944). *Art for daily living: The story of the Owatonna art education project.* Minneapolis: University of Minnesota Press.

RUDOLF ARNHEIM (JULY 15, 1904 -)
A Living Legend

Sylvia K. Corwin

Art teachers are collectors. We gather shells, driftwood, bottles, photographs, ephemera, dried flowers, bones, textured papers—anything that might find a place in a still life, a window display or a collage. I confess to huge lifetime collections. Nevertheless, when I retired from teaching in 1989, I left overflowing cartons behind. A few books were all that I took with me. Of these, my greatest treasures are those that helped me through three decades in two New York City high schools. Rudolf Arnheim authored each landmark volume!

Arnheim's theories, insights, and wisdom underlined my daily classroom approach, validated my grant writing, and inspired my struggle to maintain the integrity of an urban high school art department in the face of obstacles.

My mentor buttressed my teaching by clarifying, through his writing, why and how I should…and, could:

- use art as a tool for learning;
- stimulate students' cognitive processes while directing their creative process; and,
- nurture students' spoken and written competencies within the friendly studio environment.

The stories about D'Amico, Lowenfeld and Ziegfeld, told elsewhere in this volume have come down to us, as is the wont of all legends, from the past. Often, the passage of time and vagaries of memory tend to distort history. That is why, when writing about a *living* legend, I turned to people whose contacts with Arnheim are fresh. Wherever possible, I used Arnheim's own voice because of the precision of his language. Arnheim traces his remarkable linguistic facility, among other experiences, to the years when he worked as a translator for the British Broadcasting Corporation. As the news bulletins came in from the front in German, Arnheim, at the microphone, instantly translated them for his English-speaking listeners.

Thoughts on Art Education

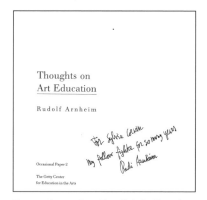

Personal notation: For Sylvia Corwin
My fellow fighter for so many years.
Rudi Arnheim.

The same year that marked the end of my 30-year secondary school career saw the publication of Arnheim's *Thoughts on Art Education* (1989). The Getty Center for Education in the Arts invited eminent scholars and practitioners to present ideas that illuminate and inform understanding about the value of art education in a series of "Occasional Papers."

In the Foreword to Arnheim's paper, Dr. Elliot Eisner, Stanford University, declared: "We have in Arnheim, at last, a psychologist who understands art and a scholar who cares about education." Eisner identifies four key Arnheim ideas "of major importance for American educational theory and for classroom practice. Coming out of Gestalt psychology, Arnheim gives us a view of art and mind wherein the perception and the creation of art is at the heart of the educational process:"

- Because the sensory system is a primary resource in our cognitive life, learning how to use our senses intelligently should be an important item in our educational agenda.
- The optimal development of a child's mind requires attention to intuitive as well as

intellectual processes.
• The paradox of perception lies in a phenomenon: humans need to recognize commonality and uniqueness virtually simultaneously. The ability to classify sameness and differ- ences, while not the exclusive purview of visual art, is often neglected in early schooling. For example, attending solely to the mechan- ics of writing— spelling, punctuation, grammar—teachers sometimes overlook what is interesting, the music of language, style, and so on.
• The forms of representation and the media to which students have access (clay, crayon, paint) influence their perception of the world and their representation of it. By increasing the possibilities through which ideas are formulated modes of thinking are formulated.

Professor Eisner continued:
"If Arnheim's ideas about art and mind were acted upon in American schools, considerably more attention would be devoted to helping children learn how to experience the unique features of the world they inhabit. High on our educational agenda would be not merely look- ing, not even seeing, but recognizing what is distinctive about an object, a person, or a field. Put another way, schools would be as concerned with fostering perceptivity as they are now concerned with the mechanics of writing."

Finally, he concludes:
"The gist of Arnheim's message is that vision itself is a function of intelligence, that perception is a cognitive event, that interpretation and meaning are an indivisible aspect of seeing, and that the educational process can thwart or foster such human abilities…What Arnheim gives us is

a sophisticated view of human capacity, one that helps us understand that the perception and creation of visual art are primary agents in the development of the mind."

FROM THE FIELD

The Journal of Aesthetic Education

Eisner is not alone in his appreciation of Arnheim's contribution to the field of art education. In the winter of 1993, *The Journal of Aes- thetic Education* devoted a special issue (Volume 27, Number 4) to essays in honor of Rudolf Arnheim. Among the authors were a psychologist, an art histo- rian, a photographer, a painter, an architect, a linguist, a musical theorist, and an art educator. I wrote "The Application of Arnheim's Principles to Interdiscipli- nary Education" (p. 155-163) for the journal. My purpose was to demonstrate to novice and experienced teachers how my professional career attempted to close the gap between theory and practice.

Improving Visual Perceptual Skills in Art Classes

I began teaching in 1957, under a provisional license, in an inner city, all-girls, magnet high school. I was granted 5 years to complete the Master's Degree required for permanent certification. By day, I shared the know-how I had gleaned as a commercial artist in an advertising agency and by night, I studied educa- tional administration. Prerequisite for students' acceptance into Washington Irving High School (WIHS) in order to major in art, were a portfolio evaluation, a teacher recommendation, plus a drawing test. The 3-year sequence included skill development in design—advertising, book, interior, fashion, tex- tile—in addition to drawing, painting, sculpture, and art history. Eighty minutes a day, 5 days a week for 3 years! Students were talented, motivated, and creative performers. But they appeared uniformly undistin- guished in their subject classes. Year after year I observed the same behavior pattern: exceptional artwork and below average academic work. Reading comprehension hovered at or below norm-referenced grade level. In *Visual Thinking* (1969/1971), Rudolf Arnheim seemed to be talking directly to me: "Once it is recognized that productive thinking in any area of cognition is perceptual thinking, the central function of art in general education will become evident. The most effective training of perceptual thinking can be offered in the art studio" (p. 296).

Just about this time the New York State Education Department, driven by statewide deficits in high school students' reading scores, threatened the termination of art instruction. The proposed mandate would bar secondary students whose level of reading was two or more grades below the norm (according to the California Achievement Test) from all elective classes. Instead, the problem readers would remain in remedial reading classes until they raised their reading scores to the grade level.

On reflection, I concluded that WIHS girls progressed in art because language was minimized. We relied on images, diagrams, sketches, photos, prints. I taught to their strengths. Remedial reading alone could never be the key for their success, neither in school nor in life.

Meanwhile, in my university night classes, Arnheim's theories became a call to arms. I could not ignore his prophetic wisdom. "The similarity of what the mind does in the arts and what it does elsewhere suggested taking a new look at the longstanding complaint about the isolation and neglect of the arts in society and in education. Art-making seemed a natural, logical tool for learning to read better and comprehend more" (personal correspondence, May 3, 1969).

Reading Improvement Through Art

The result was an interdisciplinary experiment—a cooperative effort of colleagues in 9 different New York City high schools, funded by NYC Board of Education and NY State Education Department. Reading specialists were assigned to 10th grade art classes comprised of below-level readers. Art and reading teachers were trained to collaborate, to extend, and reinforce students' language and reading experience during the daily 10th grade "required" art class.

Citations from Arnheim's research lent credibility to grant applications for *Reading Improvement Through Art (RITA)*. Arnheim's letter of support helped secure pilot funding. Officially, the project was called "Improving Visual Perceptual Skills in Art Classes in Secondary School." Teachers identified overlapping art-making skills with common visual perceptual skills: tracking, scanning, visual analysis, figure/ground differentiation, visual synthesis, visual memory, visual closures, and visual imagery. At no time were the project art teachers expected to become teachers of reading, or vice-versa. Without undermining the integrity of the art experience, reading activities included technical vocabulary, biographical and historical background information about the art processes, step-by-step instructions. An attractive reading corner was installed in each studio; students kept daily journals; teachers adopted the language experience methodology. *Reading Improvement Through Art (RITA)* encountered obstacles as the pilot plowed through the State Education Department validation process, 12 annual grant award competitions,

Arnheim is keynote speaker at New York State Art Teachers Annual conference at Kutsher's Hotel and Country Club in the Catskills, New York, 1989. Past President Corwin introduced him to an appreciative audience.

and 50 adoption/adaptation replications in high schools in and beyond the city's five boroughs.

Twice during the peak years, Rudolf Arnheim lent his gracious presence to advance RITA's implementation. He addressed a monthly meeting of New York City high school principals at The Museum of Modern Art where he argued in favor of a "reunion of sense and reason." As always, Arnheim was eloquent. Punctuating his talk at a New York State Art Teachers Conference in 1982, he guided the audience to a discovery of connections as they viewed familiar and less-known artworks with fresh eyes. In the end, he developed so strong a case for the essential role of art in our nation's schools as to bring forth a standing ovation.

The territorial challenge to the reading establishment, the resistance of the *art for art's sake* purists combined with the apathy of bureaucracies and individuals remained constant. My mentor's genteel observation on his own cross-disciplinary efforts cushioned my setbacks. Arnheim observed: "It is the nature of such an enterprise that it suggests *connections* where *distinctions* are cherished by many" (personal correspondence, 1982).

The pre- and post-reading scores in the 9 RITA pilot schools were compared with untreated similar populations in the nine locations. A team of 3 State University of New York professors subjected the data to rigorous evaluation. They concluded that the "participating

U.S. DEPARTMENT OF EDUCATION
OFFICE OF EDUCATIONAL RESEARCH AND IMPROVEMENT (OERI)
WASHINGTON, D.C. 20208

ERIC ®

REPORTS

Abstract:
The Reading Improvement Through Art (RITA) program, an interdisciplinary approach to remedial reading that combines reading and visual arts activities, was evaluated in nine New York City high schools. A total of 240 students participating in the program were pre and post-tested during the fall 1975 and spring 1976 semesters. The results of this evaluation showed that the participating students made exceptional growth in reading, growth that was beyond statistical expectations. The school attendance of the participating students also showed improvement. Based on these data and comments from reading teachers who participated in RITA, the program received a positive evaluation, with recommendations for its continuation and expansion.

VALIDATED
demonstration site

JOHN F. KENNEDY HIGH SCHOOL
99 TERRACE VIEW AVENUE
BRONX, NEW YORK 10463
PROJECT TELEPHONE: 212-562-5500
212-562-6262
NYSED: TRANSFERRING SUCCESS
SINCE SEPTEMBER, 1975

Art teachers trained in the validated NYSED methodology found the approach natural and effective. Many continued to adapt it for their classes long after the funding ended.

students made exceptional growth in reading that was beyond statistical expectations" (ED184095/ERIC). The significant results earned the coveted *validated* status; a demonstration site was opened at Kennedy High to train replicators. The demonstration classes were described in *Coming to Our Senses* (1977) by the Arts, Education and Americans Panel: "Results of tests given before and after the…combination course are impressive." Twenty-five years ago the panel raised the identical questions posed in educational circles today: "Are such learning increases due to perceptual training, individual attention, internalized motivation or emotional satisfaction?" (p. 114). Nevertheless, the panel included John F. Kennedy High School among the 14 exemplary interdisciplinary arts education programs in the United States (p. 176).

Today, it is difficult to imagine how revolutionary the RITA methodology was considered in the 1970s. Contrary to accepted school practice that concentrated on honing students' manual skills and techniques, the RITA teachers aimed to strengthen students' problem-solving ability, to sharpen their visual memory, and to improve their perceptual skills. The process of making art also served as a vehicle to apply thinking skills to a variety of challenges—including language development.

Thanks to Rudolf Arnheim, *visual thinking* has become so widespread that now it is implicit in cognitive psychology. Twenty-five years ago, when a 10th grader with problems in reading drew a diagram in his notebook to better understand an academic subject, when he recorded a visual stimulus in his sketchbook or tracked down a bit of information to successfully complete an artwork, he already validated Arnheim's legacy.

A meta-analysis of whether learning in the arts transfers to academic subjects is currently in progress at Harvard's Project Zero. The Principal Investigator is Ellen Winner, 1998-1999 Florence Ladd Fellow at the Mary Ingraham Bunting Institute at Radcliffe College. *Reviewing Education and the Arts Project* (REAP), funded by the Bauman Foundation, is pulling together hundreds of studies, including RITA, to find out what is actually known and the implications for education.

The Arts in Psychotherapy

Eight practitioners penned passionate essays in a special issue of the international journal, *The Arts in Psychotherapy*, Vol. 21, No. 4, 1994, entitled "The Life And Work of Rudolf Arnheim." Shaun McNiff, guest editor, is provost of Endicott College in Beverly, Massachusetts, and one of the pioneers of creative arts therapy education. He is the recipient of the highest award of the American Art Therapy Association for service to the profession, and, authored *Art as Medicine: Creating a Therapy, the Imagination; Trust the Process: An Artistic Guide to Letting Go, Art-Based Research; Depth Psychology of Art*, and many more books. Rudolf Arnheim supervised and inspired Dr. McNiff's early work in art therapy, "Art as a helper in times of trouble," Arnheim wrote in the journal's introduction:

> …as a means of understanding the conditions of human existence and facing the frightening aspects of those conditions, as the creation of a meaningful order—these most welcome aids are grasped by people in distress and used by the healers who come to their assistance. But the blessings experienced in therapy can reach further: they can remind artists everywhere what the function of art is and will always be.

Shaun McNiff, explains:
> Rudolf Arnheim has helped the creative arts therapy community understand how the structural qualities of images generate expressive energies and medicines that act upon the

perceiver. Therapists and diagnosticians have shown a tendency to assign meanings to images in keeping with their particular theories and these interpretations often say more about the theory than the particular art work or the person who made it. Arnheim's writings demonstrate how to look more closely at the objective qualities of an image. This focus has many therapeutic effects which include the experience of perceptual order, empathy, and the ability to relate more effectively with the outer world.

Arnheim has directly participated in the arts therapy field through his essays, the supervision of graduate level research, and three decades of service as an editorial board member of *The Arts in Psychotherapy: An International Journal*. In addition to supporting the establishment of creative arts therapy's principal journal in the early 1970s, Arnheim was a friend of Margaret Naumburg who was one of art therapy's founders in the 1940s and 50s. All sectors of the arts therapy community are continuously drawn to Rudolf Arnheim's writings which uniquely inform the search for a deeper understanding of the psychological significance of expression (personal communications, Shaun McNiff, April 1, 1998).

*Here you see Little Red Riding Hood, depicted as a bright red triangle. This is the first of a series of illustrations in *Picture This*.

The author/artist Mollie Bang demonstrates how to make the picture book look and feel increasingly scary by the addition and repositioning of simple shapes.

Picture This: Perception and Composition

When Molly Bang, a Caldecott Honor Book winner, wrote and illustrated a book about how shapes and structures in pictures affect our feelings, Arnheim wrote in it:

> When I first looked at this book I thought, with the usual vanity of professors, that the author must have been a student of mine. Instead, something better is the case: she has seen what I have seen because we all see it— provided somebody has the talent to make us aware of the magic of shapes (Foreword).

In turn Molly shares her rationale:

> I had been an illustrator of children's books for over fifteen years, but even though my work was successful in that books were selling well and occasionally winning awards, I knew I didn't understand something very basic about how pictures worked. I did know that I didn't understand what 'picture structure' meant. I also knew that my pictures wouldn't get any better until I found out…Once I saw how basic the relationship between picture structure and our emotions was, I wanted to see whether the principles couldn't be used by anyone at all to make strong, meaningful pictures.

So, readers learn to manipulate abstract shapes of colored papers and, with her guidance, come to understand how the principles work and how to make pictures that are increasingly clear and meaningful. "I had read two of Arnheim's books," she continues,

> …and was impressed both by Arnheim's interest in the psychology and physiology of vision and in the clarity of his writing. Out of the blue, I sent him a draft of *Picture This*. Within just a few weeks, I got back a delightful letter asking whether I wanted him to send it back as it was or whether I wanted to

'scribble a few notes on it.' I asked him to scribble and scribble. Two weeks later, the book came back. On every third or fourth page was a revised sentence, a question or occasionally two or three completely new sentences that added new insight. In every case his suggestion improved or illuminated the text. Later, when I had found a publisher, I asked him to write an introduction. Again, I was touched by his promptness and courtliness, and by his felicitous turn of phrase. And, all this when the man was 83 years old, with many other projects. I thought, "When I am 93—or 53—may I be as thoughtful and helpful to others who write to me! (personal communication, December 24, 1998).

First Drawings: Genesis of Visual Thinking

Heidi's Horse, Sylvia Fein's 1976 book, was a study of one child's visual thinking from age 2 to age 17. Heidi's maturing mind and draftsmanship is seen in the chronological collection of her drawings as she copes with transitions, retreats and progresses, and increases her ability to observe, think, work and communicate. Arnheim points out in the Foreword to Fein's book, *First Drawings: Genesis of Visual Thinking*, (1993) "the very fact that the work of one child can stand for that of children in general is decisive for our comprehension of art….The basic principles of all visual expression and representation, however, are evident not only in the artwork of children, but equally in that of early cultures." Fein writes: "Children draw just as did their ancestors…A unique combination of hand and brain produces pictorial ways to record thoughts and communicate them, and in the artifacts of their ancestors we see their progress from descriptive pictures to systems of numbers and language" (Preface XIII).

Wherever we look in time or place, we see our children and our ancestors forming identical configurations. We have not discovered why this is so, only that it is; and that it is important because our built world is constructed on the principles of logical relationships our children and our ancestors realize.

In these artifacts we can see the human mind and its ability to express relationships of forms, a unique human birthright.

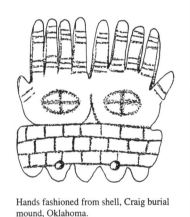

Hands fashioned from shell, Craig burial mound, Oklahoma.

From: *First Drawings: Genesis of Visual Thinking*, Exelrod Press.

The fact is that our children and our ancestors follow an identical logic, everywhere on earth. Henry Schaefer-Simmern, to whom Fein dedicated both books, was one of the first to understand the similarities. Schaefer-Simmern had done his life's work in Germany and in the United States, delineating the stages of formal development in the art of early cultures, children and lay persons. Arnheim introduced him to the principles of structural organization explored by Gestalt psychology. As Fein sees it, Schaefer-Simmern thought of artistic intuition as an inborn sureness about what is right. Fein traveled the world photographing and drawing the artifacts to show the graphic building blocks that humanity uses in its visual thinking—the universal process of artistic logic and visual order.

University Council For Art Education

University Council for Art Education sponsored a seminar, "Exploring The Legends: Guideposts to the Future," a series of Sunday events for UCAE members and their graduate and undergraduate students. Each seminar presenter strove to humanize his/her mentor via reminiscences and firsthand experiences. Inspired by Rudolf Arnheim, a *living* legend, I gathered six of Arnheim's disciples at New York University on April 12, 1992 to bequeath his legacy to an audience of art educators, students, and professors. The diverse group of academics were unanimous in their expressions of indebtedness, admiration and affection for Arnheim.

***A Life In Art:* a video documentary**

I introduced the seminar with Arnheim's autobiography—his voice-over filmed for the 58-minute video documentary, *A Life in Art*, produced and directed by José Sanchez-H with Tina Michelle Datsko. Professor Sanchez-H, a former Arnheim student, teaches in the Film and Electronic Arts Department, California State University, Long

University Council for Art Education Saturday Seminar, *Exploring a Legend: Rudolf Arnheim*, April 12, 1992. Left to right rear:; José Sanchez-H, Diana Korzenik, Susan G. Galassi, Tina M. Datsko; front: Margery B. Franklin, Sylvia K. Corwin and Charlotte L. Doyle.

Beach. (They have remastered a digital version of the program so that copies can be made to suit any video format.)

Against the backdrop of his summer cottage in Northern Michigan, Rudolf Arnheim speaks:

> I will tell you a little about myself. I was born in Berlin, Germany, and I had my education there. In 1923 I became a student at the university, and a very good university it was. At the time of the Weimar Republic the greatest scientists of our age, such as Einstein and Planck, taught there. Of particular interest to me was the psychology department. It was, you might say, the breeding place of Gestalt psychology. Gestalt psychology has nothing to do with what on the west coast is called Gestalt therapy. It is an experimental science, mostly concerned with perceptual problems and particularly with visual ones. This suited me just right, because I was especially concerned with these subjects. At that time psychology was not accepted as an academic subject but was considered a section of philosophy. Therefore, my major was in philosophy, containing psychology. My two minors were history of art and history of music.

Now Gestalt psychology was very congenial to the arts and so were the leaders of the department. Max Wertheimer and Kurt Lewin taught there and, particularly, there was Wolfgang Köhler, who as the head of the department. The very nature of Gestalt psychology found telling examples in music and art. At that time psychology was much influenced also by the works of Sigmund Freud. I remember that as youngsters we bought the classics of psychoanalysis for a few pennies. I still own some of these precious original editions.

I received my Ph.D. from the University of Berlin in 1928.

By then, however, I had gotten somewhat tired of academic matters and had begun to work as a journalist and critic for periodicals and newspapers. I was particularly interested in film. You may remember that at that time the movies were in a most crucial period. It was the time of the silent film, not yet standardized by the industry but highly experimental. So what I was concerned with was not only the critical evaluation of the single film, but the characteristics of the medium as a whole, a visual medium without sound, without color, and very reduced representation of spatial depth. This gave me the opportunity to collect the material for my first book called *Film as Art*, which was published in 1928. As a complement to this first book soon after, I wrote a second book, called *The Radio Seeks its Form*, dealing with the artistic representation of a world without vision and limited to sound. This book was first published in London in a translation by the well-known critic Herbert Read and his German-born wife, Margaret Ludwig. This was just as well, because by early 1933, the Nazis had taken over Germany, which was the end of my career in my homeland, and my books could no longer be sold there.

Therefore, in the summer of 1933 I accepted an appointment at an institute of the League of Nations in Rome, devoted to educational films. It published a periodical, *Intercine*, in several languages and worked on an encyclopedia of the cinema, to be published by Hoepli. The encyclopedia, however, never came about because Mussolini left the League of Nations when he started his campaign in North Africa. A definite change in my career also took place when Mussolini, under the influence of Hitler, decreed his so-called racial laws. This required foreign Jews to leave Italy by the fall of 1938.

In the documentary *Rudolf Arnheim: A Life in Art,* Arnheim reflects on his life and work. The video includes a biographical section and a lecture section explaining some of his theories contained in his book, *The Power of the Center.* The video is available from FACETS, 1517 West Fullerton Ave., Chicago, IL 60614. Photo credit José Sanchez-H.

I moved to London, where I was employed by the overseas service of the BBC as a translator in the German section. By 1940 I was able to obtain my visa for emigration to the United States, and this started an entirely new life and new career. In 1943, I took my first regular teaching job at Sarah Lawrence College in Bronxville, New York, where I taught general psychology and the psychology of art for 25 years. In 1968 I received an appointment at the Department of Visual and Environmental Studies at the Carpenter Center for the Visual Arts of Harvard University. When I reached the mandatory retirement age of 70 in 1974, my wife, Mary, and I moved to Ann Arbor, Michigan, where I taught at the university for another ten years. That was the end of my regular teaching; I thought "if they have not gotten it now they never will." So this is where I stand now as I'm talking to you. I thought you might like to hear about it.

Tina M. Datsko, a former student of Arnheim, California State College (Professor of Writing and Dance) created a poem for the seminar, title, "The Owl of Athena." It is drawn from Arnheim's closing entry, dated December 11, 1986, in *Parables of Sun Light* (1989).

Arnheim wrote:
The Italian *Vogue* magazine printed an interview we recorded in Milan. It ends with my saying that my life has been one of contemplation rather than of action: and since I watch the artists, who are contemplators, I am twice removed from active life *perche guardo quelli che guardano* (because I observe the observers). I am, I told the interviewer, the little owl perched on the shoulder of Athena.

And so, Datski wrote:

> …Truly, he is beloved of Athena. There
> the little owl perches on her shoulder,
> observing all. As Newton said, "if I
> have seen farther, it is because
> I stood on the shoulder of giants."
> So it must be said of Rudolf Arnheim—
> that if any of us has learned to see
> it is because the master
> has held us up beside him
> on the shoulder of the goddess.

Charlotte Doyle, Sarah Lawrence College (Professor of Child Development and the Creative Process), was never Arnheim's student. Yet she views him as inspiration, mentor and wise friend who "lit up the darkness for her." He changed her thinking about the creative process, and her teaching and writing.

> "He rejected the idea that creativity simply
> consists of coming up with unusual associa-
> tions. He went back to his roots in Gestalt
> psychology and said, "There can be no art
> without some image…a temporary or defini-
> tive notion of what needs to be achieved
> provides the tension between what is and what
> should be. The mere shuffling and reconnect-
> ing of items of experience leads…to nothing
> more than a clever game unless it is steered by
> an underlying vision of what is to be attained."
> *Picasso's Guernica: The Genesis of a Paint-*
> *ing*, (1962) pp. 8-9.

Margery Franklin, Sarah Lawrence College, an Arnheim disciple (Professor of Language Development, the Arts), investigated Arnheim's proposal that "vision is the primary medium of thought—not language" (Arnheim, 1969, p. 18) and the ramifications of this premise on teaching and writing about the development of language, the far reaching implications of *Visual Thinking*, its impact on poetry and creative writing.

Susan Grace Galassi, curator and director of education, The Frick Collection (art history, Picasso),

Rudolf Arnheim self portrait, pen and ink, June 11, 1971.

traced her route from an art history major to special assistant in the Department of Visual and Environmental Studies at Harvard to her authoring *Picasso's Variations on The Masters; Confrontations of A Painting* (1996) and *Picasso's One Liners* (1997). She said: "The quality that strikes me most about Rudolf Arnheim as a scholar and as a person is his sense of connection…I sensed a life lived in and through the visual world in his work, and the great pleasure he found in it…That sense of connection came through most emphatically, however, in his relationships with his students from undergraduate to doctoral student, he took the same non-hierarchical approach towards us that he did with the images that filled his lectures. Working with Rudi on any project or paper, at whatever stage in one's career, was likely to be the beginning of a life-long relationship" (Galassi, quoted from UCAE Seminar, New York University, April 12, 1992).

Diana Korzenik, retired chairperson, art education, Massachusetts College of Art (American art history), described her shift from the study of child art to why 19th century American mill workers practiced drawing whenever they could. Her research culminated in the award-winning book, *Drawn to Art*, 1986. Diana notes that Arnheim pointed the way to a massive revision of the art we look at, the art we study. She recalls his telling her how he uses time: "I

RUDOLF ARNHEIM
informal dialogue with Diana Korzenik

**"What is the Place of
Art Training in Education?"**

HISTORY OF ART EDUCATION – Open Class

**Thursday Eve. Oct. 20, 1983
7:30 pm**

Mass College of Art
Art Education Department
North Building Room 179
Next door to Gardner Museum
Palace Road at Tetlow Street
Boston, MA 02215

Guest appearance, Massachusetts College of Art, Boston, MA. October 20, 1983.

start off playing the violin. Then I read. Then I write about some idea that caught my interest…I've always put my writing before my teaching. It is from my private work, my own thinking and writing that I have something from which to teach" (Diana Korzenik, quoted from UCAE Seminar, NYU, April 12, 1992).

Rudolf Arnheim: Revealing Vision

When Arnheim retired from teaching at the University of Michigan, Ann Arbor, his colleagues were moved to celebrate his life's work with a collection of dialogues and essays. Editors Kent Kleinman, Associate Professor of Architecture, University of Michigan, and Leslie Van Duzer, Assistant Professor of Architecture, Arizona State University, expressed the consensus in *Rudolf Arnheim: Revealing Vision* (1997) "…These texts are oftentimes personal, but in being so they expose one of Rudolf Arnheim's most extraordinary, but perhaps lesser known accomplishments. We are speaking here of his example of a life lived fully with dignity, generosity and great warmth" (p. 5).

For instance, Dore Ashton, Professor of Art History, Cooper Union, comments: "When I think back over the decades of letters, there are three aspects—or rather values—that strike me" (p. 128). Ashton cites Rudi's lively menu of reading that includes novels and how they illuminate history. She marvels at Rudi's ability to recognize the full dimensions of poetry and create it. Finally, she describes his way of alluding to philosophy as though it were—and, it is—"a natural accompaniment of a civilized life." Ashton equates their correspondence that spans the years since she was his student at the New School for Social Research in New York with his vast oeuvre.

Revealing Vision quotes Paul Rand, whose graphic designs for IBM, UPS, ABC, Westinghouse have earned worldwide awards. Rand asks:

RAND: What do you call yourself?

ARNHEIM: When I was at Harvard they called me a professor of the psychology of art, but this one had not existed before, as far as I know. How much it is used, I don't know, either, because it is a special field. It is the application of psychology, mostly that means the psychology of perception, to art.

RAND: Gestalt psychology?

ARNHEIM: Gestalt psychology as applied to the senses: vision, hearing, touch. That is what my work was on in Berlin when I was studying psychology. I then got interested in the arts, and I wanted to apply psychology to the arts. For quite some time I did just that. In *Art and Visual Perception*, for example, I applied the psychology of perception, and then I looked for examples to illustrate it. In the last few years I sort of done the opposite. I have focused on the work of art first, and then I have looked for the psychology to apply to whatever I could.

RAND: I would be very curious to know what you think is going to happen with the computer and art?

ARNHEIM: Well, I'll tell you. It seems to me that a tool is a tool, whether it is a hammer or a toothbrush or a computer. The one thing about any tool is that although it may be extremely useful, it depends on what you do with it; it should never be in charge. What they are doing now with computer art or electronic art looks dreadful to me. It is pathetic. And that is because they think that by letting the tool do what the tool can do, it will create something beautiful.

RAND: You haven't said anything I don't agree with. I know all this, and I have written about it; it is a problem. For example, art students today can't get a job unless they know how to work on the computer, but once they develop the skill, they will never get off the computer. So there won't be any designers left. That is a serious problem (p. 75).

Another dialogue taped for *Revealing Vision* with Vincent Scully, one of the foremost architectural historians of the 20th century who taught at Yale for 44 years, begins:

ARNHEIM: I am so pleased that we have a chance to talk with one another. I have always admired your book on modern architecture. That is a real classic. Such a combination of theory and practice is very rare in theoretical writing and in architecture.

SCULLY: You are very nice to say that. Any theory I have ever had has been roughly cobbled together out of my own experience to

In his study, surrounded by his books and memorabilia, Professor Arnheim draws on his broadly based education in the humanities, his perpetual interest in philosophy, music, and literature, as well as in the visual arts. Photo credit José Sanchez-H.

help me do history. I have always felt—probably influenced by your writings—that one has to see things whole. I have never believed in enumerating parts. Though I was hardly a student of Gestalt theory, your view was one that affected me…(p. 113).

I wanted to ask you something quite different. Have you been interested in Freud's relationship to these things [Scully refers to how streets are built in Japan versus in the United States]:

ARNHEIM: Not very much. As you know, I was one of the Gestalt psychologists, and we felt very coldly about psychoanalysis for varied reasons. One was probably personal: The insistence on sex was something that didn't particularly please us. Apart from that, the Gestalt psychologists were not very interested in individuality, because we dealt mostly with general principles. Freud is interesting, of course, when he talks about general principles, which he does, and that's the way I still read him. I admire the man as a writer, and I admire the kind of steely clearness he has when he talks about principles. But I believe almost nothing of what he says in practice and in application (pp. 120-121).

In addition to Ashton, Rand and Scully, the beautiful volume includes praise from James Ackerman, Professor of Fine Arts, Harvard University, Guido Aristarco, the late founder and editor of the Italian journal,

Cinema, David Carrier, Professor of Philosophy, Carnegie Mellon University, Helmut H. Diederichs, Film and Science, University of Frankfurt, Clive Dilnot, Aesthetics and Architectural Theory, formerly faculty of the Carpenter Center for the Visual Arts, Harvard, Sir Ernst Gombrich, Art History, Professor Emeritus, University of London, Dirk Grathoff, Professor of German Literature, Oldenburg University, Gyorgy Kepes, Professor Emeritus, Massachusetts Institute of Technology, Franz Rudolf Knubel, Sculptor, Photographer, University of Essen, Daniel Libeskin, Los Angeles Architect, William J. Mitchell, Dean, School of Architecture and Planning, M.I.T., David Pariser, Art Education, Concordia University, Montreal, Quebec, Canada, Lucia Pizzo Russo, Psychology of Art, University of Palermo, Eduard F. Seklar, Former Director Carpenter Center for the Visual Arts, Harvard, Robert Slutsky, Painter, University of Pennsylvania and Cooper Union, Wilf Stevenson, Director of the British Film Institute and Thomas Strauch, Documentary Producer, Linguistics and Literary Theory, University of Essen.

Awards and Honors

During his long and fruitful career, Arnheim has been recognized with prestigious awards and honorary degrees from The American Academy of Arts & Sciences, Bates College, Kansas City Art Institute, Marquette University, Massachusetts College of Art, Oldenburg University, Rhode Island School of Design, University of Michigan, Università degli Studi at Padua and University of Palermo and more. On Arnheim's 70th birthday, academics from various disciplines gathered in the Cambridge home of Gyorgy Kepes for a *festschrift*, a custom wherein scholars present the academic papers they write to honor a colleague. Significant events marked his 80th and 90th birth year, also. The University of Michigan celebrated Arnheim Day in 1985. In 1995, German television aired a documentary produced by Thomas Strauch. Honoring Professor Emeritus Arnheim's lifetime achievement, a multi-year faculty appointment commenced in September 1999, designated *The Rudolf Arnheim Lectureship*, Harvard University, College of Arts and Sciences, Department of Visual and Environmental Studies. That year, the Film Museum of the city of Dusseldorf bestowed the Helmut Kaütner Prize to Arnheim for his work as film theorist and critic.

A GUIDEPOST TO THE FUTURE

Now, let us read what five contemporary art education leaders have to say about Rudolf Arnheim and his impact on art education—past, present and future.

Charles Dorn, Florida State University, Tallahassee, Florida

All too frequently we view a scholar's contribution to a field only at the time it is made rather than seeing it as possibly gaining even more importance over time. This is how I view Arnheim's work which has up to this time been assessed only superficially where in truth it is just now taking on even greater importance mostly because we are just beginning to understand the importance of the role of cognition in artistic forming.

Arnheim viewed the art image as the highest form of cognition. For him, it is a symbol and is not a sign that signifies the content of a thing or picture, which portray things. The image in art acts as a symbol to the extent that it portrays things that are a higher level of abstractness than the symbol itself. Therefore, a symbol gives particular shapes to things, constellations, or forces, which makes art something far removed from being a replica or something faithful to reality or likeness.

Arnheim also recognized sensory responsiveness as intelligence, which is the capacity of the various senses to obtain information about what is going on at a distance. Distance senses not only provide what is known but also remove the perceiver from the direct impact of the explored event. Because of this, the viewer is able to go beyond the immediate effect of the event, thus making it possible to probe the behavior of events more objectively. The observer is then concerned with what *is* rather than merely what has been done or with what he or she is doing.

Even more importantly, Arnheim approached perception by first looking at thinking itself, noting that thinking consists of intellectual operations on cognitive material, where material becomes nonperceptual through the act of thinking, which transforms raw precepts into concepts. Such thoughts reflect Arnheim's general view that cognitive processes, whether carried out consciously or unconsciously, voluntarily or automatically, are no different in principle.

Arnheim's work is, therefore, seminal to the profession's effort to make the case that artistic forming is intelligent activity. Without making that case in a more substantive way I believe the K-12 art curriculum will be insufficient in meeting the Goals 2000 effort. In accomplishing such an effort Arnheim's views are, therefore, critical.

Charles Dorn is Professor of Art Education and Arts Administration at Florida State University in Tallahassee, Florida. He is author of two books, *Thinking in Art: A Philosophical Approach to Art Education* (1994) published by the National Art Education Association and *Mind in Art: Cognitive Foundations in Art Education* (1999) published by Lawrence Erlbaum and Associations, Inc., Mahwah, New Jersey.

Howard Gardner, Harvard University, Cambridge, Massachusetts

I suspect that Rudi Arnheim does not think of himself as a leader. Not for him the television klieg lights, a large, flag-draped platform, an agenda, scurrying behind the scenes for votes or, in a darker time, arranging or leading a coup.

But Rudi is a wonderful example of what I call an "indirect leader." Like political or business leaders, such persons also affect the thoughts, feelings, and behaviors of others. They do not do so directly, however. Indirect leaders have their effects through the symbolic products that they create. In Rudi's case, his indirect leadership in a range of fields, from painting to philosophy, emanates from the score of books, the dozens of influential articles, and the hundreds of powerful lectures that have been his gifts to us over much of the century.

Leaders have a weapon (though Rudi would probably reject the metaphor in favor of the craftlike word "tool") of potency. It is the lives that they lead. In the long run, leaders cannot be effective if the lives that they lead are at variance with the messages—direct or symbolic—that they convey to others.

Woodcarving, one of Rudolf Arnheim's hobbies, underlies appreciation of a favorite rocking chair in his home where colleagues are warmly welcomed. Photo credit: José Sanchez-H.

Rudi's work and his life are a harmonious piece. He is an artist and a craftsman in life as well as in his writings. He is interested in the qualities of experience—of art, of science, of the imagination-and he savors such experiences for himself and recreates them for others in words and pictures and images. Most impressively, Rudi is not only the chief expositor of Gestalt ideas of our time. He passionately believes in the principal concepts and shows us, by the way that he lives, about the importance of organic unity, balance, composure, integration—and integrity—in life.

I am uniquely fortunate. I know Rudi not only from the pages of his magnetic writings. I have been his student for over 30 years and, I am proud to say, his friend as well. When he and Mary lived in Cambridge, we saw each other regularly—and I cherish the many conversations in his small study near the entrance of Le Corbusier's Carpenter Center and his comfortable art- and book-filled apartment on Garden Street. Once the Arnheims had moved to Ann Arbor, we saw them less regularly, and we savored the time that Rudi came to visit the Museum of Fine Arts or we found ourselves in the Ann Arbor area.

Recently our contact has been by those miracles of modern life—the mail and the telephone (though not, as my wife Ellen Winner indicates, by e-mail!). I treasure the literally hundreds of messages that we have exchanged over the last quarter century. Occasionally, one is asked about what one would grab from one's house were a fire to break out. Like Ellen, I keep all of Rudi's letters and notes—some a half a page, some many pages—in a special spot at my desk. Should the fire alarm sound, I will grab them and take them with me. In the Arnheim spirit, they are private communications on matters that are important to his correspondent and to himself. But I know that, in a sense, they belong to the world, and I hope that their contents will survive us both.

May that time be far off—Greetings, Rudi, and let us meet again in person and on paper many times.

Howard Gardner is the John H. and Elisabeth A. Hobbs Professor in Cognition and Education at the Harvard Graduate School of Education. He also holds positions as Adjunct Professor of Psychology at Harvard University, Adjunct Professor of Neurology at the Boston University School of Medicine, and Co-Director of Harvard Project Zero. Among numerous honors, Gardner received a MacArthur Prize Fellowship in 1981. He has been awarded 11 honorary degrees—most recently from Princeton University and from Tel Aviv University on the occasion of the 50th anniversary of the State of Israel. In 1990, he was the first American to receive the University of Louisville's Grawemeyer Award in education. The author of 18 books and several hundred articles, Gardner is best known for his theory of multiple intelligences, a critique of the notion that there exists but a single human intelligence that can be assessed by standard psychometric instruments. During the past 16 years, he and his colleagues at Project Zero have been working on the design of performance-based assessments, education for understanding, and the use of multiple intelligences to achieve more personalized curriculum, instruction, and assessment. Gardner's book, *Extraordinary Minds*, was published in 1997 for the MasterMinds Series by Basic Books. In 1999, Simon & Schuster published *The Disciplined Mind: What All Students Should Understand*. A second book is tentatively entitled *Multiple Intelligence Reframed*.

Anna Kindler, University of British Columbia, Vancouver, Canada

When I left my native Poland in the early 1980s, I landed at O'Hare airport with a small black suitcase filled with essentials to guarantee my survival in the new land. Few weeks before my departure I remember talking to my father about the choice of books that I should take along. Without hesitation, he reached to his bookshelf and handed me one of his most prized volumes: Rudolf Arnheim's *Art and Visual Perception*. My father, an industrial designer and professor of art and design, has always been very fond of Arnheim's work and, in a way, this shared fascination with fruits of Arnheim's intellect formed a special professional bond between my father and me. It is fair to say that, in our family, Arnheim has already touched and influenced two generations. The legacy of Rudolf Arnheim in psychology of art and the impact that his work has had on understanding of the nature of artistic development are probably the most celebrated aspects of the legend. Arnheim's work has afforded researchers to ask new questions that would have been difficult to pose before his time. As Claire Golomb (1992) noted, Arnheim has freed us from "the conceptual straitjacket that narrowed our vision of the nature of child art and how it can be studied" (p. 2). This gift of freedom to search for internal logic underlying development of pictorial representation has greatly inspired my own research. It has led me and my research partner, Bernard Darras, to pursue work on models of development of pictorial imagery free from concentration on realism and accounting for a wide range of iconic representations. Rudolf Arnheim's theoretical work has implications to art education practice and offers powerful support to art education advocacy efforts. By redefining artistic learning as a cognitive endeavor, recognizing the possibility of multiple solutions to problems of pictorial representation

and pointing to the cross-disciplinary connections in the functioning of the mind Arnheim has set a stage for new art education agenda. While much remains to be done to further refine this agenda, Rudolf Arnheim deserves credit for moving the field in the direction of expanding its mandate to broadly understood education in visual thinking and exploration of imagery in the context of interdisciplinary inquiry.

There is yet another part of the Arnheim legend that has received less attention in print even though it offers a legacy that research and education communities in psychology and art should never forget, for it constitutes an important guidepost to the future. I am referring here to Rudolf Arnheim's kindness, modesty, and generosity of spirit that have matched the genius of his intellect. When several years ago I embarked on the task of editing an anthology on child development in art, it was a dream of mine to include an original contribution by Rudolf Arnheim. It took me a lot of time to write my letter and gather the necessary courage to mail it. As a junior researcher with a rather modest publication record at that time, I was fully prepared for a negative response. Instead, I received a kind and most encouraging letter promising a chapter for my book. This letter and other notes that Rudolf Arnheim kindly wrote to me later on, constitute a testimonial to his gentle mentorship and generous, compassionate, and supportive attitude towards new generation of researchers dedicated to the exploration of territories that have been dear to his heart.

In the world that increasingly separates intellect from heart, genius of mind from generosity of spirit, and where modesty and humility are often replaced by arrogant assertiveness and self-promotion, Arnheim's legend offers a guidepost to professional conduct in academia and beyond. As we pay homage to Arnheim as a scholar who has charted the road to new understandings of visual perception and nature of artistic process and whose work will continue to influence art education practice in years to come, we also need to acknowledge and pay tribute to this other side of the legend that completes the image of this truly remarkable man.

Anna M. Kindler is Associate Professor of art education and teacher education at the University of British Columbia, Vancouver, Canada. Her research interests focus on artistic development, social cognition of art, multiculturalism and cross-cultural inquiry. She has published widely in national and international journals and has authored several book chapters. Her recent books include *Child Development in Art* and a monograph entitled *Between Theory and Practice: Case Studies for Learning to Teach.*

David Pariser, Concordia University, Montreal, Quebec, Canada

There is a time honored tradition of walking in nature. Such excursions do not require specialized hiking equipment, but they are immeasurably enriched by a companion who is both naturalist and poet. Such a guide will suggest that you pause to admire an uncoiling fern, a cathedral-like stump with its teeming insect life, or tell you about the biology of a great tree. Learning from Rudi Arnheim as I have done for the last 25 years has been just such an excursion, except that his itinerary has been the bosky dells, deep thickets, and occasional deserts of the fine arts. A trip in his company is always worthwhile. His scholarship in the arts, psychology, and literature and his unswerving commitment to a humane, and above all a rational outlook inform every observation. What can a person of this intellectual calibre tell us about the road that likes ahead—disappearing as it does into the impenetrable mists of post-modernism, crypto-post modernism?

Arnheim has never claimed to be a visionary, but he does demonstrate his special gifts as someone who looks acutely at the world as it is now, and who reflects with equal acuity upon the acts of seeing and making. It is on the basis of these lesser but nonetheless uncommon gifts that he delineates the forward path for art educators, psychologists and media mavens. From the first day that I saw him deliver his panoramic introductory lectures in the course on Visual and Environmental Studies at the Carpenter Center, I delighted in the artfulness, energy, and conviction with which he presented his key idea: Using our eyes is not a simple mechanical transaction—it is an act informed by intelligence and moral sensibility. And these components are as much a part of the act of vision as

they are of the act of creating an object for visual contemplation. This is the core of his message, and Arnheim has never ceased to articulate it in many forms and with the benefit of telling examples. This credo is a compass that will help us to navigate past the Cyclopean eye of the television and computer screen, and perhaps to escape the enchanting sorcery of a technology fueled by greed that Circe-like promises us sublime pleasures but in fact bestializes and commodifies us.

As Arnheim has indicated so eloquently, whatever the medium and whatever the technology, the visual artist is always dealing with the same problem: What constitutes an effective translation from the percept to a structure in a medium that functions in a similar way to its referent? What Arnheim tells us for the future is that unless we keep this basic fact about representation in mind, technological and methodological changes (sometimes referred to as progress), are a meaningless irrelevance. For example, a visual artist may have at his/her disposal the most up-to-date computer programs, software, and hardware. The fact remains that as long as that artist lacks ideas that translate effectively into images and lacks an understanding of how images are constructed, all the technology in the world cannot help. Artists have been exploring the mechanisms of perception and representation since the days of the Lascaux caves—and we ignore their accumulated wisdom at some peril. We also fool ourselves if we believe that the rules that govern the reception of expression and representation on cave walls and movie screens differ vastly. Besotted by the promise of unlimited technological power, we cling to the naïve belief that by doing things faster and by creating images that are simply "more realistic" artists will somehow be relieved of the fundamental problem which, over the ages, it has been their sorrow and joy to address. As we hurtle towards the arbitrary threshold that we have named "the new millennium," Arnheim's way of envisioning vision and visual artistry is a gift to the future. He invites all comers to walk a path through the changing landscape of the arts in the company of someone who enlightens, stimulates, and challenges without dogma. As I learned in my first encounter with him, Arnheim believes that fundamental human issues are an integral part of such "taken for granted" acts as seeing and representing. This means that our transactions with images, from inserting a photograph into our billfolds, to idly watching as tidal waves of cyberspace imagery thunder into our heads, are acts that carry cognitive and moral weight—and will always be true.

David Pariser is a Professor of art education in the Fine Arts Faculty at Concordia University, Montreal. He has taught at the Nova Scotia College of Art, The Massachusetts College of Art, and in public schools in Newton, Massachusetts and Centralia, Illinois. His research deals with the childhood graphics of great artists, and cross-cultural issues in children's graphic development. He has published articles and reviews in *The American Journal of Education, The Canadian Review of Art Education, Contemporary Psychology, The Creativity Research Journal, Leonardo,* the *Journal of Aesthetic Education, Studies in Art Education,* and *Visual Arts Research.* He is a contributor to the *Encyclopedia of Creativity.* His research on aspects of graphic development has been supported by the Spencer Foundation and Social Sciences of Canada.

FROM THE PEN OF RUDOLF ARNHEIM

Selected Reading for Art Educators

A comprehensive, international bibliography can be found in *The Journal of Aesthetic Education, Vol. 27, Number 4.* Based on two previously published compilations by Mary Arnheim, it cites not only books, but also Arnheim's essays, articles, interviews, book reviews, editorials, speeches, letters in English and in translation. Below are Arnheim's books of most interest to visual art educators, published by the University of California Press (800-822-6657).

Art and Visual Perception: A Psychology of The Creative Eye, 1954, rewritten 1974.
Picasso's Guernica: The Genesis of A Painting, 1962.
Toward a Psychology of Art: Collected Essays, 1966; paperback 1972.
Visual Thinking, 1969; paperback 1971.
Entrophy and Art: An Essay on Order and Disorder, 1971; paperback 1974.
Art and Visual Perception: A Psychology of The Creative Eye, 1974.

In July 1999, Dr. Arnheim wrote in *The British Journal of Aesthetics,* "Our mind has two means of exploring human experience, intellect, and intuition. Art makes use of both. Its subject matter covers the entire range of what is accessible to our senses and includes cognitive knowledge as well as the feelings aroused by it." Photo credit: José Sanchez-H.

The Dynamics of Architectural Form, 1977.
The Power of the Center: A Study of Composition in The Visual Arts, 1982; revised edition 1983.
New Essays on The Psychology of Art, 1986.
The Power of the Center: The New Version, 1988.
Parables of Sun Light: Observations on Psychology, The Arts, and The Rest, 1989.
To The Rescue of Art: Twenty-six essays, 1991.
The Split and The Structure, 1996.
Film Essays and Criticism, translated by Brenda Benthien, University of Wisconsin Press, 1997.
Arnheim's ever-growing bibliography, listing 12 major books, hundreds of published lectures, essays, articles and interviews, is voluminous. Sensibly, Arnheim advises art educators who seek to focus their reading on their professional responsibilities, in this way:

The elements of visual perception and expression, together with a chapter on the artwork of children, are described in my book *Art and Visual Perception* (1974). On the principles of composition see the rewritten version of *The Power of The Center* (1988). In an early essay, "Perceptual Abstraction and Art," reprinted in *Toward A Psychology of Art* (1966), I have given the theoretical foundation for perceptual concepts, more broadly discussed in *Visual Thinking* (1969). For a more recent formulation see "The Double-Edged Mind: Intuition and the Intellect" in *New Essays of The Psychology of Art* (1986) (personal correspondence, March 18, 1997).

To Arnheim's abbreviated reading list, I would add his monograph, *Thoughts on Art Education*, written for The Getty Center for Education and the Arts (1989). Taken together, these volumes substantiate the 4 key ideas noted earlier in this chapter by Elliot Eisner. The groundwork for the current interest in process portfolios probably dates back to the 1962 book, *Picasso's Guernica: the Genesis of a Painting*. In this landmark book, Rudolf Arnheim traced Pablo Picasso's aesthetic decisions, day-by-day, throughout the intense weeks while the artist created the mural masterpiece.

Visual Thinking (1969/1971)

For the art teacher whose life's demands preclude extensive reading, the 21 pages of the final chapter *Visual Thinking* (1969) are likely to trigger future investigation. In the chapter "Vision in Education," Arnheim explains,

"This book has attempted to re-establish the unity of perception and thought" (p. 294).

In his view, the purposes of art are as a fundamental means of orientation born from man's need to understand himself and the world in which he lives. This basic cognitive function parallels the means and ends of science. Art is neglected at all levels of our educational system, he reasons,

…because art educators have not stated their case convincingly enough. If one looks at the literature on art education one often finds the value of art taken so much for granted that a few stock phrases are considered sufficient to make the point. There is a tendency to treat the arts as an independent area of study and to assume that intuition and intellect, feeling and reasoning, art and science coexist but do not cooperate. If it is found that high school students know little about art history or cannot tell an etching from a lithograph, or an oil painting from a watercolor, the consequences to be drawn will depend, I should think, on how important this sort of knowledge can be shown to be. If it is claimed that the value of the arts consists in developing good taste, the weight of the argument depends on whether taste is a luxury for those who can afford it or an indispensable condition of life. If art is said to be part of our culture and therefore necessary to the equipment of every educated person, the responsible educator must ask himself whether all parts of this culture are needed for all and are accessible to all, and whether they are all equally relevant. If we hear that the arts develop and enrich the human personality and cultivate creativity, we need to know whether they do so better than other fields of study and why…Once it is recognized that productive thinking in any area of cognition is perceptual thinking, the central function of art in general education will become evident (pp. 295-296).

Comprehension of Arnheim's theoretical thinking gives the classroom/studio practitioner a pragmatic, valid approach to teaching. Proof of this claim was evident at The National Design for Thinking Institute at the University for The Arts in Philadelphia, in August 1998. Almost unanimously, design education practitioners raised their hands in answer to my question: "Who is familiar with Rudolf Arnheim's book, *Visual Thinking*?"

Arnheim's profundity and vision are deeply appreciated by a wide, cross-disciplinary audience. Every few years admirers are delighted to receive a fresh gift from his pen.

Parables of Sunlight

This is a compilation of ideas, reflections and questions about the arts, natural sciences, philosophy, religion, and psychology culled from jottings in Arnheim's lifetime notebooks. Some typical examples:

15 May 1961
As the only son and the oldest child of a family in which I experienced little hostility, I have lived my life as a friend among friends. The few persons who have ever harmed me were alien exceptions. And the basic assumption of Gestalt theory—that every dynamic whole tends toward an optimal structure—has supported my belief that every human mind struggles toward the good (p. 34).

2 December 1964
From the beginning of Western thought there has been a distinctly different evaluation of seeing and hearing in their relation to knowledge. Sight conveyed external appearance, and special efforts had to be made to defend it against the accusation that it misleads us. The Pythagoreans associated sound with mathematics. Sound penetrated the deceptive world of the phenomena—mostly a visual world—and disclosed the essence of things. It grasped the permanent truth. Sight was imagery; sound was imageless music. Any distinction of the two senses in our culture starts from this lead (p. 75).

14 February 1976
Has our sense of passing time changed since our clocks have ceased to tick? Clocks can be seen but no longer heard. Have our homes and offices become timeless—acoustically—places where nothing requires rewinding? (p. 204).

21 July 1986
Sometimes at darker moments now, I feel as though I continue playing the accustomed role of my life because I happen to be still around. It is as though the husks of things are replacing the things themselves, as though the top keeps spinning until the impulse for its rotation will cease and the top drop and stop for no particular reason (p. 363).

The Power of the Center: A Study of Composition in the Visual Arts (1988)

Arnheim confides:
> In a sense I am taking off where my earlier book *Art And Visual Perception* ended. At times I shall have to refer to matters that are more explicitly treated in that earlier book. But whereas in that more elementary study I could draw on experimental findings in the psychology of perception, the perceptual phenomena I discuss here go beyond what has been tried out in laboratories. This lack of experimental evidence may make this book seem less scientific than the earlier one and the facts less trustworthy, but for the time being that cannot be helped. Confirmation and correction will turn up in due course. Meanwhile we can remind ourselves that in the sciences, ideas are necessarily the first response to the challenging puzzles we encounter…The subject of visual composition concerns me because I believe that perceptual form is the strongest, most indispensable means of communicating through works of art (p. X-Introduction).

To the Rescue of Art: Twenty-Six Essays (1992)

We must not be deceived by the unparalleled number of art galleries, museums and art schools in our present setting, by the astonishing number of professional artists and the absurdly high prices paid for prestigious works of art. We observe at the same time an unmistakable fatigue, a lack of discipline and responsibility. The weakness shows in the design of many of our buildings, our furnishings and our garments. As its least attractive symptoms, we notice an unbridled extravagance, a vulgarity of taste, and a triviality of thought. There is too much readiness to make do with too little, to be satisfied short of the ultimate effort, without the engagement of the full resources that used to be *condito sine qua non* of respectable art. The insufficiency shows up in the poor level of much of the work produced and the low standard of what is critically accepted in the mass media (p. VIII-Introduction).

Anyone who has sat in a lecture hall with 200 students (as I did when Arnheim was a Visiting Professor in 1968 at Teachers College, Columbia University) knows the fascination of looking at art through his eyes. Part of the 26 essays, under the heading "For Your Eyes Only," discuss 7 artworks from the Boston Museum in order "to suggest ways of approaching artistic experience by what can be seen directly and spontaneously" (p. 62). In these miniature monographs, Arnheim analyzes the basic principles that give meaning to each artwork. Art educators, at every level of schooling, will find his insights indispensable in their classrooms, studios or lecture halls.

The Split and the Structure (1993)

This fourth collection of essays is comprised of 28 challenging entities, each guided by Arnheim's abiding interest in structure, order and reason. "I am trying," he tells us, "to show how artists grope for structure to shape powerful and enlightening images and how scientists' search for truth is a search for structure" (p. IX-Foreword). In a visionary piece, "Learning by Looking and Thinking," he cautions:

> Visual learning relies not only on how much ability and willingness pupils bring to their studies. Much depends also on how well the materials and conditions offered in the learning situation are suited to a ready grasp of the things to be seen and understood.

Later, he concludes:

> …we are reminded of the diagrams on the blackboard used by teachers in every field of knowledge to enliven concepts with visual concreteness. Visual thinking is the ability of the mind to unite observing and reasoning in every field of learning. Whether people spend their days on using the physical forces of their bodies as garage mechanics or surgeons or dancers or whether they labor quietly at their desks as mathematicians or poets, the principal instrument on which their minds rely will always be the same (p. 119).

CONCLUSION

We have only to look over Arnheim's lifetime, matching his courageous arguments with current enlightened art education practice to justify his legendary status. Precisely as he predicted, giant strides in cognitive

science continue to validate his theories of perception. The once revolutionary concept of "learning by looking and seeing" is widely accepted. Today, the door is open to cross-disciplinary and inter-disciplinary curricula and to implementing theories of multiple intelligences. Misconceptions about rigid stages of child development and graphic presentation about language development are vanishing. Everyday, several generations of aestheticians, artists, architects, craftsmen, critics, curators, dancers, graphic designers, educators, historians, musicians, philosophers, poets, psychologists, and others apply Rudolf Arnheim's insights in their work. Here is a recent example. Until publishing Arnheim's illustrated article on color (pp. 349-52), *The Journal of Aesthetics and Art Criticism* (Fall 1998) had *never* been printed in color.

In her article "A Feeling for Words: Arnheim on Language," Margery B. Franklin concludes:

> Many people in the fields of psychology, art education and art therapy have been profoundly inspired and guided by the work of Rudolf Arnheim. I have heard more than one visual artist remark that Arnheim is the only psychologist whose work they find relevant to their concerns…Arnheim is among the few psychologists who dared to stand outside the mainstream of American psychology in the 1940s and 1950s, to take a critical stance and to pursue the development of alternative theory. Like a naturalist or an astronomer, he held to the view that the observation of naturally occurring phenomena is the starting point of scientific inquiry and analysis (*The Arts in Psychotherapy*, 1994, p. 265).

The breadth and depth of Arnheim's influence on so many distinguished professionals is testimony to his pervasive impact on our culture. It is appropriate that Dr. Rudolf Arnheim himself should have the last word:

> As I look over my work of the last 65 years or so I find it devoted essentially to one broad theme, the human mind's coping with the experiences of living in a complex world with the help offered by the intelligent use of the senses. My analysis of the silent film had made me describe the image of a world obtained by entirely visual means, and, a few years later, a book on radio as an art of sound

presented the counter image of an exclusively audible world. This led me after my move to America to a comprehensive survey of visual perception in its application to the arts. *Art and Visual Perception*, first published in 1954, is now available in 14 languages. There followed later books with more particular investigations of composition, architecture, the creative process in a painting by Picasso, and others. A particularly adventurous excursion into a broader range of human cognition produced a study of visual thinking, an attempt to show that not only does art always involve penetrating thought, but, conversely, all truly creative reasoning in the sciences and elsewhere is based on the handling of perceptual imagery. A great reconciliation of thought and image is what I hope to have promoted during the work of a lifetime (Arnheim, quoted in *World Authors*, 1980-1985).

References

Arnheim, R. (1954/1974). *Art and visual perception: A psychology of the creative eye.* Berkeley and Los Angeles: University of Los Angeles Press.

Arnheim, R. (1971). *Entropy and art: An essay on order and disorder.* Berkeley, Los Angeles, and London: University of California Press.

Arnheim, R. (1957/1969). *Film as art.* Berkeley: University of California Press.

Arnheim, R. (1977). *Film essays and criticism.* Brenda Benthien, (Trans.). Madison: University of Wisconsin Press.

Arnheim, R. (1986). *New essays on the psychology of art.* Berkeley and Los Angeles: University of California Press.

Arnheim, R. (1989). *Parables of sun light: Observations on psychology, the arts and the rest.* Berkeley, Los Angeles, and London: University of California Press.

Arnheim, R. (1962). *Picasso's Guernica: The genesis of a painting.* Berkeley and Los Angeles: University of California Press. (Reprinted under title: *The genesis of a painting: Picasso's "Guernica,"* 1973.)

Arnheim, R. (1977). *The dynamics of architectural form.* Berkeley and Los Angeles: University of California Press.

Arnheim, R. (1983/1988). *The power of the center: A study of composition in the visual arts.* Berkeley, Los Angeles, and London: University of California Press.

Arnheim, R. (1989). *Thoughts on art education: Occasional paper 2.* Los Angeles: The Getty Center for Education in the Arts.

Arnheim, R. (1996). *The split and the structure.* Berkeley, Los Angeles, and London: University of California Press.

Arnheim, R. (1991). *To the rescue of art: Twenty-six essays.* Berkeley, Los Angeles, and Oxford: University of California Press.

Arnheim, R. (1966/1972). *Toward a psychology of art: Collected essays.* Berkeley and Los Angeles: University of California Press.

Arnheim, R. (1969/1971). *Visual Thinking.* Berkeley, Los Angeles, and London: University of California Press.

Bang, M. (1991). *Picture This: Perception and Composition.* Boston: Little Brown and Company. (2nd edition: (August 2000) *How Pictures Work.* NY: North South Books.

Arnheim, R. (1999). Art as such. *British Journal of Aesthetics*, Vol. 39, No. 3, pp. 252-254.

Coming to Our Senses: The Significance of the Arts for American Education. (1977). The Arts, Education and Americans Panel. New York: McGraw-Hill.

Corwin, S. (Winter 1993). The Application of Arnheim's Principles to Interdisciplinary Education. *The Journal of Aesthetic Education, (27)* pp. 155-163.

Efland, A. (1990). *A History of Art Education.* NY: Teachers College Press.

Fein, S. (1993). *First Drawings: Genesis of Visual Thinking.* Portsmouth, NH: Heinemann, A Division of Reed, Elsevier, Inc.

Fein, S. (1976). *Heidi's Horse.* Portsmouth, NH: Heinemann, A Division of Reed, Elsevier, Inc.

Galassi, S. (1996). *Picasso's variation on the masters: Confrontations of a painting.* NY: Abrams.

Galassi, S. (1997). *Picasso's One Liners.* NY: Artisan.

Golomb, C. (1992). *The child's creation of a pictorial world.* Berkeley: University of California Press.

Kleinman, K. & VanDuzer, L. (Eds.) (1997). *Rudolf Arnheim: Revealing vision.* Ann Arbor: The University of Michigan Press.

Korzenik, D. (1985). *Drawn to art: A nineteenth century American dream.* Hanover, NH: University Press of New England.

Mortensen, E. (1977). *Improving visual perceptual skills in art classes in secondary schools: School year 1975-1996.* New York City Board of Education. ERIC ED 184095.

McNiff, S. (Ed.) (1994). Rudolf Arnheim's life and work: special issue *The arts in psychotherapy* (21). NY: Pergamon.

Smith, R. (Ed.) (1993, winter). Essays in honor of Rudolf Arnheim: special issue. *The Journal of Aesthetic Education* (27). Urbana-Champaign: University of Illinois.

World authors 1980-1985. (1991). Bronx, NY: H. W. Wilson Company.

VICTOR D'AMICO
(1904 - 1984)

A life dedicated to humanizing the arts. A lifetime devoted to development of creative power of children, young people, and adults.

Prabha Sahasrabudhe

A Brief Biography

Victor D'Amico

Victor D'Amico was born in 1904, he was at Cooper Union between years 1920-1922 and then at Pratt Institute 1922-26. He started his teaching career in 1925 in the Child Study Association sponsored settlement house Summer Play Schools. He was teaching in ten schools in Manhattan and the Bronx a week, a different one each morning and afternoon, "traveling around with two suitcases of supplies, perspective charts, color-wheels, and packaged lesson plans but these teaching aids don't work," he says, "What worked was walks in the neighborhood, talking to children about their interests, looking at the Brooklyn Bridge, wondering what's holding it up?" Here was the beginning of Victor D'Amico's credo: "...stimulate a child to explore his own expressive idea once he has been motivated by a theme or his own environment. The art experience should be a problem solving situation with the end product an individual result" (Lerman and Govencheck, 1979, p. 2).

Because of the Summer Play School work in 1926, the Ethical Culture Society asked Mr. D'Amico to join the newly established Fieldston School in Riverdale, New York,

It is my belief that the arts are a humanizing force and that their major function is to vitalize living; to make each child and man the richer for having taken part in them. The effectiveness of art is also measured by the way it serves the most urgent need of its time and our greatest need today, I believe, is to discover the dignity of man, to help him find his self- respect and to enjoy this greatest natural endowment, the power to create.

D'Amico, 1979

as the Head of the Art Department. The late 1920s, early 1930s was an era of celebrated independent schools such as Horace Mann, Lincoln, Walden, and Dalton experimenting with Progressive Education ideas, for D'Amico Ethical Culture Schools provided perfect environments to explore, experiment, test, refine, revise ideas about art, and methodologies for art teaching. As William Rubin, a former Director of Painting and Sculpture at MoMA, and a student of D'Amico's at the Fieldston School, testifies, "Things were done in the class that were far beyond the methods employed at the time [by other teachers]...I could spend hours outlining the inventive, original ways of approaching art which Victor pioneered ...his immense exuberance and love for artistic study was extraordinarily infectious..." (Lerman and Govencheck, 1979, p. 2).

Victor D'Amico stayed at Fieldston through 1948; however, during these years particularly after 1932, he was also involved in teaching at Teachers College, Columbia University, working with study groups on committees for the Progressive Education Association, and for the Rockefeller Foundation. This led to his being invited by Alfred Barr to develop an educational project for the Museum of Modern Art. The next ten plus years (1937-1948), D'Amico worked five evenings a week at the MoMA developing and implementing his signature museum art education programs: the Young People's Gallery, The New York City High Schools' program, studio classes and circulating exhibitions. These were formative years for D'Amico's philosophy.

It was at the Museum of Modern Art, where with Alfred Barr and Rene d'Harnoncourt, his professional allies and personal friends, that Victor achieved his prominence in art and museum education. He was the director of a one-of-a-kind education department in a major international institution dedicated to Modern Art for over 30 years. He retired in 1969, and during this period "the experimental project which began with a gallery of exhibitions for children and young people of high school age, and with a circulating program of exhibits for New York City schools" had grown into projects, programs, and philosophy which have had national and international impact. Through his writings, his books, his conference addresses and other pronouncements, D'Amico influenced and shaped the landscape of art education in the 1930s, 1940s, and 1950s. His educational programs at The Museum: The War Veterans' Center, The People's Art Center, The High School Programs, Children's Art Carnivals at MoMA and around the world were legendary, and living concrete showcases for art education philosophy and pedagogy. The walls of art studios at the People's Art Center and of the Children's Art Carnival had portholes, one way mirror/windows for adults, parents and teachers-in-training to view art education in practice. This is the story of this man, his philosophy and pedagogy, his projects and programs. He was clearly one of the four giants—D'Amico, Lowenfeld, Read and Arnheim—who "...helped conceptualize modern art education" (Hausman 1995, p. 54). He retired from the MoMA in 1969. In 1972 when the Museum of Modern Art closed its art center, some of the people who had worked with Victor D'Amico chartered The Napeague Institute of Art, where he continued to teach children, young people, and adults almost till his death in 1984. Among the awards given him in recognition of his work are the Honorary Doctorate of Fine Arts from The Philadelphia College

> D'Amico was a remarkable man who left an indelible mark on many of us and on a field which has had few such visionaries...there are few people whose convictions remain valid after sixty years which have been so full of change... he was a charismatic, charming, clear-headed man, absolutely driven by beliefs about the usefulness of art in people's lives, and in the making of art not only as an essential human activity but also the key to understanding arts made by others.
>
> *Yenawine 1995, p. 29*

of Art (1964), and Distinguished Service to Education in Art medal, awarded by the National Gallery of Art, The Smithsonian Institute, Washington, DC (1966).

VICTOR D'AMICO'S PEDAGOGY: SOURCES AND INFLUENCES

Victor D'Amico was associated with Teachers College, Columbia University from 1932-1942 (as a graduate student and later an adjunct faculty). These were the days of Progressive Education. John Dewey's *Art as Experience* was published in 1934. This book along with Harold Rugg and Ann Shumaker's *The Child Centered School* (1928) probably were two significant influences on D'Amico's thinking. As Morgan notes, Dewey's influence is evidenced in D'Amico's insights into people and his ideas about art (Morgan, 1994). Involvement with Progressive Education and Teachers College were the credentials which led to his being asked to undertake the 1935 National Survey of Art Education project for the Rockefeller Foundation.

This impressive document is almost the earliest recorded critique of the status of art education, and I surmise that Victor used this experience, his classroom observations from across the country, and critical discussions with art teachers working on their own convictions for revising, refining, polishing his own ideas and philosophy of teaching art.

> This survey report (D'Amico, 1935) of 94 schools from 23 states of the union from across the country, a carefully typed manuscript, a narrative based on site visits, classroom observations and interviews with teachers on quality of instruction, equipment, facility and art teacher's philosophy is perhaps the only document on art education of its kind. D'Amico visited 48 different towns, held discussion with many more art educators all in three spring months of 1935. The document presents clear vignettes of art programs in Shady Hill School in Cambridge (MA), The Community School in St. Louis (MO), Merril-Palmer School in Detroit (MI), Public Schools of Atlanta (GA), and 89 others. And consider the names that jump out at you from these pages: Rosabell McDonald, Belle Boas, Thomas Munro, Count Rene d'Harnoncourt, Sallie Tananhill, Mary Albright, Joseph Albers, Florence Cane, and (yes) Grant Wood, Rudolph Schaeffer, Hale Woodruff, all of them pioneers in our field.

Towards the end of this report D'Amico articulates an art in education position (12 typewritten pages in the Report to the Rockefeller Foundation). The salient points of this early 1935 art education posture were: Art education was to be dedicated to the fullest development of the individual creative powers, to sensitizing the individual to aesthetic values, to the development of seeing and working like an artist, to seeing oneself as part of the society, to maintaining self-integrity, and to living life at the fullest level of appreciation. Thus, I suggest that the time— the progressivist/expressionist era in education, and the place, the New York City environment—were indeed significant shaping influences on D'Amico's philosophy of art education.

THE PROGRESSIVE ERA AND ARTISTIC EXPRESSIONISM IN EDUCATION

What was the social/intellectual climate of the times? Victor D'Amico cites John Dewey, Progressive Education, the Child-Centered Pedagogy, and Modern Art as his inspirations and sources, which nurtured the development of creative self-expression as a central theme of D'Amico's work (D'Amico, 1967).

Cremin (1961) has discussed the impact of artists and writers on progressive education, the work of Harold Rugg and the child-centered school movement, the play school philosophy and practice of Caroline Pratt as the intellectual forces of the era. These are clearly reflected in the above 1935 articulation of D'Amico pedagogy. These influencing ideas, as well as the unique intellectual and artistic environment of Greenwich Village, and educational excitement that was Teachers College of the early 1930s shaped young D'Amico's philosophy and ideas on art, schools and education. This conceptualization, fundamentals of practice of creative art education, came to fruition as he worked through his ideas into programs and projects at the Ethical Culture Schools and in the exhilarating and a supporting environment of Museum of Modern Art.

Wygant (1993) described the period as having achieved a mythos, as an especially significant decade. The "Jazz Age," the decade of the "flaming youth," the "flapper," a period described by Scott Fitzgerald as "the greatest and gaudiest spree in history."

Cowley, 1934, p. 5

In many respects these were the times of unprecedented affluence, of mobility and an attitude of moral independence. This era of economic well-being also produced affluence of ideas, for there were intellectual and cultural ideas in the environment which were changing the course of human discourse. During the 1920s, as the intellectual avant-garde became fascinated with arts in general and Freudian thought in particular, the earlier focus on social reformism was virtually pushed into the background by rhetoric of child-centered pedagogy. A strand of progressive education movement which Cremin has identified as artistic expressionism in education, had become a defining influence. It was the artistic intelligentsia "artists and literati" of New York, Chicago, and San Francisco who were largely responsible for creative and conceptual base for child-centered pedagogy (Cremin, 1961, p. 201).

This expressionist era was dominated by a set of ideas shared by the artistic and intellectual culture as well as the progressivist educators. Cowley, in his collection essays (Exile's Return 1934) on writers and authors of "the lost generation" of 1930s lists: The ideas of salvation of the child proposing that they be allowed to develop their fullest potentialities; the idea of self-expression through creative work as the purpose of life; the idea of paganism leading to worshiping the human body as a temple; the idea of living for the moment, extolling the virtue of living intensely and to seize the moment; the idea of liberty, demanding rejection of every rule, law, convention that interferes with human freedom; the idea of female equality, requiring equal treatment of women; the idea of psychological health suggesting that all maladjustments are results of social repression; and the idea of changing place, promoting the notion that they do things better in Europe. *(Cowley, 1934 p. 60-61). The Progressivist educator who personified this position was Harold Rugg.*

In his *Transformation of the School* (1961) the story of progressivism in American education 1876-1957, Cremin talks about progressive education as a part of a vast humanitarian effort (in some respects part of a worldwide response to industrialism) dedicated to applying the promise of American life— the ideal of government by, of, and for the people to the puzzling new urban-industrial civilization that came into being during the later part of the 19th century.

Harold Rugg and The Child-Centered School

In the post World War I years radicalism in progressivist education eclipsed under the weight of this Rousseauian child-centered pedagogy championed by the likes of Harold Rugg. In *The Child-Centered School* (1928), an appraisal of the New Education, written with Ann Shumaker, Rugg undertakes to document efforts of new schools across the country. These schools were dedicated to freeing the creative mind: "First [from] the rise in inductive science and objective measurement and their applications in the Industrial Revolution; Second [from] the perpetuation of the puritan attitude of mind, Third [from] the taking over the control of government by the Puritan leaders" (p. iv). Identification with creative artists was so strong in Rugg's new education that he firmly believed that, "To comprehend the significance of the child-centered schools, one would need, indeed, to understand the attempts of creative artists to break through the thick crust of imitation, superficiality, and commercialism which bound the arts almost throughout the first three centuries of industrialism" (p. v).

Rugg and Shumaker equated progressivism in schooling with the historic battles of the artist against superficiality and commercialism of American society. The key to the modern creative revolution, they argued, was the triumph of (creative) self-expression, in education as well as in art; hence in creative expression they found the quintessential meaning of progressive education movement (Cremin, 1961, p. 183). D'Amico was familiar with these new child-centered schools. Several of these schools and their artist-teachers were included in D'Amico's (Art in American School 1935) *Survey of Art Education*, a fact that supports a conjecture that young D'Amico as a student at Teachers College, and teaching art in settlement

The Child Centered School (Rugg and Shumaker, 1928) devotes over 200 pages to discussions on the arts: dance, music, theater, and visual arts in schools. New schools in this book are schools where arts have become a central feature of the curriculum. Rugg and Shumaker cite several artists-teachers who support these ideas: Hughes Mearns (1925) of the Lincoln School says of literary materials, "Poetry cannot be summoned, it can only be permitted." For Peppino Mangravite (1932) an artist-teacher at Washington Montessori School, "A teacher must comprehend what the child wants to do... The idea, the mental picture must be the child's. Once he is started, a teacher can help." Willy Levin of City and Country school proposes that "You have to feel the thing the child wants to do, to think his thoughts, in short to become a child yourself" [whereas]...Florence Cane (1926) of Walden School talks of her method as "having given the child his materials I trust him to do what he wants and let him continue to draw or paint as long as his interests last. To the extent that he is content with his work I am assured the thing projected corresponds with the image within."

Rugg and Shumaker, 1928, p. 229

houses just south of Greenwich Village was more than familiar with this Rugg and Shumaker work, and had made use of it in his own teaching.

Efland's (1990) history of art education attributes the beginnings of this creative expressionist credo to Franz Cizek in Vienna, Marion Richardson in England, and Rugg and Shumaker in United States. As Rugg and Shumaker have noted, art education of the child-centered schools did not come from the professors of art education but from artist-teachers. Most self-expressive art teaching was advocated and practiced by artists who were deeply imbued with conviction that a natural affinity existed between the activity of the artist and the graphic expressions of the child.

Several artist-teachers wrote about their work in progressive education literature, but it was Victor D'Amico who through his writings, his work at Fieldston and at the Museum of Modern Art, refined this progressivist self-expressionist approach into a definitive pedagogy of art education. A philosophy and pedagogy which via the agency of the membership of the National Committee on Art Education became a major national influence.

Caroline Pratt and the Play School Practice

Caroline Pratt (1924) wished to devote her efforts to improve school practice from ground up. Her desire was: To serve children of tradesmen, laborers, and white collar workers who would normally be found in New York City's public schools. To study interests and abilities of the growing child as they are manifested. To supply an environment that step by step shall meet the needs of his development stimulate his activity, orient him in his enlarging world...and afford him effective experiences in social living (pp. iii-vi).

Among the artist-teachers who applied this progressivist self-expression to their teaching on a broad scale were Hughes Mearns (Poetry), Satis Colemen (Music) both of the Lincoln School, Lucy Sprague Mitchell (maps/writing/field trips) of Bank Street, Willy Levin of the City and Country School, and Florence Cane (visual art) of the Walden School.

However "what had begun as an effort to build a richer life for slum children was slowly transformed into a classless experiment in creative education" (Cremin, 1961, p. 204). It was fortuitous indeed that Pratt's school was located in Greenwich Village because most of the support and patronage for her play school idea came from the artists and writers who were moving into the neighborhood. Caroline Pratt's experience of living in Greenwich Village before World War I can be tied directly to her emphasis on creativity, the art curriculum, imagination, and self-expression (Carlton, 1986). Caroline Pratt spoke of the child as artist, each with an intense desire to express or externalize what he/she had seen, heard, felt, each with his/her own personal perception of reality.

In play school perspective, children are understood to play for their own purposes of giving form and shape to their experiences in life. Pratt connected play to creative art in a fundamental way. She approaches play as preparatory to creative expression; she proposes that factual elements of art are acquired in first hand experiences, in playing with elements of line, color, texture and form. Art and imagination are integral to each other and they are irreducible, and cannot be dealt with separately (Carlton, 1986, p. 38).

The Greenwich Village

Carlton (1986) describes the Washington Square area as the hub of activity for the movers and the shakers of the day. The Liberal Club was next door to the new Provincetown Players on McDougal Street just off Washington Square south. The arts reigned supreme in the Village, and progressive thought had a bubbling, intoxicating effect on the participants (p. 208).

What is interesting here is an assertion (Cowley, 1934) that it was the artistic intelligentsia of the "Greenwich Villages" of New York, Chicago and San Francisco who were largely responsible for inventing the conceptual base for a child-centered school. The village was the center of this drive for creativity and experimentation, and nowhere was this more evident than in the arts. The art world was being defined by John Marin, Isadora Duncan, Max Weber, and Alfred Steiglitz who emphasized originality, individuality, private and personal visions, experimentation with forms and quest for self-expression. The doctrines of self-expression, liberty, psychological adjustment combined to place the creative confident individual at the center. This train of thought developed its own pedagogical thesis: "the notion that each individual has unique creative potentialities and that a school in which children are encouraged freely to develop these potentialities is the best guarantee of a larger society truly devoted to human worth and excellence" (Cremin, 1961, p. 202). D'Amico does not make any reference to the Greenwich Village and its ethos in his writings or lectures. There are only indirect conjectural references to literature on child-centered schools. Yet we ask, is it possible for a young innovator involved in progressive art education, working at one of the progressive schools, studying the state of art education in schools not to have been influenced by this environment? Particularly when we know that he was at the center of educational innovation the Teachers College, Columbia University.

Teachers College, Columbia University

Teachers College was never a "one-idea" institution. Teachers College, as the then Dean William F. Russell has maintained, had no single point of view and no single institutional philosophy. The College had in fact always attempted "to assure representation for all points of view, ...insuring a healthy intellectual divergence" (Cremin, et. al. 1954, p. 147). Yet "There is no denying that its hospitality to all major streams of progressivism in education quickly made it the intellectual crossroads of the movement" (Cremin 1961, p. 175). As the Director of Research for the newly established Lincoln School at Teachers College, Rugg was a spirited member of the Progressive Education Association, and also a member of a group of leading lights of Greenwich Village.

Cremin, Shanon, and Townsend (1954) describe the years 1927-1935 as optimistic years for Teachers

College. By 1934 the College reorganization had regrouped the original Faculty of Education, and Faculty of Practical Arts into five new divisions. The Fine and Industrial Arts programs under Professor Sallie B. Tannahill were now included under "Instruction" in Division IV. During these years Victor D'Amico was head art teacher at Fieldston School. During 1936-1943, Victor taught methods courses and had worked on the editorial board of the *Art Education Today*, an annual publication sponsored by the faculty of Fine and Industrial Arts devoted to problems and issues in art education. It was this environment and John Dewey who defined and shaped an intellectual space that D'Amico had entered and it was their ideas hovering in that space which D'Amico pedagogy echoes.

In a way the primary mission of the founders of the modern art was not collection and preservation but education. Artemas Packard, an art history professor with pronounced sympathy for Progressive Education and Chairman of the Department of Art at Dartmouth College, was asked by Nelson Rockefeller to develop a recommendation on the question of how to identify and educate a wider audience for this new museum. His major recommendation was to establish an education department which would play a significant part in a program of art study consistent with the interest of contemporary art.

Morgan, 1993

Modern Art and The Museum of Modern Art

This confluence of educators and artists of the era who found common cause in ideas of progressivism and the work of the artists made possible the conception of child-centered perspective which granted each child the right to pursue his/her own desires to express what he/she has seen, heard and felt. Identification with creative artists, and equating their "studio" efforts to break through superficiality with creative self-expressions provided legitimacy to art education in schools dedicated to originality, individuality, personal visions, experimentation with forms and quest for self-expression.

The Museum of Modern Art in New York City was founded in 1929 (a week after the stock market crash) as a rebellious dream of three far-sighted women— Lillian Bliss, Mary Quinn Sullivan and Abby Aldrich Rockefeller, they created a museum to show modern art, work of living artists. "...They had the courage to advocate the cause of modern movement in the face of widespread division, ignorance, and suspicion that the whole business was some sort of Bolshevik plot...their museum was to introduce the public to newer and more

experimental work being made" (Gollin 1995. p. 6). This mandate led to the selection of Victor D'Amico to develop a modernist pedagogy to bring about cultural change in American society, to improve their taste, foster an appreciation of progressive tendencies in art. We need to remember that in 1930s thru early 1950s modern art was far from being an acceptable art form for general public and D'Amico's educational activities were seen as an instrument to gain credibility for modern art in American cultural scene. Art for Victor D'Amico was modern art, and in the progressivist perspective, he saw modern artists' engagement in experiments with media and materials that dealt with new experiences, visions and possibilities for expression, as a worthy model for art education of students—children as well as adults. The road to modern art was engagement with artists materials and artists' worlds.

VICTOR D'AMICO'S PEDAGOGY: THE EVOLUTION

The following review of D'Amico's ideas as reflected in his major activities, writings, and lectures is organized in three time periods. Chronologically, I have borrowed Efland (1993) suggested time categories, however the captions and the content of D'Amico literature discussed herein is my own. These are: *The Formative Years: 1929-1940*, the years bracketed by the Great Depression and pre-World War II America, *The Influential Years 1941-1958*, a middle period which included both World War II and post-World War II years. These were pinnacle years for D'Amico. During these years The Museum of Modern Art became a respected force within American cultural establishment. Its People's Art Center, the new home of the Museum's Education programs, was acclaimed by Nelson Rockefeller as

> ...an accomplishment of major importance and one which is entirely due to your vision, ability and leadership...the Board of Trustees are particularly proud and happy in our association with you...

and we share with you in the deep satisfaction of your achievements. (Memo to D'Amico, September 1951).

The Challenging Years 1958-1984. Victor D'Amico retired from MoMA in 1969. By then both art of the day and the dominant educational paradigm had shifted significantly, as had the social and political circumstances. In his later writings, Victor reflects his disillusionment. His anguish is reflected in sometimes bitter critique of the direction where art education seemed to be headed.

The Formative Years: 1929-1940

As early as 1930 D'Amico seemed to distance himself from the then progressivist self-expressionist art educators who wanted teachers to keep 'no interference' stance in children's creative activity. He writes "...She (teacher) cannot dictate, she may only suggest, she does not pull the child after her but stands behind him directing his steps..." (D'Amico 1930, p. 25). The teacher is ever present in D'Amico's creative art teaching. When discussing his way for helping students with 'outdoor painting' he writes "...the objective is not at all for realistic landscape; no mention is ever made about the similarity between the picture and the specific objects represented but the concern is in the appropriateness of every part in the picture as a whole...this method has advantage over the creative work produced by merely the imagination in the classroom, and may be termed creative effort plus" (D'Amico, 1931a, p. 18). This surely is not the laissez-faire (hands-off or no-teaching) approach of the other progressivist art teachers.

I contend that this reference to the social function of art and the need for art education to be involved in all curriculum is not an integrationist/reconstructionist view, as Efland suggests. There is another way of reading this and the interpretation I offer (which I

D'Amico was a progressivist with a difference. Efland (1993) cites D'Amico in The New Art Education (1933) to suggest D'Amico's alignment with the progressivist-reconstructionists group (such as George Count, William Kilpatrick and others): The old formal school sinks deeper and deeper into the rut of academic art; art of the progressive schools, too in most cases become pampered and anemic through over-indulgence in self expression and individualism...the new education in art will not be a pampered or fastidious art, but a new born art born of the wisdom and fire—experience cleansed by the fire of hardship [perhaps he is referring to his experience of working in settlement house schools]... the new education in art will be strong in human interest and will have a social function....The more I study the problem of art education, the more I see it involved in every subject in the curriculum and sense it as a formative power in building the life and character of the child.

D'Amico, 1933, p. 461

believe is much closer to D'Amico's views, as borne in a private conversation with D'Amico in 1970s). D'Amico's teaching and his curriculum at Fieldston School in Riverdale, NY involved interdisciplinary work but it was, as he would say, always based on 'making art' as the medium of confronting social issues. In the sidebar quotation what is critical is the phrase "sense it [see art making] as a formative power [for creative and aesthetic sensibility]." This was not Kilpatrick's "Project Method" or Leon Winslow's *Integrated School Art Program* (1939). Rather, it used the creative power of the arts to tackle any subject in the school curriculum. My point of view is further confirmed by a student of D'Amico at Fieldston. This curriculum called Arts High, she says, "was designed for those who were visually oriented and prone to reinforcing our learning through drawing our observations, thus enhancing our findings visually" (Muriel Silberstein-Storfer, 1993).

Victor D'Amico's great sensitivity to the aesthetics of classroom and studio environment is spelled out in an article he did for *Progressive Education* in 1931. He writes that "An art room designed and planned can be as invigorating as a landscape of rolling hills in sunshine. A modern art room will be beautiful and efficient" (D'Amico, 1931).

The two very significant D'Amico works of this period are: A survey report, *Art in American Schools* (D'Amico, 1935), for the Rockefeller Foundation and his 3 year study for the Progressive Education Association (PEA) Committee on the Function of Art in General Education published in 1940, as *The Visual Arts in General Education.*

The survey report discussed earlier contains a rather intriguing and optimistic piece that appears in that document as an epilogue. D'Amico was always taking stock and looking ahead. This need for continually asking where are we, where have we been, where are we going, is endemic for people with global visions, individuals convinced of their mission on this earth.

This early framework for art education considers creative act and appreciation as two integral aspects of the art experience, and the motivating engine which promotes creative expression. Motivation is an important piece in Victor's creative teaching methodology. It is a matter of setting up an environment for evoking interest, engagement and stimulating individual expression. Creative teaching uses art fundamentals (techniques and processes) not as ends in themselves but as means for meeting students' expressive needs.

The PEA committee report, published in book form as *The Visual Arts in General Education* (D'Amico, 1940) focuses on the value of art in secondary school. This committee work was done in collaboration with several leading progressive art educators, among them Belle Boas, Rosalind MacDonald, and Thomas Munro. The writing of the report was primarily D'Amico's responsibility. The book articulates a comprehensive and well considered philosophy and a pedagogy, which Foster Wygant (1993) calls a landmark achievement of the time and considered by some as the "bible" for students of art education in early 1940s.

The Influential Years: 1941-1963

The middle period years, the World War II and post War era, were pinnacle years for D'Amico. He was working full throttle writing and refining his ideas, developing action programs to carry out his ideas. *Creative Teaching in Art* (1942) epitomized his work to date: it drew heavily upon his association with progressive education, his work on the Committee on the Function of Art in General Education, his Rockefeller Foundation survey experience of art in

What was D'Amico's hopeful view of the art education beyond 1935:
- Art has placed all subjects on creative level
- Art has become the nucleus, and means of integrating school life
- Art education has come to stay. Creative teaching has become the educational method
- Curriculum is organized in three cores: Arts, Social-physical sciences, and information, and skills
- Art experiences for all students/specialized classes for gifted
- Greater use and development of leisure time
- Art becomes socializing force
- Art for the handicapped in therapy and creative settings
- Evaluation of creative expression on the basis of individual response, growth and development, rather than on fixed standards and group norms.

How would you assess where we are today with reference to these hopes? Were these reasonable hopes for the future we are in now?

schools across the country, his own teaching experience at Fieldston, and of course his art classes with children and teachers at MoMA. This book articulated a pedagogy for D'Amico's "art as a humanizing force" credo developed earlier. The thesis is that the children should be permitted to work as artists, pointing out that given the right school environment the child can be helped to create to the fullest of his potential, in the same manner that the artist approaches his media and materials (Sahasrabudhe, 1991). Do we not hear echoes of Bruner's 1960s thesis that *The Process of Education* will be enhanced if the structure of a discipline, and the methodology of its practitioners are considered as shaping influences for school curriculum. D'Amico was almost 20 years ahead of the 1960s Woods Hole conference.

The book is organized under chapter headings such as: "The Child as Artist," "The Child as Painter," "The Child as Sculptor," "The Child as Stage-Designer," etc. Freundlich (1979) considered the book as one of the most sensible and intelligent books ever written in the field of art education. Fred Logan (1955) wrote, "D'Amico's conviction that the artist is one of the most valuable members of the society, that the artist's approach to his work...as the model to propose ideas, motivations, and instructional strategies for creative teaching in art is the inspiration and foundation for the book" (p. 234).

The book was a godsend for art teachers looking for new ways of doing things in the classroom. It went through seven printings leading to its second revised edition, which appeared in 1953. In his autobiographical lecture at Miami University of Ohio, D'Amico spoke of 1942 as "a good year." In addition to publication of his book *Creative Teaching in Art* (1942), the Committee on Art Education was also founded the same year. Fred Logan (1955) writes of years 1940-42 as a period that brought a sort of culmination, a clear

"...given the right environment the child can be helped to create to the fullest of his potentiality..." Victor D'Amico at the construction/ collage table with a child.

and thoughtful summation to conceptualization of art education and cites D'Amico's *The Visual Arts in General Education* as the book that articulated that "comprehensive and well considered philosophy" (p. 209). From the hindsight of history one might add that along with D'Amico's *The Visual Arts in General Education* (1940) and *Creative Teaching in Art* (1942), Herbert Read's *Education through Art* (1945), Viktor Lowenfeld's *Creative and Mental Growth* (1947) and Rudolf Arnheim's *Art and Visual Perception* (1954) are the seminal works that conceptualized art education of the modern era.

If the 1950s are claimed as the Lowenfeld years, the 1930s and 1940s were certainly the D'Amico decades. His tenure began in an era when the Museum of Modern Art (MoMA) under the leadership of Alfred Barr and Rene d'Harnoncourt, (both teachers in their own right) dedicated to making modern art—the art of their complex-times—available and accessible to the American public. In D'Amico's pro-active programs they found an art educator whose vision was rooted in the art studio, committed to modernism, to individual creativity and to the expression of meaning in formal aspects of art (Yenawine, 1995, p. 30). His sphere of his influence went beyond the museum, his charisma was contagious, his ideas compelling.

In 1942, a group of art education professors, artists and museum educators joined him in founding the National Committee on Art Education (NCAE). The enthusiasm of a national leadership group of outstanding art educators, and their dedication to D'Amico's ideas is described by Howard Conant (1995) "The outstanding quality and accomplishments of NCAE over 30 (sic) [1942-1963] years of life was achieved by zealous dedication of many members, governing councils and boards, but most of all by astonishing ability, insight, energy, courage, profound commitment, and incredible persistence of its long time chairman, Victor D'Amico (p. 50). As The National Committee on Art Education (NCAE) became an influential national force, a vehicle for D'Amico philosophy shaping the art education dialogue; the Children's Art Carnival which opened as Children's Holiday Carnival on MoMA premises (D'Amico, 1974, p. 22), became reason for the international reputation achieved by the education department at the Museum of Modern Art. The Carnival was a sensation in Barcelona and Milan in 1957, a major hit in Brussels World Fair in 1958, and a most welcome United States gift to India in 1962.

The Challenging Years: 1958-1984

Victor D'Amico retired from MoMA in 1969, and the Museum of Modern Art closed down D'Amico's The People's Art Center in 1970. By then both the museum culture and the dominant educational paradigm had shifted significantly, as had the other social and political circumstances impacting art education. MoMA in the late 1960s was "The ship that was not only rudderless, it had neither pilot, nor lookout and was short of crew" (Brown 1979, p. 79). In the later 1960s D'Amico's support at the museum began eroding as was the influence of both his mentors Alfred Barr and Rene d'Harnoncourt, both of whom retired in 1967. The museum education in the country was moving away from the experiential methods of D'Amico, focused on learning to appreciate art by making art, to educational programs that highlighted the art object and what people need to know about it, in order to understand and appreciate art. Information had gained supremacy over experience. By the early 1970s a new brand of university-trained museum curators had replaced educators of D'Amico variety.

On the educational front, the year 1957 is generally agreed upon as the year that marks the end of the progressive era in education. This was the year when the Russia's launching of Sputnik served as the catalyst for a curricular reform movement. A movement lead by the scientific community suggesting the scientist/professional specialist scholar as the disciplinary model for conceptualizing curriculum structure. Jerome Bruner's report of The Woods Hole conference of 1959, the *Process of Education* suggested "discipline" as a field of inquiry to be pursued as the professional scientists and scholars do. This led to Professor Manuel Barkan's (1962) paper "Curriculum Problems in Art Education" introducing the notion that the disciplines of the aesthetician, the art critic, and art historian are as important as the artist for the structure and content of art education curriculum.

Art education was in a paradigmic transition and Victor D'Amico never caught up with it. His writings of this late period reflect his disillusionment, his bewilderment, his anguish and sometime bitter critiques of where art education seemed to be headed. In an environment where the art education world seemed to have mounted an increasingly sustained campaign against "creative self-expression" D'Amico seems to be sole defender of creative art education against ominous attacks. In an address to the sixteenth annual conference of the National Committee on Art Education, *A reappraisal of art education: coming events cast their shadows* (D'Amico, 1958) he attempts an open objective review of his differences "with my colleagues." He lists 26 "wrongs" with art education as practiced in the late 1950s. He is appalled by the decline in quality of children's work. He refers to research as attempts to over-psychologize the child and creativity. He cites limitations of experimental research methods to study creativity, and he calls the idea of subordinating the end product in the overzealous emphasis on process as misplaced. He cautions against the notion of treating the child as an artist as if the child is already accomplished and needs no training. Even today, the questions about aesthetic quality of child art, limitations of psycho-educational models for experimental research, and the notions of child as the artist remain open debates. D'Amico never lost his conviction about the centrality of the experience of creative artmaking in the process of children's growth and development. He saw historical contexts and children's critical ability as entwined parts of the experiential-creating activity, as he has written:

"... individual expression of any child or adult can be enriched by appreciation of our art heritage and ...without this he must remain an impoverished isolated person" (D'Amico, undated, pp. 4-5).

Victor D'Amico's 1960 publication, *Experiments in Creative Art Teaching* is a comprehensive report of MoMA's Department of Education and 22 years of its activities. This document is a presentation of an educational philosophy "... not merely a theory: it is result of practical experience over an extended period of time." Though this is an internal institutional report probably prepared as D'Amico was battling the beginning winds of change at the museum [my conjecture] the report is also intended to be "of service to educators and museums in extending or developing their programs... and a resource for the art teacher as he[she] carries on the his important work of developing creative individuals" (p. 6).

For D'Amico art had become a human necessity. "If the aim of art education were to be expressed in a few words," he said, "it would be to seek the highest development of the creative spirit of every man, woman and child" (D'Amico, 1960, pp. 2-3). He was speaking to the 18th annual conference of the National Committee on Art Education in the auditorium of the Ethical Culture Society in New York. This is where the Society held its Sunday prayer meetings under an inscription "The Place Where Men Meet to Seek the Highest is Holy Ground." For D'Amico, the art room was the holy ground for art teachers seeking the growth of the child's creative spirit— the ultimate goal, "... which I believe is as close to holiness, or Godliness, as we mortals will ever get" (p. 5).

Viktor Lowenfeld died in 1960 and Victor D'Amico was left alone to defend child-centered, experience-centered approach to art education. His address to an InSEA conference in Montreal 1963, D'Amico talks about those looming shadows. The ominous clouds make him wonder whether art education is returning to its decadent past, "...has world turned backwards?" with this seeming return of all those strange and distressing ideas once considered harmful and obsolete. His target, the sponsors of these new ideas are young teachers in their twenties and thirties. He declares that they have no idea about what creative education is about, but then he holds the generation of the creative self expression era responsible for it.

In his 1965 paper presented at the University of California's Symposium on Child Art, D'Amico asks "...when we talk and think of children, do we see children of the world or do we see particular children ...children are not abstractions, mere digits and numbers. They are individual human beings all over the world, and they all need art." Here, he extends his idea of art as a human necessity and creative art teaching as a humanizing influence, to art as "...an integrating human force...[therefore our obligation and our means]...for developing [every child's] creativity...[and thus make] an important and vital contribution to the world community" (p. 2). This lecture he says, is quite hopeful because of the [then] recently passed Education Act [to strengthen Elementary and Secondary Schools] of April 1965, and suggests that these new federal dollars ought to address needs such as providing competent and trained art teachers for every school, and making available resources and support materials for quality teaching for all school which would make museum and gallery art works accessible for schools, and undertake a campaign for public education for understanding the role the arts in American life. But then, he also appeals, "Let us focus on the real child and not spend so much energy on theory and generalization, and so much research couched in tables and graphs, that has nothing to do with the child" (p. 8).

These are themes that reoccur in his address to the Pacific Regional Convention, Monterey, California (May 1966). The address "A Millennium or Mirage: Art Education Today" reviews art education trends against an overarching "need of today, [which for him]... is to discover the dignity of man, to help him find his self respect and enjoy his greatest natural endowment, the power to create" (p. 27). The disturbing trends he speaks about include obsession about categorizing and classification of children in gifted and non-gifted, talented and untalented, culturally privileged and underprivileged. This emphasis on grouping on statistics and mechanical organization has lost sight of children as human beings. He talks of lack of leadership of rugged individuals the pioneers who seek new frontiers. Current leaders he suggests are cultivating "group minds," seeking political power, and involved in bureaucratic grantsmanship. Art education he thinks, requires rebels who oppose status quo and the tendency toward group leadership. He

decries a trend which downgrades art educator/art teachers in opposition to artists, historians, critics, writers. As you read this address you understand that the major target of this critique is what passes as research "much of it worthless and even harmful." D'Amico was not against research per se, yet he was not convinced that considerable amount of scant resources available for art education ought to be frittered away on poorly conceived research problems and questions. However this address, as his other outspoken commentaries of this period, have been perceived in the field as attack on all research. One needs to heed to his recommendation for "research-in-action" in this address. Consider that action research was not a generally available methodology for art educational research in 1966 and then read, what D'Amico is saying here: "The research [articulated insight] I recommend most highly is that which is produced day by day in many schools throughout the country by art teachers...there is a goldmine here, available for research... That [this] research be done by experienced teachers, that research projects be directly related to actual teaching situations, not contrived one..." (p. 31). "We never had its so good," he says, "let us not turn it into a 'mirage'.

The 1974 D'Amico address for Center for the Study of The History of Art Education at Miami University, Oxford. Ohio, is a genuine first person story of D'Amico's contributions to art education, but the tone of this address also creates an impression that Victor D'Amico somehow knew that his days were done.

VICTOR D'AMICO: MoMA's ART EDUCATION PROGRAMS

The Young People's Art Gallery (1937-1948)

I was sixteen years old when I came to The Museum of Modern Art [MoMA] and was admitted to the program for adolescents, called The Young Peoples Gallery. In that gallery, which was centrally located on the first floor of the museum, young people were to curate shows and write accompanying materials...I remember Victor's smile. We, students, never could figure out whether he was approving or disapproving...I experienced and participated in many 'authentic projects' worthy of students participation...they

built self esteem as well as provided skills…
Victor, through this project brought many adolescents from the city schools into the world of art (Churchill, 1991).

The Young People's Art Gallery was one the first programs undertaken by D'Amico as an art education experiment. The gallery provided a place for adolescent young people in an adult museum—a vehicle for multi-dimensional experiences in artmaking, exploring and discussing modern art, making aesthetic judgments, organizing, installing exhibitions of their own work, as well as work of artists which reflected their attitudes and preferences. The gallery space, and art studios were designed by Victor D'Amico. The Studio also became a gallery where students planned and installed exhibitions.

New York City High School Programs (1937-1960)

New York City schools were amongst the first to sign up for the museum's education program. The museum offered visual materials to the New York City Public Schools to enrich their teaching of creative arts and appreciation. By 1960 there were over 130 sets of exhibitions, films, slide sets, and color reproductions circulated to schools. Some were mounted as "Teaching Portfolios" and "Teaching Models." These units, boxed-in cabinets with wheels, which might include panels of photographs and texts,

All the studio furniture, and fittings, adjustable work tables and foldable easels were designed by Victor D'Amico. A modern art room will be beautiful and efficient. A prototype for a studio-classroom. *(D'Amico 1931)*

three-dimensional objects/models for the study of architecture, painting, sculpture, theater, graphics and other topic of interests to the adolescent. Olive Riley, the then Director of Art at New York City Board of Education was an early colleague and admirer of Victor D'Amico.

The War Veterans Art Center (1942-1948)

In 1942 during World War II, MoMA's education department at the request of Mrs. John D. Rockefeller Jr., began providing art activities for veterans returning from World War II. This was rather a natural thing to do, a socially conscientious museum leadership sharing the civic responsibility of reorienting returning soldiers to civilian life. The Center's programs however did not become an occupational activity but remained focused on "making art," helping veterans explore their creative abilities so they might feel a sense of fulfillment, whether they intended to use art as a profession or an avocation. For many this was a therapeutic experience "as good as a good night's sleep."

The People's Art Center (1949-1969)

By 1948, the War Veterans Art Center had accomplished its goal. "The Museum grew and the demand became greater than the facilities and the programs…. One of the most exciting of these was Victor D'Amico's art education programs which reached the young people, the old people… all people…so we had a build a new building" (Nelson Rockefeller on fund raising dinner October 2, 1962). The new "21" building was to be The People's Art Center and new home of the MoMA's education program, two floors of the building designed by Philip Johnson were devoted to studios, a research center, and a gallery. All the studio furniture, and fittings, adjustable work table and foldable easels were designed by Victor D'Amico. Studios had adjoining viewing rooms so that parents and teachers-in-training could watch classes in session. The Center opened on September 24, 1951, an art education center for people of all ages dedicated to the purpose that art education should contribute to the living needs and interest of all, with classes for children, for parents and children together, and for adults.

THE D'AMICO PHILOSOPHY ON DISPLAY

The Children's Art Carnival at MoMA (1942)

The Idea. The first Children's Art Carnival was installed in a tent in the museum garden on Fifty-third Street, New York City. The purpose of this carnival was to introduce parents and the museum community to MoMA's education program, but D'Amico was also offering the MoMA administration a demonstration of what creative art education can render. "The Children's Art Carnival was a new venture, based on the concept that children comprehend better through their senses, especially their tactile, visual and kinesthetic sense, than only through words" (D'Amico, 1968. p. 23). The carnival, presented in a uniquely designed environment (A Buckminster Fuller geodesic dome housed it for first few years) dramatically appeals to the child, the parent, and the educator. For a child it is a world of fantasy created for him alone. For the parent it is private window looking into the child's creative life, a window through which to watch and observe the art process unfold; for educators, it offers new ideas and methods of teaching and shows new and varied material and equipment.

> The entrance gate shaped as contour of a 4 year old and 12 year old establishes the developmentally defined outer limits for application of D'Amico's ideas. Carnival is a place for encouraging children ideas and imaginations without adult interference, or influence. Presence of too many adults can be often confusing for the child and can cause conflicts that get in the way of the children's own imagination. The only adults who enter the carnival area are teachers, and sometimes the press (because this was after all a demonstration). Adults could watch, what went on inside the carnival's two areas through portholes, glassed-in unobtrusive windows.

The Significance. No other single activity of the Museum's Department of Education received so much public notice consistently year after year, over the sixteen years that the Carnival played at the MoMA. Through visiting teachers and the press, the Carnival—the ideas, methods, and equipment of the Carnival has been

adopted entirely or in parts all over the world (D'Amico, 1960, p. 40). Conceived as a magic world for children, the Carnival was divided in two areas. Over the years, through its growth and its international presentations the basic arrangement of the areas and the ideas they represent has not changed. Everywhere the Carnival plan has consisted of two galleries. An inspirational area, and a studio-workshop area.

The Two Galleries/Two Areas. The first area is for motivating the child, the second for participation in an art activity. After being motivated or inspired through play invited by different toys and games and perhaps relieved of some of the cliche's and stereotypes "with which his/her (child's) mind is often burdened" the child enters the studio-workshop, which is the participation area. Here the children are invited to indulge their imaginations through painting, making a collage or a construction, guided in their efforts by sensitive and experienced MoMA trained teachers.

Inspirational Area. The motivational area with its variety of toys encouraged the child to experiment with color, motion and design through operations of buttons, switches and pedals. This semi-darkened room usually painted in deep blues and greens, with lighted windows and spotlights which revealed the many attractive "toys" [this was the inventive D'Amico—these toys were D'Amico's kinetic sculptures with built in pedagogical and play dimensions, over the years Victor worked with known designers and fabricators working with his ideas for Toys] in pools of light from within, giving the whole area a jewel like effect. The Color Player with its piano keys and pedals allowed projection of color, moving shapes on a screen. The Furry Cat invited touching, The Magnetic Picture maker—a magnetized panel made it possible to arrange free form metallic shapes in provocative picture compositions. Jigsaw puzzles made from reproductions of modern paintings enticed and cultivated a sense of art of the world. The environment created a mood of magic and fantasy, a friendly forest beckoning the child from every direction to its delightful surprises. The cheerful mood was emphasized by a continuous background of musical recordings (selections from: *The Nutcracker Suite, Swan Lake* (Tchaikovsky), *Grand Canyon Suite* (Ferde Grofe), and *Hansel and Gretel Suite*, (Humperdinck)). In India, Western classical music was changed to

"Presence of too many adults…get in the way of children's own imagination….Adults could watch what went on inside the Carnivals two [here studio] areas." Children's Art Carnival, "El Festival de Arte de los Ninos." Barcelona, Spain 1957.

Indian light classical music. The Inspirational Area provided stimulation to think creatively, play with exciting materials and visual, sensual, tactile play elements providing experiences that engaged children in thinking, imagining in shapes, colors, textures, and rhythm. (D'Amico, 1960; see page 39 for a complete listing and descriptions of Toys and Games in the Inspirational Area.)

Studio-Workshop Area. Was quite a contrast. Children moved from the dimly lit toys and games in pools-of-light, inviting, motivating imagination and contemplation—to the brilliantly lighted, brightly painted studio-workshop area. This was an activity area. All the furniture was meticulously designed for children, with specifications evolved through years of D'Amico experimentation at People Art Center studios. The

cantilevered, low-hung, adjustable, primary color painted easels against the perimeter walls and the color coordinated stools were integral to the pedagogy. Tempera paints dispensed from easy-no-clog "pourable" jars, glass coasters which served as paint holders, large bristle brushes, sponges, arranged on aluminum trays, each item representing a carefully considered decision. The 18" x 24" paper-size, rounded out prescribed painting paraphernalia. Then there were the collage and construction work tables: round tables with a revolving lazy-susan-turntables in the center. The turntable with pie-shaped compartments were each filled with select and chosen materials for collage and construction: feathers, pipe cleaners, buttons and beads, colored and textures papers, pieces of cork and wood, and so on. There is no specific list of materials; depending on where the Carnival is, lazy-susans can be filled with local materials (That is what we did when the Carnival was on tour in India and we had exhausted first batch of supplies imported from America). What D'Amico demonstrates here is the need to carefully select materials "...never considered junk but selected and organized for visual qualities and possibilities for exploring color, shape, texture, solidity, pliability, and other qualities of materials ..." (Lois Lord, 1954). Construction and collage roundtables had work stations for 6 to 8 children and were equipped with staplers, scissors, child-safe adhesives, and sometimes hole punches. Above the roundtable hung a hoop, to suspend mobiles, and other art work which the child fancies should be hung.

Children work about 20 minutes in the Inspirational Area, and some 40 minutes in the studio. There is no set sequence or order for students to follow in the motivational area, teachers help to see that all children get a chance at all the toys they want to explore and work with. In both areas children are encouraged to work independently, teachers provide help when needed in operating a toy, or on getting started with painting, collage or construction.

The Children's Art Carnival in Barcelona and Milan (1957), Brussels (1958), and India (1963)

Tucked away on the balcony of the cylindrical building of the United States pavilion at the Brussels World's Fair (1958) was a small structure with portholes and a sign saying Children's Creative Center.

This was a demonstration of creative art education, Dr. D'Amico's philosophy and pedagogy on the world's stage. *Omnibus,* the Ford television program, devoted 15 minutes of its May 4, 1958 telecast to a tour of the fair. The Children's Creative Center was a centerpiece of this broadcast. Alistair Cooke in his introductory remarks, described the essence of this children's creative oasis in the maelstrom of sophisticated adult exhibitions as one American triumph which will rock no headlines is a play hall that is heaven for the children of all nations and, except as you become a little child, you may no wise enter therein. This is place where any child may find new uses for a length of string, where he may indulge very simple sensations, like the movement of a caterpillar, like the feel of the cat. Once they have loosened up their imagination, they move into the inner room [the studio-workshop] (D'Amico, 1960, p. 34).

The Belgian educational liaison office recorded a total 16,472 school children and 2,000 teachers as having had the experience of working at the center which a Belgian reporter for the daily STAR called an American art school for children (Letter/Reports form American Staff to MoMA Education Department. D'Amico papers: Special Collections, The Milbank Library, Teachers College, 1958).

In addition to the recognition it received at Brussels fair, the previous year in 1957, the Carnival under the auspices of the United States Department of Commerce was the focus of attention at the International Trade Fairs in Milan and Barcelona. In Italy it was called "Il Paradiso dei Bambini" (The Children's Paradise), and in Spain it was "El Festival de Arte de los Ninos" (A festival of arts for children). In both these places the Carnival was a distinct success. The press, television, and other media in these countries gave special attention to the Carnival as an outstanding contribution of United States. An Italian reporter wrote: "In a world where there are so many devices being invented and tremendous machines built for

---

Two findings of educational importance: D'Amico emphasizes two important findings that emerged from various experiments of the Children's Art Carnival, 1) that children can develop creatively regardless of their previous background. The freedom and dynamic quality of the creative approach is able to overcome and compensate years of academic and indoctrinated methods of teaching; and, 2) that ethnic and national background has no bearing on the child's creativity. "Creative children are the result of a creative education that develops creativeness; uncreative children are the victims of indoctrinary teaching. It is that simple."

D'Amico, 1960, p. 40

---

destroying both people and property, what better way can there be to foster a feeling of brotherhood between nations than to develop the creative possibilities of their children" (see MoMA press release—on reporting by Brussels' newspapers—April 1958, No. 29, Special Collection).

Children's Art Carnival in India

It was in Brussels World's Fair in 1958, that Ms. Indira Gandhi (Then the President of

"....the collage and construction tables: round tables with revolving lazy-susan/turntables in the center…filled with select and chosen materials for collage and construction…" Children's Holiday Carnival at MoMA. Undated.

The Indian National Congress, the premier political party of India) along with Mrs. Dorothy Norman, first saw the Children's Art Carnival. She was so impressed by the Carnival and its philosophy and so convinced of its great beneficial significance for Indian children that she asked Mrs. Norman to investigate the possibility of acquiring the Carnival for India. At the time, Mrs. Gandhi was the chairperson of an autonomous government organization called The Bal Bhavan Board, dedicated to developing and creating a string of Bal Bhavans. My doctoral dissertation at New York University conceptualized these Bal Bhavan children's centers as national institutions devoted to creative and recreational development of children (Sahasrabudhe, 1961). Mrs. Gandhi wanted the New Delhi Bal Bhavana to be the host institution for D'Amico's Creative Art Center. Between the years 1958 and 1962, when Mrs. Jacqueline Kennedy symbolically presented the Children's Art Carnival to Mrs. Gandhi, many important people at the Museum of Modern Art, the Kennedy White House and Asia Society of New York, were involved with Victor D'Amico and Mrs. Dorothy Norman in making a gift of this Carnival to India a reality. Fortunately, I happened to be in the right place at the right moment. I had known Victor D'Amico; I had been selected by him and The National Committee on Art Education as one of the Committee's Junior Leaders, I had taught at the Peoples Art Center, I was a teaching-fellow at New York University and had nearly completed requirements for an Ed.D. degree at New York University. Victor D'Amico introduced me to Mrs. Gandhi, as possibly the person who could direct the Carnival in India after the departure of his American staff. During the years (1958-1962) that the details this gift were being worked out, I did a study for Mrs. Gandhi

developing a conceptual framework and organizational detail for Bal Bhavans in India (Sahasrabudhe, 1961). In 1961 I was appointed the Director of the first Bal Bhavan and National Children's Museum in New Delhi, and assumed that position in Fall 1961, and by winter of 1962 this institution was ready to receive the Children's Art Carnival from the Museum of Modern Art, New York.

This was the first time this Carnival, a philosophy and the practice of creative art education was being presented by the United States to another nation. Also, the first time the Carnival was to be housed entirely in its own structure. This housing for the Carnival was to be designed so that it was portable, movable from one site to another. The structure was fabricated in New Delhi from designs by Dr. D'Amico and working drawings by Mr. Frank Vitullo.

The Children's Art Carnival Opened in New Delhi on October 28, 1963 for a 6-week (6 days a week) run through December 7, 1963. During this Carnival stay in New Delhi, 5,403 children from 141 schools participated in creative art education. Sunday was reserved for non-school community groups. Sunday visitors accounted for another 1,875 young people from non-school settings. Dr. D'Amico and his staff conducted all classes the first 3 weeks. During the second three weeks the Bal Bhavan staff members who had interned with the American staff the first 3 weeks took over the entire operation under my supervision. After its New Delhi stay, the Carnival went on tour of Hydrabad, Madras, Banglore, Bombay, and Ahmedabad. Five trucks loaded with 73 "seacrates" containing the entire carnival structure, and equipment left New Delhi for Hydrabad on January 4, 1964 and returned after 3 1/2 months to New Delhi in mid-April. The entire story of this travel and tour—packing and unpacking, advanced preparation staff and the installation crews, the local responsibilities undertaken by local authorities and organization, participation by school systems and state education agencies makes another exciting story. *(Sahasrabudhe, 1964).* During these 3 1/2 months in five Indian cities, Carnival worked with 546 school groups, 10,057 children, 3,997 adult visitors (looking in through the windows) and our Carnival staff trained 285 primary school teachers in D'Amico pedagogy.

The Children's Art Carnival in Harlem, New York

"...[P]erhaps the last stage of Children's Art Carnival was established in Harlem in 1969, the year of my retirement from the Museum...[where] Mrs. Taylor has produced a triumph of her own with the Harlem Carnival..." (D'Amico, 1974) This Harlem experience transforms the Carnival from its museum context to that of the larger context of a community, however the Carnival in Harlem stands as a tribute to D'Amico's manifest desire to see the creative experience as a vitalizing force able to change the lives of young people and their communities.

In 1968, Trustees of Museum of Modern Art began considering outreach. The question of sharing its educational programs with underprivileged youth of

Children's Art Carnival may have changed its shape and its housing, however the credo that drove D'Amico philosophy survives and still drives the efforts of the staff at 62 Hamilton Terrace, Manhattan, New York, 10025.

the this city became a priority item on the Board agenda. Also on hand were all these returned materials and physical equipment that made up the Childrens Creative Art Centers in Brussels and Milan World Fairs. So the Children's Art Carnival in Harlem (CAC in Harlem) was opened in March, 1969 in a 50' x 50' garage at Harlem School of the Arts (Taylor, 1979). Ms. Betty Blayton Taylor served as the Director, the fundraiser, instructor, purchasing agent, and receptionist. CAC in Harlem began as an after school program, but soon became an over-subscribed regular school-day integrated art program. CAC in Harlem staff created innovative art activities based upon students personal stories, and neighborhood locales with such a positive effect on visiting school students that their host school teachers were quite impressed. This led to CAC in Harlem's collaboration with Dr. Gilbert Voyat (a Piagetian educator) of City College and created a much celebrated and validated Title 1 Creative Reading Through the Arts program (Taylor, 1979).

The CAC in Harlem was incorporated as an independent community based school in 1973, and moved to its present site in September 1974. Still grounded in D'Amico's fundamental belief that development of creative expression in children fosters creative thought process which revitalize all life, CAC in Harlem continues to provide innovative visual and communication arts programing for minority and disadvantaged youth of ages 4-21. Its activities have moved into an enlarged scope, and include pre- and after-school programs, classes for handicapped children, career training for teenagers, reading through the arts, projects in teenage employment in cooperation with Jobs for Youth, Mayor's Volunteers, The Human Resources Youth Corps, and Career Training programs. Many of these remain individually funded programs.

Today (Taylor, 1995b) the Children's Art Carnival (CAC) in Harlem is an independent, non-profit community based organization providing children free creative learning experiences (free in terms of expression as well

as costs). CAC in Harlem continues to provide art workshops in painting, collage, puppetry, construction, drawing, photography, cartooning, video production, illustration, drama and movement, writing, photojournalism, screen printing and computer graphics. Its school day programs reach some 45 plus public schools and "...over the past twenty-five years...has involved some 275,000 children" (Taylor, 1995 p. 1). CAC in Harlem through its extensive theme-based arts activities, projects and collaborations with other New York City arts agencies (Arts Partners, Artists-in-Schools) has been a leader in integrating creative arts expressions with schools' curricular subjects, and with reading programs. CAC in Harlem has become a model, cited for its success by the National Endowments for the Arts, for alternative education serving 6,000-15,000 students at in-school sites in Manhattan, South Bronx, and Queens, New York.

Through the Enchanted Gates (1952-1953)

In 1952 and 1953 MoMA's Department of Education produced a successful television series, *Through the Enchanted Gate*, under the joint sponsorship with National Broadcasting Company. This series, available as 26 kinescopes models creative teaching as demonstrated in the Children's Art Carnival like environment. The two sets (Children 3-10 yrs, and Art for the Family) of 13 half-hour shows each were produced in NBC studios and filmed live by Peoples Art Center staff. For each segment the camera opened with children going through "The Enchanted Gate" contour gate of the Children's Art Carnival fame. This was an experiment in teaching art to children at home via the television screen. Kinescopes of all the programs are now available for circulation through the MoMA's Film Library.

The Art Barge, The D'Amico Art Institute in Amagansett, New York (1960)

Victor D'Amico retired from the Department of Education at MoMA sometime in 1969, but his work was not done. In 1955 the Museum of Modern Art and D'Amico instituted summer art classes in East Hampton at the Ashwagh Hall, Springs, New York. But what Victor D'Amico was looking for was "some place more dramatic and reflecting the character of Hamptons environment—sky, sea and salt air—either a boat or something resembling one" (Lerman and Govencheck, 1979, p. 14). Imagine floating a sea-going navy barge from the New Jersey coast and having it towed to Long Island. D'Amico did just that. Now, that barge is beached on the pine-barrens of Amagansett in Napeague Bay between East Hampton and Montauk as The Victor D'Amico Center for Art Education in Amagansett NY. The Barge is now a thriving community of young and old, painting away through the summer months. In 1972, some of the group of adults who had worked with D'Amico for several years chartered Napeague Institute of Art. In the 1990s the institute was renamed The Victor D'Amico Institute of Art, an active art center year-round for adults, for artists, and for art teachers.

"...After its New Delhi stay, the Carnival went on tour of Madras, Hydrabad, Bangalore, Bombay and Ahmedabad." Girls from a Bombay (Mumbai) School after having spent 90 minutes in D'Amico's Carnival, 1964.

VICTOR D'AMICO ON A LARGER CANVAS

Victor D'Amico and Art Education

The University Council on Art Education held the first of its legends seminars in tribute to Victor D'Amico, in May 1991. In his address Hausman uses "the larger canvas" metaphor to talk of D'Amico, "...as I stand before you with my reducing glass turned towards my view of Victor D'Amico...I will try and cast this view on the larger canvas of what was happening in art and art education" (Hausman, 1991). Earlier in this paper I suggested the period of 1941 through 1958 as D'Amico's most influential years when he was actively and demonstratively involved in shaping the philosophy and practice of art education. Whereas, Hausman seemed to suggest that "...what was happening in the late 1940s and 1950s was the emergence of a profession devoted to the theory and practice of the teaching of art...," and "...that D'Amico somehow was not a part of it" (p. 17). This is disturbing to me. I would suggest that Hausman has gotten his chronology mixed. This is a misconception that needs to be corrected. D'Amico and the National Committee on Art Education exercised a significant influence on both theory and practice of art education through late 1950s, and

the years when the so called paradigm shift seems to have occurred at the end of that decade into early 1960. What is important here is to point out that Hausman's presentation somehow seems to "echo" the establishment view of Victor's contribution to art education. Progressivist and self-expressionist ideologies of the 1940s held their central position in art education through the mid-1950s and, as noted, D'Amico was a progressivist with a difference.

Victor D'Amico was indeed a person with national aspirations and global vision. He truly believed that creative activity has the potential to influence humanity. In his 1961 address to the National Committee on Art Education Eighteenth Annual Conference, he speaks of art a human necessity:

Art may therefore be the salvation of modern man, but only if children have the benefit of true aesthetic experiences and if the average man seeks the real reward of creative endeavor, which is aesthetic satisfaction. Art is more than a fad or a frill, more than just cultural enrichment. It is, in these days of hot threats and cold wars, a human necessity (D'Amico 1961).

This part of my D'Amico story is about D'Amico's

Victor D'Amico made hands on activities in museum rather a rule than exception. The mission of the famous MoMA was to educate the public to the understanding and appreciation of modern art. The issue still continues to be whether: the route to understanding and appreciating art and culture is the first-hand experience with art making and hands-on involvement in the media and method and materials of the artists, or it ought to be based on the second-hand information and knowledge acquired via lectures, critiques and discussions. D'Amico's emphasis on making of art objects as central to public understanding of art was not lost on museum people. His multifaceted model for a museum education department is perhaps the greatest legacy to the museum education field.

indelible and profound imprints on that larger canvas of art education. What follows is his impact on museum education in American art museums, his stewardship of National Committee on Art Education, the Victor D'Amico/Viktor Lowenfeld dialogue that never took place, often referred to "experience to information" paradigm shift of the late 1960s early 1970s, and the university-based art education.

When asked: Why was this committee formed? D'Amico cited three reasons: First, the founders did not plan to start an organization, but they were brought together when they found restrictions in freedom of expression in a meeting of the annual conference of a large art organization. Second, they desired an organization free of compromises that had to be made when organizations depend for support on business interests. Third, when the group is devoted to education and excellence in creative teaching at all levels.

D'Amico 1960, p. 51

That Victor was cognizant of his role and significant influence, and that the museum world was keenly aware of his work is attested to by the fact that in the early 1950s, the National Committee on Art Education developed and conducted several seminars on museum education. These events for museum educators dedicated to explore the role of art museums in education were attended by well

D'Amico's Influence on Education in Art Museums

The first art museum educator has his/her beginning in the Great Colombian Exposition of 1893 at Chicago's Museum of Science and Industry, speculates Susan Mayer (1995). That is when some public school art teachers met and museum education was born. Now today, museum educators are not only active in the affairs of the National Art Education Association, but they have also become a recognized voice in the world of American museums. It was not always so. Art museums were then (and in some ways continue to be) conservative organizations, dedicated to acquiring art and artifacts, studying, preserving and conserving the past. Museum educators, therefore, have traditionally thought of themselves as scholars, curators, docents; and their methodology has been that of historians and critics. Their universe is the academy. In this environment, when D'Amico, an art teacher and an art educator, gets the job of running an education department, and proposes alternative ways of fulfilling his responsibility for educating the public to understand and appreciate modern art, this is revolutionary! We know that D'Amico's influence was greater in the field of art education than in museums, yet what his vision and success did for museum education is still being assessed. However it is necessary to say that his approach rooted in the art studio a commitment to individual creativity, and the inventive spirit of the modern artist, and his insistence that children find their meaning the content of their expression in their experience are propositions very welcome in the museum education world.

"...So the Children's Art Carnival in Harlem (CAC in Harlem) was opened in March, 1969 in a 50' x 50' garage at Harlem School of The Arts." Ms. Betty Blayton Taylor, the director, in her 'CAC-in-Harlem' studio area (1969).

known representatives of most major east coast museums. Included among these were E. M. Benson of Philadelphia Art Museum, Belle Boas from Baltimore Art Museum, William E. Wolfenden from Detroit Institute of Art, Katherine Bloom from Toledo Museum of Art, Hanna Toby Rose from The Brooklyn Museum, and Gertrude Hornug from the Cleveland Museum.

National Committee on Art Education (1942-1964)

This was D'Amico's national forum. One of his MoMA mandates was to study problems in art education and suggest how to solve them. D'Amico also needed a sounding board. Artists and art educator colleagues who shared his progressive assumptions provided a means of finding validation for his ideas and programs. The need for peer and public approval is a recognized leadership trait. His charisma and his integrity brought together such a group of his peers who served the MoMA's education department as an advisory committee—planning publications, conferences and research agendas. The group become the founding members of the National Committee on Art Education, a working group that would identify, "tackle and solve problems and not one that merely discovers and discusses them" (NCAE Newsletter, Jan. 1964).

D'Amico and this group believed that commercial interest in selling art materials played a significant role in deliberations of the existing art teacher organizations of the time and therefore desired to form a group that could pursue its educational ideals without deference to commercial interests. They needed an influence and self-interest-free environment for discussion about issues of art education. The Museum of Modern Art administration, because of its commitment to D'Amico's program, was quite sympathetic to the committee's objectives and agreed to become its sole sponsor for life (through 1964). Thus MoMA sponsorship gave the National Committee on Art Education a commercial interest-free-space, financial security, and solidly linked creative art education to modern art. D'Amico announced, "we hope to follow its (MoMA's) example by promoting creative art education in the United States as effectively as the museum has promoted modern art throughout the world" (Morgan, 1993).

This was D'Amico's organization, and except for five later years when the committee conferences were held at university sites, all other 16+ NCAE's annual conferences were held at MoMA. These conferences had become an annual event eagerly awaited by aspiring art educator membership from across the country, which during the first decade 1942-1952, had grown to over 1,000, and the attendance at museum conferences averaged near 2,000. Conference addresses,

Kenneth Wienbrenner valiantly challenged the membership to affirm that: Recognizing many possible advantages in newer teaching techniques, automation in schools, as well at home, work and culture...somebody still needs to ask what becomes of the child in the process...does art, by its very nature, have something to offer education as an antidote to the effects of standardization, conformity, and new authoritarianism of the machine.

Morgan, 1993

panel discussions, and presentations concerned themes such as (among others): opposition to laissez-faire art education; importance of guided creative teaching; new techniques, aesthetics and aesthetic values; art history and creative teaching; creative education as investment in peace; the artists as free human beings; perception, reality and symbolic reality; what makes a good film? Conference programs brought major speakers to the NCAE stage which included: philosopher Archibald MacLeish, anthropologist Margaret Mead, editor Milton Kox, historian Horst W. Janson, sculptor Jacques Lipchitz, architect/designer George Nelson, and painters Stuart Davis, Ben Shahn, Max Weber, and Robert Motherwell.

The consensus that governed the Committee in the 1950s, and its mission to bring together educators interested in formulating a basic philosophy of art education and promoting creative teaching at all levels had began to be shaky by the later years. Some have called the emerging paradigm shift discussed in this section later as the reason for this loss of cohesion in the leadership. D'Amico remained steadfast in his belief in power of the creative expression, and was quite his skeptical about issues such as: the uses of psychological interpretations of creative expression as end in themselves and the informational significance of art history. Fissures in the leadership of the NCAE widened and with the growing influence of Lowenfeld on university based members of the National Committee on Art Education, these rifts continued to widen. The first annual conference outside the museum at Pennsylvania State University in 1956 was hosted by Viktor Lowenfeld. The theme of this conference was the new psychological research in art education. The attendance at the conference was a disappointing 250, compared to the usual near 2,000 when the event was held in New York City. D'Amico was not happy and demanded that the Committee on Art Education take an unequivocal position and declare that art education was being jeopardized by various factors extraneous to teaching of art (Morgan, 1993). The next 5 years, as various university based leaders attempted to patch things together, the Committee's annual conferences were held at various universities. Fred Logan coordinated the conference at Michigan in 1957, Robert Iglehart at Wisconsin in 1956, at The Ohio State University in 1961, and Kenneth Wienbrenner at Buffalo State College in 1963. In 1957 the organization had a new constitution and had become the National Committee on Art Education.

Finally in a 1962 editorial column for *The NCAE Newsletter*, D'Amico seems to accept the inevitable:
> I cannot imagine that what my own progress would have been without the Committee. It has been both an inspiration and a discipline. It has pushed my sights far beyond what I could have perceived alone and it has increased my activity and energy manifold. I am sure the Committee has not done less for others (Morgan, 1993).

In June 1965, NCAE Newsletter announced the birth of the spin-off organization, the Institute for the Study of Art Education (Freundlich, 1985) now to be headquartered at New York University. This was the end of MoMA's relationship with, and role in, organized Art Education. The University Council on Art Education is a later version of the Institute for the Study of Art Education.

D'Amico and Lowenfeld

> As young students of art education our visions of practice were shaped by two colossal figures: D'Amico and Lowenfeld. Lowenfeld's influence has been recognized in the history of art education, but D'Amico's work, though not forgotten, has yet to be fully acknowledged (Sherman and Efland, 1997).

Looking back at the era of the two—Victor and Viktor—one thinks that D'Amico and Lowenfeld, both dedicated to allowing children a full measure of freedom to explore their world via art experiences and art materials should have been natural allies and should have found great comfort in each other. D'Amico's populist charisma, and Lowenfeld's professional charm, D'Amico's relationships with artists and influence in the world of art and museums, and Lowenfeld's achievements in the academic university circles could have complemented their respective domains. Indeed it was D'Amico who introduced Lowenfeld to American art education. He invited Lowenfeld to lecture in his classes at Teachers College. In his Miami University address in 1974, he recalls: We became fast friends and were sometimes called two Victors in art education. Lowenfeld gave his first lecture in the United States in my methods course at Columbia [University]. We later disagreed in educational philosophy. I was opposed to his concept of visual and haptic types on grounds that children should not be classified and that a child is the product of his environment and education, capable of being made into any form determined by the teacher. There is no such thing as the "talented" child. There are only potentially creative children. Lowenfeld and I parted ways, but I regard him as one of the greatest leaders in art education of all time (D'Amico, 1974).

This was just one of the differences in their approach to art education. Two strong-willed individuals came from very different orientations to art education. Lowenfeld with his European background in psychology, saw art education as a means to foster the creative and mental growth of the child. Art was the means not the end. A healthy, well-adjusted, creative child was Lowenfeldian aim, and aesthetic quality of his work counted for less (Efland, 1993). D'Amico would not allow "psychology" to influence his view of the child. He did not want art educators to value the expressive content of children's work over its aesthetics and turn art making into some sort of therapy. D'Amico was an art educator whose ideas about teaching came from art itself. For him art education was about providing students the experience of making art, engaging in and enjoying one's creative potential.

D'Amico and Lowenfeld wrote influential books which became standard "text books" for art teachers. "While Lowenfeld's 1947 book, *Creative and Mental Growth* was the text for my undergraduate course in art education, D'Amico's *Creative Teaching in Art* (1942/1953) was my bible for practice," writes Arthur Efland. "This was more than a how-to-do manual. He called attention to the body of knowledge as well as to techniques to be taught, he provided clear presentation of studio processes and illustrations of what good child art was supposed to look like" (Efland, 1995, p. 6). However, by 1955, the Lowenfeld book had replaced the D'Amico text (a popular textbook for a decade) as the primary resource for art education.

D'Amico invited Lowenfeld to be on The National Committee on Art Education. This was an organization that welcomed open expression and debates of honest professional differences and over the years there had been instances when the two Victor/Viktor openly clashed but I do not recollect an articulated debate over views on art education. Leah Sherman mentions a specific incident: the question of who should teach art? For Lowenfeld, if the teacher knew the child (and that meant a classroom teacher with credentials in educational psychology), he or she could under supervision of an art consultant teach art. D'Amico would not have any of that. His orientation required an art specialist (grounded in the experience of art making) trained as a teacher. (Efland cites a conversation with Leah Sherman and Jerome Hausman, in Chicago in 1993.)

Perhaps a larger explanation of the ever increasing gulf between D'Amico and Lowenfeld was grounded in the domains of their professional activity, and resources and support structures available to them. D'Amico worked in a museum: museum education had not as yet become an organized influencing network. However, in the late 1960s museum education was changing too, and curators had taken over, with studio activities at museums replaced by emphasis on visual literacy. Perceptive and viewing had become a priority over creative expression as central means for developing understanding audiences (Yenawine, 1995).

Lowenfeld, on the other hand, led a university art education department with legions of graduating students, who were to become the burgeoning faculties of art education around the country, bringing along with them *Creative and Mental Growth*, which by the late 1950s had become "the" book. Art education was emerging as a profession with shifting emphasis toward more organized and knowledge based theory and practice for the teaching of art. Art education was becoming a discipline. This was part of the paradigmic shift referred to earlier. By 1955, the Progressive Education Association had dissolved and a new educational paradigm replaced the person-centered, experience-centered art education with discipline-centered art education. By the end of the decade, the university art education departments were a growing force and the research orientation of art education (at

"...to allow them [children] to give free expression to their experiences, to find form for their discoveries is fundamental." Children's Holiday Carnival at MoMA. Undated. (Note: many photographs in this collection have no individual attribution. All credit to be assigned to D'Amico Papers, Special Collections, Milbank Memorial Library, Teachers College Columbia University.)

the expense of more open ended exploratory practices of the studio) was providing models for practice. D'Amico was disturbed by the trend. His rhetoric, "The principal aim of teaching art is to develop each individual's sensitivity to the fundamentals of art and thus to increase his creative power and his awareness of vast heritage of contemporary art and that of the past" (D'Amico, 1960, p. 9) had begun to sound repetitive.

In his 1960 speeches, D'Amico talks laudably about the Johnson Era education acts. However during the early 1960s, the U.S. Office of Education sponsored some 18 plus major conferences and research initiatives in art education. Victor D'Amico was not a presence in these evolving scenarios. Except for the New York University's federally sponsored Seminar on Elementary and Secondary School Education in the Visual Arts, directed by Howard Conant, Victor D'Amico was ignored by the broader community of art educators. One of these conferences was the renowned Penn State Seminar of 1965, an art education landmark which sort of completed the shift to discipline-centered view of art education. Victor D'Amico did neither attend nor was he invited. Victor D'Amico's era in art education had come to an end.

GUIDEPOSTS TO THE FUTURE

The following is essentially a series of paraphrased statements drawn from D'Amico's various writings, carefully structured together to present Victor D'Amico's view of art education.

The arts as a humanizing force

The principal aim of creative teaching is to develop each individual's sensitivity to the fundamentals of art and thus to increase his creative power and his awareness of the vast heritage of contemporary art and that of the past (D'Amico, 1960).

"It is my belief that arts are a humanizing force and that their major function is to vitalize living, to make each child and man the richer for having taken part in them. I believe that people are more precious than products, and that effectiveness of arts can be measured by the zest that they impart to society. Even though an artist may give his life to art, he gives it on behalf of those who will live to enjoy it. The effectiveness of art is also measured by the way it serves the most urgent needs of its time, and our greatest need today, I believe, is to rediscover the dignity of man, to help him find his self respect and to enjoy his greatest natural endowment, the power to create" (Lerman, 1979).

Fundamentals of art teaching

What is meant by "fundamentals?" Not, as most people believe, such criteria as elements and principles of art, not skill or good draftsmanship, neither technical know-how nor color harmonies and rules of perspective, neither factual data on the history of art nor verbal ability to describe, analyze and interpret a work of art. These are not fundamentals, but at best, only means to a particular expression or achievement. They are incidental to the actual fundamentals, more vital and dynamic, i.e. the development of individuality and sensitivity to aesthetic values in the works of art, in human relations, and in one's environment. As Jane Bland (1957) writes: "Giving a child opportunity and time to explore their world of experience, to create situations and environments where they could do so with the help of art materials and media, to allow them to give free expression to the experiences, to find form for their discoveries is fundamental. It is fundamental to provide young children with opportunity and encouragement to express freely. Acceptance and respect of what the child creates is fundamental. It is fundamental to learn techniques as they are needed" (D'Amico, 1960).

What does creative teaching in art do for young people?
- Has to do with helping young people develop artistic sensitivity, and helping them increase creative power.
- Has to do with understanding and enjoying the vast heritage of past as well as contemporary art.
- Has to do with helping young people see and wonder about what life means.
- Has to do with helping young people recognize that each person is unique and different from everyone else.
- Has to do with helping young people expand their vision beyond their self, and realize that there are others with equally unique visions.
- Has to do with helping young people become aware of the aesthetics of where they live (D'Amico, 1968).

What is creative teaching in art?
- Demands positive and constructive teaching by an able and skilled teacher.
- Requires planning and direction with reference to process and procedures.
- Requires teachers who motivate activity toward a specific goal, and create an environment which stimulates positive response.
- Requires children to have freedom, but not permissive free-for-all undisciplined environment

which makes no demands, sets no limitations, and provides no means for going beyond the set parameters.

- Proposes problems that are within the scope of the abilities, interests, and needs of the students' age level group: problems which result in real solutions, stretch students' imaginations, encourage exploration, provoke effort, and recognize students achievement in terms of his/her own realization and expression (D'Amico, 1963).

A creative teacher:

- Has a mastery of creative arts, and is trained in understanding of creative behavior, and cultural background of children.
- Has field experience, and some understanding of the psychological and creative growth of children at various age levels.
- Develops, stimulates and sustains creative interests, and communicates aesthetic values.
- Inspires feeling towards art, respects individuality of expression, is devoted to excellence of design and craft and has basic human warmth (D'Amico, 1966).
- Does not subscribe to the "laissez-faire" instruction but considers stimulating child's imagination, motivating ideas and setting a stage for discovery of qualities of materials as his/her primary responsibility.
- Gives great importance to the aesthetics of the learning environment and organization of instruction. Considered ways of presentation of media and carefully chosen materials are an integral part of caring creative teaching (Bland, 1957).

The baking tins, furniture coasters filled with red, yellow and blue primaries, large bristle brushes, 18" x 24" paper have become standard equipment in all elementary school art today. It would be neither be an exaggeration to claim that, that carefully thought through paraphernalia is indeed a presence of D'Amico's ideas, nor would it be far fetched to suggest that the enormous do-it-yourself movement has had it genesis in D'Amico's work, his classes and his publications. His approach, his philosophy, and his pedagogy does prevail.

References

Barkan, M. (1962). Transition in Art Education: Changing conception of curriculum content and teaching. *Art Education,* 15(7), 12-27.

Berggren, L. A. (1984). *Victor E. D'Amico: His sources and influence.* Unpublished Masters Thesis, Massachusetts College of Art, Boston.

Bland, J. C. (1957). *Art of the young child.* NY: Museum of Modern Art.

Brown, M. W. (1979). From an evangelical tent show into a modern museum. *Art News,* 78(8), 77-79.

Bruner, J. S. (1960). *The process of education.* Cambridge, MA: Harvard University Press.

Cane, F. (1926 April/May/June). Art in the life of the child. *Progressive education,* pp. 150-162.

Carlton, P. (1986). *Caroline Pratt: A biography.* Unpublished Doctoral Dissertation. Teachers College Columbia University, NY.

Churchill, A. (1991 March). *Reminiscences.* Paper read at Exploring the Legends: Guideposts to the Future, The UCAE Conference on Victor D'Amico.

Conant, H. (1995). Remembrances of Victor D'Amico and the National Committee on Art Education. In Victor D'Amico: Art as a human necessity. A catalogue: *Victor D'Amico Exhibition.* (pp. 47 - 54). Tokyo: Child Welfare Foundation of Japan.

Cowley, M. (1934). *Exile's return: A literary odyssey of the 1920's.* NY: Viking Press.

Cremin, L. A., Shanon, D. A. & Townsend, M. E. (1954). *A History of Teachers College Columbia University.* NY: Columbia University.

Cremin, L.A. (1961). *Transformation of the school: Progressivism in American education 1876-1957.* NY: Alfred A. Knopf.

D'Amico, V. E. (1930 February). Teaching art to the home child. *American Childhood.* MA: Milton Bradley Co.

D'Amico, V. E. (1931a, March). Outdoor painting for children. *American Childhood.* MA: Milton Bradley Co.

D'Amico, V. E. (1931b, November). The modern art room. *Progressive Education.* pp. 575-577.

D'Amico, V. E. (1933). Toward new art education. *Progressive Education.* (XX). pp. 461-465.

D'Amico, V. E. (1935). *Art survey-schools visited.* [Art in American Schools]. A report to the Rockefeller Foundaion. Unpublished manuscript. Victor D'Amico Papers. Special Collections, Milbank Memorial Library, Teachers College Columbia University, NY.

D'Amico, V. E. (1940). *The visual arts in general education: The report of the progressive education Association committee on function of art in education.* NY: Appleton Co.

D'Amico, V. E. (1943). The arts in therapy. *The Museum of Modern Art Bulletin.* X (3).

D'Amico, V. E. (1942/1953). *Creative teaching in art.* Scranton, PA: International Text Book Co.

D'Amico, V. E. & Duncan, J. H. (1947). *How to make pottery and ceramic sculpture.* NY: The Museum of Modern Art.

D'Amico, V. E. & Martin, C. (1949). *How to make modern jewelry.* NY: The Museum of Modern Art.

D'Amico, V. E., Bassett, K. & Thurman, A. (1951). *How to make objects of wood.* NY: The Museum of Modern Art.

D'Amico, V. E. (1951). Creative Art. *The Museum of Modern Art Bulletin.* XIX (1).

D'Amico, V. E. (1954). Art for War Veterans. *Museum of Modern Art Bulletin.* XIII (1).

D'Amico, V. E. (March 1958). *Children's Creative Center: Brussels World's Fair.* Typed article prepared for The Book of Knowledge. Victor D'Amico Papers. Special Collections, Milbank Memorial Library, Teachers College Columbia University.

D'Amico, V. E. (April 1958). Children's Creative Center in The U.S. Pavilion at the Brussels World's Fair. MoMA press release. No.29/April (also lists, Toys in the inspirational area, and the Staffing at the center). Victor D'Amico Papers. Special Collections, Milbank Memorial Library, Teachers College Columbia University, NY.

D'Amico, V. E. (no date). *Appreciation as an integral part of art education.* Unpublished manuscript. Victor D'Amico Papers. Special Collections, Milbank Memorial Library, Teachers College, Columbia University, NY.

D'Amico, V. E. (1960a). *Experiments in creative art teaching: A progress report on the department of education 1937-1960.* NY: The Museum of Modern Art.

D'Amico, V. E. (1960 b). *Art a human necessity.* An address (18th Annual Conference Report). NY: National Committee on Art Education. Victor D'Amico Papers. Special Collections, Milbank Memorial Library, Teachers College Columbia University, NY.

D'Amico, V. E. (1963). Does creative art education have a future? An address (to International Society for Education Through Art, InSEA Conference, Montreal August 1963). Unpublished manuscript. Victor D'Amico Papers. Special Collections, Milbank Memorial Library, Teachers College Columbia University, NY.

D'Amico, V. E. (May 1965). Developing creative children for a creative world. An address at The University of California Symposium on Child Art. Unpublished manuscript. Victor D'Amico Papers. Special Collections, Milbank Memorial Library, Teachers College Columbia University, NY.

D'Amico, V. E. (1966). A millennium or mirage: Art education today. An address, NAEA Pacific Regional Convention, Monterey, CA. *Art Education,* 19(5), 27-32.

D'Amico, V. E. (1967). Notes for an autobiography.

Unpublished manuscript. Victor D'Amico Papers. Special Collections, Milbank Memorial Library, Teachers College Columbia University, NY.

D'Amico, V. E. (1968a Fall). Some statements on art education, *NCAE Bulletin.* Museum of Modern Art. Special Collection, Millbank Library, Teachers College Columbia University, NY.

D'Amico, V. E. (1970, April). The progress of an art teacher.
   Arts and Activities, pp. 404-412.

D'Amico, V. E. & Buchman, A. (1970). *The art of assemblage.* NY: The Museum of Modern Art.

D'Amico, V. E. (1972). Teaching is an art. Unpublished manuscript. Victor D'Amico Papers. Special Collections, Milbank Memorial Library, Teachers College Columbia University, NY.

D'Amico, V. E. (1974). Autobiographical reminiscences: An Address: Miami University of Ohio at Oxford. Center for the Study of History of Art Education. Unpublished manuscript. Victor D'Amico Papers. Special Collections, Milbank Memorial Library, Teachers College Columbia University, NY.

Dewey, J. (1934). *Art as experience.* NY: Minton, Balch and Company.

Eisner E. W. (1989). The efflorescence of the history of art education: Advance into the past or retreat from the Present. *Proceedings of the second Penn State conference: The history of art education.* NAEA, pp. 37-41.

Efland, A. D. (1990). *A history of art education: intellectual*
   and social currents in teaching the visual arts. NY: Teachers College Press.

Efland, A. D. (1993). Child Art, Modernism and the Legacy of Victor D'Amico. Unpublished manuscript. Columbus, OH: The Ohio State University.

Efland, A. D. (1995). Victor D'Amico's Children's Art Carnival and Modern Art. In *Victor D'Amico: Art as a human necessity.* A Catalogue: (pp. 59-72). Victor D'Amico Exhibition. Tokyo: Child Welfare Foundation of Japan.

Freundlich, A.L. (1985). The (National) Committee on Art Education, *Proceedings of the Penn State conference: The history of art education.* Reston, VA: NAEA.

Freundlich, A.L. (1979). Statements about Victor D'Amico. *In Victor D'Amico: 50 Years of Humanizing the Arts.* A Catalogue Exhibition Tribute to Victor D'Amico. East Hampton, NY.

Gollin, J. (1995). The Museum of Modern Art Years. In *Victor D'Amico: Art as a human necessity.* A Catalogue: Victor D'Amico Exhibition. Tokyo: Child Welfare Foundation of Japan, pp. 5-18.

Hampton, G. (1985). Welcoming remarks. *Proceedings of the Penn State Conference: The History of Art Education.* Reston, VA: NAEA.

Hausman. J. J. (1991, March). Victor D'Amico on a larger canvas. Unpublished paper presented at "Exploring the legends: Guideposts to the future," The UCAE Conference on Victor D'Amico, NY.

Hausman. J. J. (1995). The continuing argument for art in education. In Victor D'Amico: *Art as a human necessity. A catalogue: Victor D'Amico exhibition,* (pp. 55-58). Tokyo: Child Welfare Foundation of Japan.

Lerman, D. & Govencheck, T. (1979). *Victor D'Amico: 50 Years of humanizing the arts.* A catalogue: An exhibition tribute to Victor D'Amico. East Hampton, NY.

Logan, F. M. (1955). *Growth of art in American schools.* NY: Harper and Bros.

Lord, L. (1954). *Collage and construction.* Worcester, MA: Davis Publications.

Mangravite, P. (1932). Artist and the child. In G. Hartman & A. Shumaker (Eds). *Creative expression.* NY: John Day.

Mearns, H. (1925). *Creative youth.* NY: Doubleday, Doran & Co.

Morgan, C. (1993/1994). From modernist utopia to cold war reality: A critical moment in museum education. Unpublished manuscript. Victor D'Amico Papers. Special Collections, Milbank Memorial Library, Teachers College Columbia University, NY.

Morgan, C. (1995). Victor D'Amico at MoMA: A shifting paradigm in museum education. In *Victor D'Amico: Art as a human necessity. A catalogue: Victor D'Amico exhibition.* Tokyo: Child Welfare Foundation of Japan, pp. 34-40.

Mayer, S. (1995). Victor D'Amico in the Context of Art Museum Education. In *Victor D'Amico: Art as a human necessity. A catalogue: Victor D'Amico exhibition.* Tokyo. Child Welfare Foundation of Japan, pp. 41-46.

National Children's Castle, (1995). *Victor D'Amico: Art as a human necessity. A catalogue: Victor D'Amico exhibition.* Tokyo: Child Welfare Foundation of Japan.

National Committee on Art Education: *NCAE Newsletter* (January 1964). NY, Museum of Modern Art Education Department. Victor D'Amico Papers. Special Collections, Milbank Memorial Library, Teachers College Columbia University, NY.

Pratt, C. (1924). Experimental practice in the city and country school. (Based on copious notes by Lula Wright). NY: E. P. Dutton and Co.

Read, H. (1943). *Education through art.* NY: Pantheon.

Rockefeller, N. A. (October 1962). Speech at fund raising dinner, MoMA Bulletin.

Rubin, W. (1979). Statements about Victor D'Amico. In *Victor D'Amico: 50 years of humanizing the arts. A catalogue: Exhibition tribute to Victor D'Amico.* East Hampton, NY.

Rugg, H. & Shumaker, A. (1928). *The child-centered school: An appraisal of the new education.* NY: World Book Co.

Sahasrabudhe, P. (1961). A conceptual framework for a children's art education center in New Delhi, India. (DAI *Carnival In India, 1963-64.* New Delhi, India: Bal Bhavan and National Children's Museum.

Sahasrabudhe, P. (March 1991). Victor D'Amico: A Legend and A Legacy. Unpublished paper presented at Exploring the Legends: Guideposts to the Future, The UCAE conference on Victor D'Amico, NY.

Sahasrabudhe, P. (1994). Victor D'Amico: Expressing the creative. *School Arts,* 93(2), pp. 34-36.

Sahasrabudhe, P. (1995). The Expressionist Era in Education: The Grounding for a Victor D'Amico Pedagogy. In A. Anderson, & P. Bolin (Eds). *Proceedings of the Third Penn State International Symposium: History of Art Education.* The Pennsylvania State University/NAEA. pp. 495-503.

Sahasrabudhe, P. (1995). The children's art carnival: windows on creative art teaching. In *Victor D'Amico: Art as a human necessity. A catalogue: Victor D'Amico exhibition,* (pp. 19-28). Tokyo: Child Welfare Foundation of Japan.

Sherman, L. & Efland, A. (1995). Educational discourse and visual documentation of practice: Victor D'Amico, modernism and child art. In *Proceedings of the third Penn State international symposium. History of art education,* (pp. 486-494). The Pennsylvania State University/NAEA.

Silberstein-Storfer M. (1995). Comments on Victor D'Amico. In *Victor D'Amico: Art as a Human Necessity.*

A Catalogue: Victor D'Amico Exhibition, (pp. 76-77). Tokyo: Child Welfare Foundation of Japan.

STAR, A Brussels Daily Newspaper (1958, June 7). Montreal playland world fair model: Victor D'Amico Papers. Special Collections, Milbank Memorial Library, Teachers College Columbia University, NY.

Taylor, B. B. (1995a). 25th anniversary: The children's art carnival. Annual benefit catalogue. NY: CAC in Harlem.

Taylor, B. B. (1995b). The children's art carnival: 1994 1995. Report: Objectives, Activities, Outcomes, Plans for the Future. In-house unpublished manuscript. NY: CAC in Harlem Archives.

Taylor, B. B. (1979). The children's art carnival: A Brief History. Unpublished manuscript. NY: CAC in Harlem Archives.

Times (London) (April 21, 1958). Play—the new way. Victor D'Amico Papers. Special Collections, Milbank Memorial Library Teachers College Columbia University, NY.

Winslow, L. (1939). *The integrated school art programs.* NY: Macmillan.

Wygant, F. (1993). *School art in American culture 1820 1970.* Cincinnati, OH: Interwood Press.

Yenawine, P. (1995). Approaching Art, Changing Styles: Victor D'Amico and Philip Yenawine at MoMA. In *Victor D'Amico: Art as a human necessity. A catalogue: Victor D'Amico exhibition,* (pp. 29-33). Tokyo: Child Welfare Foundation of Japan.

LOWENFELD AT PENN STATE:
A REMEMBRANCE

Robert J. Saunders

CONTEXT OF THE LEGEND

Viktor Lowenfeld's place in the history of art education is well established. *Creative and Mental Growth*, first published in 1947, had seven revised editions, the last four edited posthumously by one of his graduate students, William Lambert Brittain. The eighth and last revised edition was published in 1987, almost 27 years after Lowenfeld's death in May 1960.

Lowenfeld's theories and practices are given serious discussions in histories of art education, such as: Arthur Efland's, *A History of Art Education: Intellectual and Social Current in Teaching the Visual Arts* (Efland, 1990), and Peter Smith's, *The History of American Art Education: Learning about Art in American Schools* (Smith, 1996). There have been shorter biographical pieces, the first, a two part piece, appeared in *Studies in Art Education* (Saunders, 1960, 1961). When Stephen Dobbs was editor of *Art Education,* Michael Youngblood guest edited a special issue on Lowenfeld (Youngblood, 1982). Peter Smith wrote his Doctoral Dissertation on, "An Analysis of the Writings and Teachings of Viktor Lowenfeld: Art Educator in America" (Smith, 1983).

When *Creative and Mental Growth* appeared in 1947, elementary art education textbooks dealt briefly with modified stages of growth based upon the American Child Study Movement (1891-1903), described a variety of artmaking activities usually in separate chapters for each, drawing, painting, design, lettering, printmaking, etc. Some were based on integrated and Progressive Education concepts, and others looked at children as little artists. Some of these factors could

The world extracts a price for calling teachers wise: it keeps discussing the paths they recommend, but few men follow them. *Walter Kaufmann*

Buber, 1970, p. 10

be found in *Creative and Mental Growth*, but Lowenfeld dealt more in depth on psychoanalytic concerns, and the aesthetic, social, physical, intellectual and emotional growth evident in the art of children. Where, for instance, Margaret Mathias, in *The Beginning of Art in the Public Schools*, adapted the stages of the Child Study Movement (manipulative, cataloging, narrative and ideational) fostered by G. Stanley Hall, to the manipulative, symbolic, and realistic stages of artistic development (Saunders, 1971). Lowenfeld derived the stages of growth in art from the German and Austrian Child Study Movements taught by Kirshensteiner. Lowenfeld's stages were: (1) Scribble: uncontrolled, controlled, naming of scribble 2-4 years; (2) Pre-schematic 4-6 years; (3) Schematic 7-9 years; (4) Dawning realism/the gang age 9-11 years; (5) Pseudo-realistic/age of reasoning 11-13 years, and (6) Period of decision/crisis of adolescence 14+ years. Lowenfeld did not originate these stages of growth but adapted them from previous studies. He told me once when talking about them, that his main contribution was the "naming of scribble stage" which indicated that the child was able to find meaning in his or her own scribbles. This was an important step in the development of the child's imagination. Where other elementary art texts taught linear perspective, Lowenfeld taught the value of x-ray, fold-over, and over-lapping as stages in the natural development of the child's three-dimensional space concepts. Lowenfeld's chapter on "Abnormal Trends as Seen in Creative Activity" featured astounding examples of the art of mentally and physically challenged students (called "handicapped" then) with pictures of figures and heads modeled by blind children. His application of visual and haptic orientations explaining differences in the

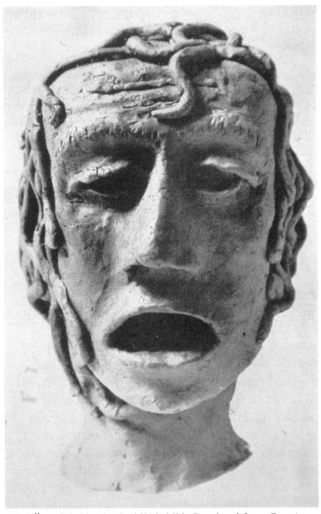

"Pain" modeled in clay by blind child. Reprinted from *Creative and Mental Growth,* 1947 Courtesy of John Lowenfeld.

I discovered *Creative and Mental Growth* in the art education section of the library stacks in San Diego State College (now University) in 1948 while taking a course in "Methods in Elementary Art." My twin brother Earl, Marcia Chamberlain (a friend since 8th grade art classes), and I were going for California certification in art. Earl and I, like other followers of Lowenfeld, were returning servicemen after World War II. We were all using the G.I. Bill to help us through college, as Efland noted above in this volume's historical introduction. Earl and I had enlisted in the Naval Reserve just before graduating from Herbert Hoover High School in San Diego, California. Our elementary art methods class had a reading list, but no assigned textbook. After finding *Creative and Mental Growth,* I asked our teacher, Tanci Sion, to put it on the textbook list, so we could buy it on the G.I. Bill. Which she did, and some of us did. In our course for "Methods in Teaching Crafts" we used Faulkner, Ziegfeld, and Hill's, *Art Today* (Faulkner, 1941).

But it was several years before I finally got to Penn State. First, I spent a year for additional certification in English and Social Studies at Chico State College, in northern California. California had no elementary art certification at that time, and all art positions were on the secondary level. The openings were few. I spent a year substitute teaching Art, English and Social Studies in the San Diego Public Schools. I

I was one of the blessed to learn under him (Lowenfeld) as well as his theories. My life was changed permanently as a result of our pathways crossing (altho I didn't realize it at the time).

Bonnie B. Schry, Boca Raton, FL. Letter to author, December 10.

first met Viktor Lowenfeld in the summer of 1952 when he was a guest professor at Long Beach State College.

Lowenfeld at Long Beach State College

During my college years I kept a small journal rather sporadically. The details and dates for what follows as memory are based upon those journals. An artist friend from San Diego, Dr. John Olsen, was head of the art department at Long Beach State. He had invited Lowenfeld to be guest professor for the summer session in 1952. Olsen and I had discussed *Creative and Mental Growth,* and visual-haptic

representational styles of children's art had not been dealt with in the literature before. He also answered some questions I had from my high school days about why some kids drew well and others didn't. These were the things which the first generation of Lowenfeldians responded to and which led them to go to Penn State to study under Lowenfeld. They came from all parts of the United States, a few from Canada, Egypt and Chile. They would write to Lowenfeld, or talk with him at one of his lectures. He was a warm, popular speaker, whose enthusiasm and Austrian accent added to his charisma. He invited them to come to Penn State, where he embraced them as a father. They had all found *Creative and Mental Growth* on their own, had it for a textbook in an undergraduate class, or first lent to them by a teacher or advisor. For some, he changed their lives.

orientation of artists, so he suggested I come as Lowenfeld's graduate assistant.

Lowenfeld was a large man, over 6 feet tall, salt and pepper hair even at 49 years (born 1903, Linz, Austria) a big warm smile, and heavy Austrian accent. He had fled Austria two days before Krystalnacht, with his family (wife: Margaret/Gretl, son: Johann/Johnny). His older brother, Berthold, preceded them by a year, and was then Superintendent of the California School for the Blind in Berkeley. They were able to leave Austria with the assistance of Sir Herbert Read, who aided in the publication in English of Lowenfeld's first book, *The Nature of Creative Activity* (Lowenfeld, 1939).

> Lowenfeld was having us draw full, free-flowing, non-representational lines with huge black marking crayons in order to become aware of the kinaesthetic origin of expressive lines. ...He was having us make drawings of ourselves carrying a heavy load on our back and pulling down on a rope as if ringing church bells and bending over with a pitchfork to gather up hay.
>
> *Duke Madenfort, 1982, pp. 22-23.*

Our textbook for the course was the second edition of *Creative and Mental Growth,* which had just been published that year, 1952. Lowenfeld taught from the textbook, demonstrated techniques, and instructed his students (art and elementary classroom teachers) in the drawing activities used as examples in the text. I recall at one time half the floor space given over to a long mural on 3-foot or 6-foot wide butcher paper of a circus made with all sorts of materials, fabrics, cut outs images, and colored or metallic papers. He was strong on murals in the classroom as projects for integrating with other subjects, and in teaching children to share space, to give and take when putting together the mural. I also recall watching him demonstrate what became known as the "Lowenfeld Motivation" by having the class act out what he wanted them to draw. He used motivations to involve the children so they would want to do the activity he had in mind for them to do. His favorite might have been eating hard candy. He gave a piece of hard candy to each student (teacher). He asked: "How does it taste? How does it feel in your mouth? Is it hard? Is it soft? How do you eat it? How do you feel when you eat it, happy? Glad? Now draw a picture, I am eating a piece of hard candy." The final statement was always to repeat the name of the picture to be drawn or painted. He always distributed materials (this time, crayons and paper) before the motivation, and kept the students busy with the motivation. This way they

could move right into the picture, instead of being distracted away from the momentum of the motivation by passing out materials. The purpose behind the motivation was to activate children's passive knowledge about themselves and stimulate self-identification. In this case, it activated learning about their faces, mouths, teeth, so they would include these details in their drawings. It was to enrich their self-images. Other motivations dealt with running, jumping, combing hair, brushing teeth, etc. doing things with parents, pets, favorite toys or playing games on the school ground. They could be drawn with crayons, painted, or modeled in Plasticine (Saunders, 1982).

The summer session ended the middle of July. On July 15th (1952), I entered in my notebook, "Dr. Lowenfeld asked me about coming to Penn State this fall to get an M.A., and eventually a Ph.D. He thinks I may be able to do the M.A. in two semesters, and arrange things as far as my program and required credits are concerned. I told Viktor it was too soon, I still need to find out what I want to do as an artist, a writer, or what? Later this morning Mrs. Lowenfeld phoned me at the department office, told me Viktor had told her how pleased he was with my assistance, apologized for not inviting me over, and hoped I would come to Penn State. I thanked her, told her I'm not yet sure what I want to do, but think I probably will be going to Penn State."

My Wunderjahre: New York City 1952-53

I spent the rest of the summer painting scenery for a production of "Carousel" with the Star Light Opera in San Diego, and in September left for a year in New York City, to try out the options. I lacked the $250.00 needed to join the stage painters union. My portfolio from a liberal arts college art department was no competition to those from professional art schools. I wasn't about to be a messenger for an art agency, carrying the artwork by agency artists back and forth in the snow. My slides of oil paintings and work were well received by those who saw them, but I still needed to support myself and find studio space. At the time, I was earning $37.50 a week minimum wages working in the receiving department of Saks Fifth

Avenue, living at the Westside Y.M.C.A, within walking distance of the Museum of Modern Art, the Whitney when it was behind the MoMA, the Frick, the Metropolitan, and the Guggenheim when it was still in a townhouse on Fifth Avenue. In March I wrote Dr. L. about a fellowship. He wrote back that he could arrange a working scholarship as a graduate assistant. At the end of the summer in 1953, I went to Penn State.

LOWENFELD AT PENN STATE

During one of the first interviews with Dr. L. we set my goal, for a Master of Science in Art Education degree, with a general minor, so I could choose my own classes in psychology, history, philosophy, and summer painting classes, plus the usual required subjects in tests and measurements, history of education, and education research. Edward Mattil, Assistant Department Head to Lowenfeld, taught a course in Secondary Art Education with Victor D'Amico's, *Creative Teaching in Art* (1953) as our textbook. Dr. Mattil emphasized exploring with crafts and materials, with some activities from his own textbook, *The Meaning in Crafts,* which was published later (Mattil, 1959). Sybil Emerson taught the design course, with her textbook, *Design: A Creative Approach* (Emerson, 1954). Kenneth Beittel taught the ceramics courses, and Art Ed. 586 "Art Education Research." Yar Chomicky taught sculpture and watercolor painting. Lowenfeld taught Mural Painting, Art Ed. 487, and seminars on Wednesday evenings, in the fall, Art Ed. 534, "Therapeutic Aspects of Art," and in the spring, "A History and Philosophy of Art Education." These two seminars were probably unique at that time, and may not have been taught in art education programs other than at Penn State.

The education courses were taught in the Education Department in Burrows Building, where Lowenfeld had his office. The Art Education classes were taught in "Temp" a wooden frame structure left over from the War, when the U.S. Army was on campus. It was rectangular with a corridor bisecting the center leaving two courtyards inside. The Fine Art Department was in the front half, and Art Education in the back half. The walls of the corridors of both sections were covered with murals by students in Lowenfeld's mural painting classes. The first semester murals were personal and had a therapeutic purpose in which

students confronted problems and conflicts in their own lives. Lowenfeld led the class around the halls, and chalk marked an "X" on those murals which could be painted over. New murals were painted over older murals as students in each succeeding class chose the space they would use, and paint out the mural before it. At first walking through these halls was a bit unnerving, to see the angst, anxieties, weeping faces, clutching hands, figures hidden in trees, some representational, others abstracted. One day, walking through them, I thought a poem: "Mural, mural on the wall; tell us all, tell us all!"

Perhaps more than any other of Lowenfeld's students, John Biggers has carried on his tradition with his own murals, and those of his students on the walls of the Art Education Department at Texas Southern University in Houston. Olive Theisen's, *The Murals of John Thomas Biggers* (Theisen, 1996) provides pictures of the outlines and drawings with which Biggers plans his murals, very much in the process taught by Lowenfeld and used by his students in "Old Temp." John Biggers came to Penn State from Hampton Institute (now University), where Lowenfeld had taught and refined some of his theories before going to Penn State. John Mack, who was a teacher at Hampton, also followed Lowenfeld to Penn State. While Lowenfeld was at Hampton, Charles White completed his mural, "Contributions of the Negro to Democracy in America," Elizabeth Catlett, married to White at the time, taught sculpture, and Samella Lewis also worked with Lowenfeld then (Theisen, 1996). One Sunday afternoon when I was at Penn State, we all drove down to Bucknell University in Lewisburg, Pennsylvania, to hear Jacob Lawrence, whom Lowenfeld also knew from Hampton, talk about his work for an exhibition, which I recall as his series of prints on John Brown, the Abolitionist.

Lowenfeld's Mural Classes I and II

Lowenfeld lectured the first few weeks of class, Monday and Wednesdays, 9:00-11:00 a.m. Between classes we wrote down ideas for murals from past issues and problems in our lives, discussed them with Dr. L., chose one, wrote a narrative about it (verbalizing was important to the process), and listed secondary events related to it, which we then sketched on separate sheets of paper. We used, as Lowenfeld called it,

The halls of old Temp were like secular wailing walls for the ailing spirit. They were not murals in the usual sense. One couldn't even back off to see them. You were caught in a whirlpool of personal reconstruction.

Kenneth H. Beittel (Beittel, 1982, p. 21).

a "significance sequence" in which the size of each sub-issue or event was large or small according to how significant it was in our lives. We then organized the events in a left to right chronological sequence according to the narrative. Next we traced over the whole gestalt of the mural, and prepared the wall by painting over the previous mural with white Texolite. We scaled off the drawing and the wall, and re-drew the images larger on the wall, without changing them in order to maintain the spontaneity and expressive line of the sketches. (Adapted from my notes, September 23, 1953.) Lowenfeld's lectures covered his philosophy about mural painting, and the techniques for painting them. He taught us that the difference between the fine arts and art education was that in the fine arts, the emphasis was on the product, and in art education it was on the process. The difference between the artist and the non-artist, is that the non-artist can only identify with himself (this was 1953, before gender correct terminology was established), while the artist can identify himself both with his subject matter and with that which is outside himself. Because murals are less intimate (more public) than paintings, they lack the spontaneity of painting since they must communicate. Through painting we learned to own the experience, have control over it, and clear it from our lives. Lowenfeld demonstrated different stages in the process and how to separate the egg yolk from the albumin and mix the egg tempera which we used with dry pigments. He taught us an *al secco* technique, in which we applied color, then rubbed the brush strokes down to reveal the texture of the wall. Lowenfeld felt that the mural should enhance the wall not violate it with painterly techniques. Rather than use white, we let the wall come through, and "de-materialized" the paint by rubbing it down to reveal the white of the wall.

Lowenfeld had a moralistic philosophy about murals, that they should enhance the wall by remaining on the surface, not violate it by showing three-dimensional form or penetrating the wall with deep space illusions. He felt that moral and ethical cultures produced murals sensitive to the walls, as during the early Renaissance in Giotto's murals for the Arena Chapel, but that the Baroque, and Mannerist murals exhibited a decadent society during which murals denied the existence of the wall with the trompe l'oeil, (fool the eye) effects, false architectural features, columns, railings, and skies on ceilings.

The mural I painted covered a wall 7 1/2' high and 11' long, with a door on the left end, around which I fitted smaller figures. The theme was my leaving home, the trek to study under Lowenfeld at Penn State, and self-discovery in which the final image was a giant ego Howard Roark-like Existential figure of myself, holding a smaller image of myself in my open hand exalting in being free. (In the Navy I had read, Ayn Rand's, *The Fountainhead,* in college, Andre Gide's novels about gratuitous acts, in New York City, Gide's journals, and books by Jean-Paul Sartre.) When the mural was finished we wrote our signatures, rather than lettered our names, because these were therapeutic works of art. In signing them, we took responsibil-

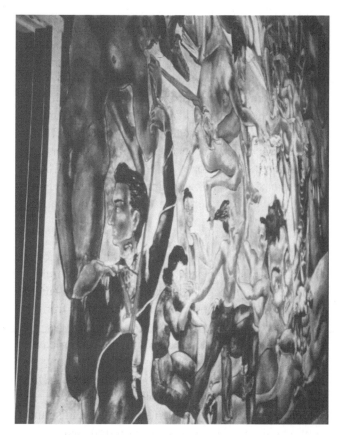

"Mural by author for Lowenfeld's course in Mural painting (1953), in hallway, 'Old Temp.'"

ity for this part of our lives. We took slides of the murals, but over the years many of them have been lost or misplaced.

In the Advanced Mural class, we did not paint about ourselves. Heads of different departments might ask Lowenfeld for a mural describing their department. Lowenfeld told us who wanted murals, we chose one, and then visited the department to see what they wanted. I chose one for the U.S. Naval Torpedo Testing Laboratory. They wanted a mural for their reception area that illustrated what they do, which was test torpedoes in a water tunnel. I chose the assignment because I had been in the Navy during World War II, and at one time seriously thought of volunteering for submarine duty. I visited the laboratory, sketched the water tunnel and the engineers standing looking at it with clipboards; researched the diagrams and history of torpedoes, found pictures of the interiors of submarines, and saw a couple of movies about submarine warfare. I made my drawings, following the same process as before, and told the story of testing and using torpedoes. But, I couldn't get it right. Dr. L. and I struggled and fretted about it. After a couple of weeks, I told Viktor that the mural didn't say what I wanted to about torpedoes. He gave me permission to do it my own way, implying it would be all right if the Laboratory chose not to accept it.

Within one class period, I finished my drawings as I wanted them. I built a frame for the muslin or sheeting for the mural, primed it with Texolite. It was 4-1/2 feet high, and 7-1/2 feet long. The difference between these murals and our therapeutic murals, was that we painted them separately and installed them on the walls, and we lettered rather than wrote our names when finished. This maintained

their objectivity from our lives. On the left end of the mural was the water tank with a torpedo inside. The engineers stood around looking at the tank, its gauges, and holding clipboards. On the far right end, sailors on a submarine had just loaded a torpedo which was being fired, while a sailor with a hard face and black hair called for another torpedo. He was also shown sleeping peacefully in a bunk bed, while below him, in another bunk bed, a blond haired sailor lies awake visualizing in the center of the mural a Japanese ship's captain pointing down at a torpedo headed for his ship, and the explosion. Dominating the center, a large face of the Japanese ship's captain, water flowing out of his open mouth, reaching his arm up grabbing air in his hand, as he drowns.

When finished, we took the mural to the Testing Laboratory, and left it to be installed. A couple weeks passed, and we did not hear from them. We called and they said they were going to put it in their board room instead of the reception area. A week or so later we phoned again. The person we spoke to said the colors were wrong. They didn't go with the walls. We said with their gray concrete brick walls, the color was all right. Finally, he asked, "Would you like to know what the real problem is?" "Yes," we said. "It reminds us of something we would like to forget," he said. We said we knew that would be a problem. They asked if they could return it, we said yes, and went to get it. I took pictures of it in their offices. We took it back to "Temp" and hung it over a door in stock room of the art education department. The summer after Lowenfeld died, I was on campus for my doctoral defense of thesis and went to get it. It was gone. Nobody knew where. It had probably been painted over by someone who needed the canvas for another mural.

"Torpedo mural" by author, painted for U.S. Torpedo Testing Laboratory. Penn State Campus. Never installed. 1954.

Lowenfeld's Seminars

Dr. L. taught two graduate seminars on Wednesday evenings, 7:00-9:00 p.m.; "Psychotherapeutic Aspects of Art," in the fall semester, and "The History and Philosophy of Art Education" in the spring. They were required courses, but we wouldn't have missed taking them. No matter where Lowenfeld was on a lecture trip, he always, always, returned in time for these seminars. His lectures were well written out, he read and extemporized on them, and didn't stop from the beginning of the class to the end. His voice was strong but soft, and expressive. His Austrian accent was only a slight problem at times, but his slowness of speech made note taking easy. We asked questions and he answered them thoroughly. We had no break in the middle of the class as in other evening seminars. Ken Beittel mentioned one time, early on, when Viktor was first at Penn State, that he talked for three hours, until someone said to throw in the towel. He asked what that meant. He was told he had been lecturing for three hours and it was time to quit. After that he kept himself to two hours. We all sat around a group of tables arranged in a large rectangle, with Dr. L. seated at one end. Although he was not arrogant, he had an imposing manner in spite of himself, which may have come with the Prussian academic tradition in which he grew up. In the Grad office we joked about sometimes feeling we should stand up when he entered the room.

Dr. L. dramatized his lectures. When telling us about the problems of the partially seeing, he leaned over, held a picture against his eye as if trying to see its details. He opposed copying but when working therapeutically, said it might be necessary. He told about a partially seeing boy who, because of his narrow visual range, was copying a painting of a tree from a postal card in which the tree overlapped the sun. When the boy discovered that, he got very excited to see that a tree could cover the sun. Dr. L. also told us about his research and work with some of the cases described in his chapter, "Abnormal Trends as Seen in Creative Activity." This chapter appeared in the first three editions of *Creative and Mental Growth,* but was removed from the posthumous editions. William Lambert Brittain, who edited them, told me years later, the decision was Macmillan's. Their plan was to have a separate publication with that

chapter and other related writings, but it never came about. In this seminar, Dr. L. also made it clear that we were not to act as therapists, but only recognize symptoms and traits if they are revealed in children's art so as to get further guidance. He also recommended we take the "Introduction to Exceptional Children" course taught in the Special Education Department.

The seminar on "The History and Philosophy of Art Education" was taught during the spring semester, entirely from lecture notes. Most of the sessions dealt with the European origins which Lowenfeld knew well, beginning with Corrado Ricci, Maria Montessori, Johann Pestalozzi, Frederick Froebel, Georg Kerschensteiner, Max Verworn, and Gustave Britsch, Franz Cizec, and others. It was from Kerschensteiner that the stages of growth were developed in the German Child Study Movement, and later the Visual-Haptic continuum was developed. Dr. L.'s knowledge of art education history in the United States was less comprehensive, and here he filled in the gaps with assignments and papers which we presented to the class. He was always pleased with any research that supported his own theories and practices, but encouraged other research as well.

Lowenfeld was also adamantly opposed to the use of coloring and copying books. He said that Fascism began in the kindergartens of Germany, where children were trained at an early age to stay within the boundaries set for them, like lines of their coloring lessons. I prepared a paper tracing the origin of color-ins to Frederick Froebel in *The Education of Human Nature* in 1826 (Fletcher & Welton, 1912). Froebel described ways to teach children about nature by having them draw leaves, then suggested they could draw around the leaves for their outlines first, or use patterns of leaves. Finally, he suggested the teacher could save time by drawing around the leaves first, and have the children fill in the outline. At Christmas time in 1955, Bellefonte Chamber of Commerce in the *Centre Daily Times* serving Bellefonte and State College communities, initiated a coloring contest with drawings of Santa Claus. Lowenfeld wrote a letter of protest, which was reinforced by other Penn State art education students and faculty. It turned into a campaign which was finally picked as a news item by both the *Pittsburgh Press* and *Newsweek.* Tom Slettehaugh, one of Lowenfeld's students, saved the clippings (Slettehaugh, 1955).

Lowenfeld: Speaking Autobiographically

In one seminar session, Lowenfeld told about his own life and background. In 1958, Ellen Abel taped this session, and John Michael edited and had it transcribed at the Miami Center for the Study of the History of Art Education (Lowenfeld, 1958). Several questions often arise about Lowenfeld's life: (1) Did he study under Franz Cizec, and Oskar Kokoschka? (2) Did he know Sigmund Freud and Martin Buber? He answered some of these questions in his autobiographical session.

RE: Franz Cizec: Lowenfeld, in his autobiographical lecture, refers to being "exposed" to Cizec when they were both at the Kunstgewerbeschule, where he was studying and Cizec held his children's classes. At the same time, Lowenfeld studied painting with Oskar Kokoschka, in the evening classes at the Kunstgewerbeschule, about which Dr. L. said, "expressionistic art was in all of our living" (Lowenfeld, 1958, p. 17). What Lowenfeld learned from Kokoschka about expressionism must have been in conflict with what he saw when he visited Cizec's classes.

Cizec taught children only. He did not teach the older students how to teach, but they did visit his classes to observe his methods. Lowenfeld was one of them. In the class that Lowenfeld told us about, Cizec demonstrated at the slate board how to draw a horse, beginning with a rectangle, then adding two triangles for the neck and head, and again for the legs. The children followed step-by-step; it was the traditional method of teaching children how to draw in the 19th century. Lowenfeld was critical of Cizec's methods, and read us a passage from Viola's book, *Child Art* (Viola, 1944), about Cizec's methods for releasing the imagination of the child. But as Dr. L. described them, Cizec's methods differed from what he was saying. Lowenfeld read this passage with a highly critical and devastating sarcasm.

We had never seen this side of Lowenfeld before, and were greatly disturbed. We even talked about it the next day in the graduate students' office, a room set aside for our use with a couple of desks and chairs. The next week, Lowenfeld began the seminar by apologizing to us for his treatment of Cizec in his

reading. He said, it was wrong, it bothered him on the way home and he worried about it during the week. He said, in effect, that Cizec could only advance so far, he was held back by his own training and background. He said Cizec saw what should be done, but could not do it, even Christ was able to achieve just so much and go no further. Cizec had freed children from the rigid subject matter of the past (probably geometrical shapes and linear perspective taught in Prussian schools in the 19th century), and gave them things to draw which interested them, such as animals and children playing games. To some extent Lowenfeld may have been talking about himself. For all the freedom he allowed us, he was quite adamant about his beliefs and in encouraging our self-expression. This may have been why we had that feeling about his Prussian academic tradition and joked about standing up as he entered the seminar room.

Lowenfeld's Salad Days (Formative Years)

Lowenfeld was about 18 or 19 years old when he studied in the Kunstgewerbeschule. However, in 1920 when he was 17, and had just graduated from the Realgymnasium (the equivalent to the high-school and community college level in the United States), Lowenfeld became involved in a youth movement which, as he said, "no longer differentiated between Catholic youth movements, Protestant youth movements, or Jewish youth movements, or Pathfinders or Scouts. All went under one big heading, the Youth Ring, Jugendring." (Lowenfeld, 1958, p. 10). With Martin Buber, Rabindranath Tagore, and other education leaders less well known in this country, Siegfried Bemfield, Gutave Wynecken, they started an experiment on Ryckfohr (or Fohr), an island in the North Sea.

There, in the town of Wyckfohr, they founded, what they called, a Jungend Republik (Youth Republic), in which youths governed themselves. Lowenfeld said he was "only a small wheel." He was an intermediary between the children and the leaders, and many others could meet with them. He described it as "a most wonderful time of learning—of romantic learning. Don't ever look down at romanticism because it is romanticism which probably brings together (your) emotions and your intellect and your senses. You become much more open-like. When you are in love, you see things more sensitively and experience them more intensely... There is nothing wrong about it. These are some of the very decisive stages in my development" (Lowenfeld, 1958, p. 11).

Repeatedly, when Lowenfeld's students and members of his staff speak about him, they tell about that feeling of being the only one. We may have waited outside his office to see him, but when he talked to us we had his full attention. He made us each feel as if we were the only one. It was more than just part of his charisma, it had an intensity which seemed to come from inside. It was not practiced or rehearsed. This might be what Buber called the *"Ich und Du"* relationship. Buber had finished the first draft of *Ich und Du* in the fall of 1919. The Jungendring was founded the following year, 1920. Buber published, *Ich und Du* (Trans. *I and Thou*) (1923), so this could have been very much a part of the philosophy he taught in the youth ring (Buber, 1970).

> The island Lowenfeld called Ryckfohr, is probably Fohr, one of the North Frisian Islands in the North Sea. Off the coast of Schleswig-Holstein, it was the property of the Duchy of Schleswig until 1864, and was the property of Denmark and now Germany. Fohr is 32 sq. miles in area, with a population of 9,800 in 1990. Its main city, Wyk auf Fohr, was chartered in 1910. Now, it sports tourism, a bathing resort, shell fishing, airport, ferry terminal, and a Romanesque church.
>
> *Cohen, 1998*

It may have been from both Buber and the sacredness of all life in the Hindu beliefs of Rabindranath Tagore that Lowenfeld learned or developed his love of nature, of letting natural things grow naturally, whether they were people, animals, plants or weeds. As Lowenfeld, said, "I remembered always from the youth movement, as part of our growing up, that we should use all our senses to become more sensitive to nature. See! This is what Buber said. This is what Rabindranath Tagore said. This is what we had been exposed to. Only man who uses all his refinements of his sensitivities grows up a refined human being in a world of peace." (Lowenfeld, 1958, pp. 12-13.) Ed Mattil tells of walking with Lowenfeld in the yard of his home, and starting to pull out weeds, dandelions, chickweeds, and thistles. Lowenfeld was pained to see him do it, and told him how beautiful they were and that he should leave them (Mattil, 1982). I too,

recall one day when the Lowenfelds were moving into their new house, which they had designed and built on Franklin Avenue. Viktor asked me to come over and help him transplant a cherry tree. We were going to move it from outside the kitchen door in their place on Atherton, to a similar place in the new house. He had the tools. I took the pick, and the spade and started to dig vigorously when he stopped me. "No," he said, "Stop. You are approaching it like an intellectual. You must be gentle and sensitive to its roots so it will grow." So, I stopped, surveyed the trunk (like a thinking type), moved out to give the roots more space, and went at it less vigorously. We transplanted it, and it was still growing the summer after Viktor died. It may grow there still.

Lowenfeld's Experiments with the Blind

Lowenfeld taught art in the elementary schools in Vienna for 5 years while attending the Art Academy in Vienna, which he found "very dry and academic." He then transferred to the Kunstgewerbeschule, which he likened to a "Vienna Bauhaus," where he studied for several years and received his diploma. There he also studied sculpture under Edward Steinberg, who required his students to blindfold themselves when working with clay. This "revolted" Lowenfeld. He felt we should use all our senses, and not deprive the use of the visual sense when sculpting. He confronted Steinberg, but was told, "You get your visual experience in your painting class" (Lowenfeld, 1958, p. 13). This was incompatible with what he had learned in the Jugenring, so he decided to visit the Institute for the Blind, to find proof that Steinberg was either right or wrong.

> Whenever I went to see Dr. Lowenfeld in his office, he always made me feel as though he was there just waiting for me to come, as if I were his only student.
>
> *John Michael (Michael, 1982, p. 14).*

> With Viktor you felt that there were only two people on earth, and you were one of the two, and you were equals.
>
> *Edward Mattil (Mattil, 1982, p. 9).*

At the Institute for the Blind, Lowenfeld approached the Director, Dr. Burkle, who had published a book, *Psychology of the Blind,* and was a professor at the University of Vienna. Viktor presented Burkle with some of Steinberg's concepts, and suggested the possibility that blind people, because they were deprived of the sense of sight would produce the "best sculptures or at least the purest three-dimensional sculptures." Dr. Burkle opposed the idea on the basis that "blind people cannot have simultaneous images" and do not have an imagination in which symbols can be organized into a simultaneous image—into a whole" (Lowenfeld, 1957, p. 14). Burkle refused to let Lowenfeld experiment, but suggested that he read his book, and enroll in the University of Vienna, to "study some of the perception of blind people, and get some of the psychological knowledge" (Lowenfeld, 1957, p. 15). Lowenfeld continued his studies at the Kunstgewerbeschule, and also attended the University, studied art history, psychology, and minored in mathematics which fascinated and "interested (him) in the laws in nature" and "some of the old laws of proportions (which) you can only understand if you study mathematics, especially trigonometry..." (Some of these old laws very possibly were the sacred geometry of Pythagoras with the geometrical structures of nature and natural phenomenon, popular during the 19th century.) Lowenfeld was also teaching art in elementary classrooms, and later would teach both art and mathematics in the Realgymnasium or secondary schools.

> Three are the spheres in which the world of relation arises. The first: life with nature. ...I contemplate a tree. ...I can feel its movement: the flowing veins around the sturdy, striving core, the sucking of the roots, the breathing of the leaves, the infinite commerce with earth and air—and the growing itself in the darkness.
>
> *Buber, 1970, pp. 56-57.*

Lowenfeld still wanted to experiment with blind children in making sculpture, so he visited them on Sunday afternoons at the Institute for the Blind, without informing Dr. Burkle. He made friends with three of them, two boys and a girl, and talked with them about art and sculpture. They asked if they could do some too. He stole some clay from the Kunstgewerbeschule and had them make clay heads and masks, which he carried out of the Institute in his briefcase so nobody would see them. He braced the sides of the briefcase with small sticks, so the sculptures wouldn't be mashed. After he had quite a collection, he took samples to Dr. Burkle, who objected to his doing this without permission, and sent him from the office, saying, "Out! Out! This can be the downfall of education for the blind if it is known. Blind people will think they can become sculptors,

artists. This is misleading! This is a crime! Out!" (Lowenfeld, 1958, p. 19.) Lowenfeld was 19 years old. It was 1922.

At that time, Lowenfeld was reading a monthly pamphlet, *Die Fackle (The Torch)*, published by the poet, Karl Kraus, with poems, literary articles, satire, drawings, and poetry by the insane. Viktor wrote Kraus about his work with the blind. Kraus asked to see the examples, and found them to be, "fundamental works which should become known." By then, the Institute for the Blind had a new Director, Dr. Siegfried Altmann, who was an admirer of Karl Kraus. Kraus brought Lowenfeld and the sculptures to the attention of Dr. Altmann, who immediately introduced modeling into the school curriculum, and made Lowenfeld "responsible for all creative teaching there" (Lowenfeld, 1958, p. 21). At that time, he also received his secondary teaching certificate, and taught art and mathematics in the Realgymnasium This was 1924. Lowenfeld remained at the Institute, and continued his studies at the University. In 1925, Lowenfeld designed and made the stained glass windows for the giant Concert Building at the Paris World's Fair.

About 1926-1928, Lowenfeld published an article in a medical magazine about his work with the blind. Sigmund Freud read it and phoned Lowenfeld. He would like to see the work. Lowenfeld replied that he would be honored by such a visit, after which Freud visited frequently to observe what he was doing. At the same time, Freud was revising his book, *Totem and Taboo*. As a result, Lowenfeld became more seriously involved in research as a scientific venture. He read Carl Jung's typologies, psychological types, as well as those by Danzels, Nietzche, and Schiller (Lowenfeld, 1958, p. 24).

Young Lowenfeld had already been observing differences, and gathering data. This led to the writing of his first book, *die Entstehung der Plastik* (The Genesis of Sculpturing) published in Germany in 1932. It was also his Doctoral Dissertation title and dealt with parallels between sighted and blind individuals who had never sculpted/modeled before. Later, he met through Karl Kraus, "a very wonderful art historian," Ludwig Munz, a Professor at the University of Vienna, who had already published a book on Goethe and his art. Munz became fascinated with the sculptures of the blind. Together, he and Lowenfeld published, *Plastiche Arbeiten Blinder* (Sculptures of the Blind), in 1934 in Germany. This was followed with *The Nature of Creative Activity* (1939) based on similar research. Written in German, Lowenfeld sent it to Sir Herbert Read, who had it translated and published in England.

There has been a feeling among some education researchers that Lowenfeld's research methods were not empirical enough to be solid research. If we look at Lowenfeld according to his psychological type, empirical research would not be his way of investigating learning processes. In looking at Lowenfeld's typologies from the Jungian point of view, which Lowenfeld had studied, I think he would have been an Intuitive-Feeling type. Carl Jung defined four personality types: Thinking, Sensation, Intuitive and Feeling, which paired off into whole types. Lowenfeld's feeling functions would explain his warmth and love, and charisma of which he gave of himself. But it is with his Intuitive functions that he handled his knowledge and learning. He analyzed and synthesized very well, but he was not an academic in the same way as the Thinking-Sensation type of intellectual. This was in evidence in his early years. As a child from about 4 or 5 years, to 10 years, his Intuitive-Feeling preference showed up. Lowenfeld was "very much drawn to music, played the violin, and was considered a child prodigy because he could 'play almost anything out of mind, including whole concerts.'" He played "with the symphony—even difficult pieces." Upon one occasion he played before the Archduke, for which he was given a violin as a gift. Lowenfeld goes on to say, "I was called Gypsy because I played everything out of mind." His parents thought he should "become educated and learn to play the violin from music." His teacher made it "very serious, too serious, and made (him) play very exacting according to sheet music, and that stopped (him)" (Lowenfeld, 1958, pp. 3-4). One Sunday evening at the Lowenfeld's we discussed intuition and a statement by Albert Einstein, in which he talked about knowing intuitively something that is way out somewhere (Viktor reached out with his arm) and then having to do the research to prove it.

Lowenfeld did not consider himself a researcher as such, but he was one of the first to really advocate research in art education against much criticism from other art educators, especially those in the National Committee on Art Education. He encouraged his graduate students to conduct research in areas where he saw lacunas in our knowledge about creativity, learning to make art, and differences between artists and non-artists. He was always glad to recognize and support studies and reports which supported his own theories that provided new evidence for the visual-haptic continuum, stages of growth, and so forth, but he was equally supportive of students who wanted to follow their own direction.

Lowenfeld and Doctoral Dissertations

For my Doctoral Dissertation, I had no interest in doing test-and-measurement types of research. My real interests, in addition to art, were in history and creative writing. We decided early on, that my Master's Thesis would be a pilot study for a larger history of art education to be developed further as my doctoral dissertation. My master's thesis was rather presumptuously titled, "The Parallel Development of Art Education in the United States and Canada, with Emphasis on the History of Art Education in Canada" (Saunders, 1954). With the thesis finished, Viktor and I began planning a history of art education in the United States for my Doctoral, when we each received a brochure that a history was already being published, Frederick Logan's, *The Growth of Art in America's Schools* (Logan, 1955), which had been Logan's dissertation. We realized after reading Logan's history, that a Doctoral Dissertation should go into depth on a single phase of history, rather than try to do the whole thing. Lowenfeld invited Logan to teach a summer course at Penn State, which I was to attend. Afterwards, Dr. L. asked me to suggest some areas of study. I found three. One was Lowenfeld himself, which he said was not appropriate. Another

He (Lowenfeld) was, in any event a classic Type A personality who traveled the rubber chicken circuit endlessly and willingly spoke to any group who would invite him, often saying, 'I go to preach the Gospel' as he boarded a plane for Boston, or Boise, or Keokuk, or Kalamazoo or wherever.

Harlan Hoffa, 1998, pp. 21-22.

was John Dewey and his philosophy on art and education, and the third was Horace Mann. He was mentioned in Logan's book, and I had recently read Louise Hall Tharp's, *The Peabody Sisters of Salem* (Tharp, 1950). Such a study would gave me a family narrative of three people, each of whom had different approaches to teaching art and drawing in 19th century Boston.

As a dissertation, it was more appropriate for a Ph.D. degree, than an Ed.D., which focused on tests and measurements. Dr. L. said the main academic difference between the two degrees, is that the Ph.D. required knowledge of two foreign languages, and the Ed.D. required knowledge of tests and measurements. The Ph.D. must be on an original topic, but not necessarily make a contribution, and the Ed.D. could build on someone else's research, but it had to make a contribution to our knowledge of learning. A history was, therefore, more appropriate for a Ph.D. topic than an Ed.D. topic. While we were talking about it, Lowenfeld phoned Dean Trabue, Dean of the College of Education, and said he knew that Doctoral Dissertations in education were supposed to be based on educational and applied research, but that he had an Ed.D. candidate who was not interested in tests and measurements, but in historical research and we were in need of historical research in art education. Thus, he was given permission for a historical study for a Ed.D. degree. My dissertation title was, "The Contributions of Horace Mann, Mary Peabody Mann, and Elizabeth Peabody to Art Education in the United States" (Saunders, 1961). Looking back on Lowenfeld's phone call, I can imagine him making a similar call to Dean Trabue for permission to have John Biggers make a mural for his dissertation, which was, I think, the first time a mural was acceptable for a Doctorate. Biggers' written dissertation became the documentation of his research and drawings.

That was in March 1956. We were in his office, which was more like a cubby. Afterwards I wrote in my notebook: Lowenfeld said, "All research should

The mural John Biggers painted for his Doctoral Dissertation (1954) was "The Contribution of Women to American Life and Education" for the Blue Triangle Branch, of the YWCA, Houston.

Theisen, 1996.

contribute to better teaching. An Ed.D. is a professional degree, as is an M.D.; a Ph.D. is not a professional degree and is not used to show new knowledge in the field... If a dissertation does not become a deeper experience in the search for new knowledge then and only then should it be abolished... Publishing is not necessary for a Doctoral Degree, nor afterward. Having fallen deeply in love once, is it necessary to do so again?... When a doctoral candidate gets hold of his dissertation and it holds him, he becomes pregnant, and remains so until he has given birth. Even those who have given birth more than once or loved more than once—the first time is the most decisive" (From my notebook, March 1956).

It took 4 years to research and write my dissertation. I left the Penn State campus for 4 years of public school teaching, also required for the Ed.D. Degree. I found a position teaching art in the Junior-Senior High

Last photograph of Viktor Lowenfeld, while listening to Mozart's *Quintet in F,* the Sunday afternoon before his stroke, (April, 1960).

School, North Arlington, New Jersey. It was near my main sources of research, 20 minutes by bus from the New York Public Library, and several hours drive to the Massachusetts Historical Society in Boston. Lowenfeld asked us to send our dissertations to him chapter by chapter, so he and our other advisers, could keep abreast of the research and find possible errors before too much had been built upon them. This was especially important for those doing test and measurement research. It was while I was in New Jersey that Lowenfeld died. I had sent him my final chapters several weeks before, a longer time than usual had passed. I phoned him at home on a Saturday morning, April 9th (I think). Johnny, his son, answered telling me of Viktor's stroke. It happened while he was making an impassioned plea to the Board of Trustees on the need to keep the elementary art education program. He never recovered, and died May 25, 1960. There was an obituary in the *New York Times* on May 26th. Viktor was dead. The lion had left the field. In German, Lowenfeld meant, "Lion in the field." With that, and a given name like, "Viktor" how could he not become a victor in whatever field he ranged.

Lowenfeld opened his autobiographical session by asking, "Who has not become involved in the creative process so much that he felt that his only desire and wish would be to finish this only and one product and then he may die? But, may I say, there is always a first love. And this first time, when you begin to feel a spark which hits you, is probably one of the decisive moments in your whole life the first love always remains young because it remains with the past and does not grow older with you as you grow older" (Lowenfeld, 1958, p. 1). For Viktor, I think, the Jugenring was a first love, as were his experiments with the blind children, and the aura of German Expressionism in which he grew up and painted. He in turn, and Penn State, became, for many of us, one of our own first loves.

Margaret/Gretl and Viktor/Vikle at Home

I completed the revised draft of my dissertation, and returned to Penn State that summer for my defense in July. Gretl asked me to stay with her while I was there. We sat in the kitchen and she told me of the stroke and Viktor's days in the hospital. It is not possible to think of Lowenfeld at Penn State, without

Photoportrait of Gretl, taken by V. L. Courtesy of John Lowenfeld.

remembering Gretl. Viktor would invite his graduate students over for an evening of sometimes music, or talk, he might play the guitar. Although Gretl sang, but not for guests. She gave recitals of German Lieder at Hillel, the Jewish Center, to raise funds in support of the center or other causes. Gretl and Viktor were warm, gracious, and caring hosts. The first time I was their guest, we listened to recordings, talked, and Viktor showed me the manuscript for *Creative and Mental Growth,* written in long-hand on lined paper, with only minor spelling and punctuation corrections. Other times they encouraged us to dance spontaneously to Mozart, or some other chamber music.

In their new house, they held a reception for the members of the Penn State Graduate Club in Art Education, which Lowenfeld had formed, after we had held our annual summer conference on campus, during which the grad students gave reports on their research findings, dissertation work, and learned to plan conferences. We looked at Viktor's paintings, a few portraits of Gretl. A painting of a black man bent down by a great white bundle carried on his back hung on the wall over Gretl's grand piano. In Viktor's room, his painting of a blind man in pale colors holding a plant and feeling the leaves with his fingers, sat on an easel. There were several earlier works in his study, and downstairs in the family room. But that posthumous summer, Gretl and I would sit in the kitchen while she asked repeatedly, why it happened, this was the house Viktor planned to retire to and live out their lives. At the end of that summer I left North Arlington, for an elementary art position on Long Island.

APPLICATIONS: LOWENFELD A LA CARTE

From 1960-1966, I taught art in Commack, Long Island, New York. At the time it was the fastest growing school district in the country, the result of suburban expansion from the New York City area. We built 16 schools in 5 years. That made it possible to add an art teacher to each new elementary school as it was completed. We had no art rooms, and for me this had its advantages. I found it easier to integrate art with other subjects in the classroom, especially when making murals of Indian life on Long Island, or the discovery of America, or leaving student's self-hardening clay pots in the classroom for social studies units to dry before painting them the following week, or building a puppet stage. I could leave a mural, puppet stage, or other incomplete works in the classroom so the children could complete work on it before the next art class.

They also worked with Plasticine, which I used to prepare them for working with self-hardening clay in later grades. Each child from Kindergarten to second grade had his or her own 1/4-pound ball of Plasticine in a small milk carton

to use in art class or in free time. Lowenfeld recommended Plasticine for children to learn about the body as an aid to drawing. He said that if children had trouble drawing certain things, then change the materials. Instead of drawing it, have them make it in Plasticine, which frees them of the problem of drawing. For instance with 1st and 2nd grade students, I had a lesson to develop their left-right body concepts, by drawing themselves pledging the allegiance to the flag. I used Lowenfeld's method of having the children act out pledging (activate their passive knowledge), by asking them to look at how the flag hangs, notice how their right arm bends and the clothes they were wearing. After which I would say, "Now let's draw, I am pledging allegiance to the flag." Their materials, crayons, and 18 x 12 inch brush manila paper, was distributed before the motivation.

At Penn State, we were taught in the Saturday morning lab classes, with children from the State College community, to assess all artwork after a lesson to identify their problems in doing the assignment, then decide what the next lesson should be to solve that problem. For instance, if I found that many students had trouble drawing their arms bending, or showed confusions about their left and right, I would give them a similar problem in the next art lesson, perhaps with Plasticine so as to actually bend the arms, and to make clay figures stand up without support. Then later, I might give them another drawing activity requiring the arms or legs to be drawn bending.

For older students, on the day they had a gym class, I would

Terrace side of Lowenfeld house, during a reception for graduate students following summer conference, 1956. Courtesy of John Michael.

The Lowenfelds are the two most sincere individuals I have ever known....Viktor was the individual he was because of Gretel [sic]; and Gretel [sic] was the individual she was because of Viktor. They were a beautiful team, thoroughly devoted to each other. It was always a joy to visit them for an art education party or just stopping by for a chat.

Derwin W. Edwards, 1982, p. 39.

Painting of slave bent under the White burden. by Viktor Lowenfeld.
Photo by author (with flash).

activate their passive knowledge about the game they
played, with questions about how they played, and
have them act out throwing, jumping, catching, etc.
Then I asked them to draw themselves playing the
game in the gym. They could solve the problem of
drawing the walls of the gym any way that worked for
them. Or, I would ask them to select a game and
model themselves playing it in Plasticine. Using an 18
x 24 inch sheet of paper, I asked students at each table
what game they were playing, then I drew a baseball
or football field, or basket ball court on the paper.
They then put their figures on the paper in positions
for playing these games. The finished pieces were
placed on the counter in the room and remained as
table top scenes until the next week's lesson.

The problems of drawing three-dimensional space
begins when children first put in the base line in a
drawing in kindergarten or before. Various drawing
activities helped solve these problems, such as, "We
are playing tag on the school grounds." "I am walking
down the hall at school" after taking the class for a
walk in the hallway, encouraged the drawing of fold-
overs. The problem of drawing "Washington Crossing
the Delaware" and showing both sides of the river,
produced in one 4th grade class, 9 different approaches to the problem. Drawing activities, such as
climbing a mountain, or standing in a crowded eleva-
tor (to show overlapping), etc., drew on the children's

natural ways to draw spatial concepts, before they
were taught linear perspective in the upper grades.
Lowenfeld said that when a student began to draw two
sides of a building, even if it was incorrect, it indicated
readiness to understand linear perspective, which is
not a naturally developed stage in drawing but a
cultural solution to delineating three-dimensional
space on a two-dimensional plane.

In my elementary art classes, we did other things,
printmaking, sculpture, assemblage, collage, art from
scrap, mobiles with wire hangers, stage decorations,
etc. but the purpose here is to relate ways I applied
Lowenfeld's techniques and methods. By emphasizing drawing, I focused on that which was the essential
criteria for artmaking before Abstract Expressionism,
and the ability which children and adults fear the most
when they say, "I can't draw." I also found that, with
my cart loaded with crayons, paper, brushes, paints,
and a bucket of Plasticine balls, I could meet any
challenge that faced me in the classroom when I
arrived. The easiest thing to change, was my mind.
For instance, once when I arrived in a kindergarten for
the art session, the teacher said, "Oh! I forgot to tell
you. We can't have art today, we are testing hearing."

Painting of blind boy feeling a flowering plant. By Viktor Lowenfeld,
kept on easel in V. L.'s bedroom. Photo by author.

I said, "That's all right, we'll draw pictures of taking the test." I passed out the crayons and paper, and asked the children draw pictures of the audiometer while they waited their turns, and then put themselves in the picture after being tested. They could make up ways to draw the beeps they heard coming out of the ear phones to indicate sounds. This was still a form of self-identification by making self-imagery.

I survived teaching 700 kids a week from a cart, because Lowenfeld and I pushed the cart together. Later, in the district, some of the other elementary art teachers were given art rooms. We had one art teacher, James Jones, who also used Lowenfeld's methods, and was given an art room, but he never gave up the cart. When an art activity in his art room was going over time, he would leave it with the classroom teacher, phone the next class and tell the teacher not to come to the art room he would go there. He also was able to do more integrating that way, instead of everything being done in the art room.

Applied Research Techniques for Report Card Grades

During my last two years in Commack, I finally devised a child-centered method for grading art for their report cards. Based on the methods of applied research, I had the students in each class draw the same subject matter for the first art lesson of the year, then again mid-year before the first report card, and then a third time at the end of the semester. Each one was numbered 1, 2, or 3 on the front, and names, dates, grade level and age on the back. For grades K-3, the topic was, "I am jumping for an apple in a tree." It gave me an example of their full figure concepts, arms

Saturday morning lab school, at Penn State. Teacher, Mary Filer, with author, two unidentified students, and children. Note the segments of a mural on the wall behind artwork. Photographer unknown (1955 or 1956).

and legs bending, relation of hand to apple, clothes they wore, and their tree concept, trunk, branches, leaves, and fruit (it could be an apple, orange, pear, or tutti-frutti, an all kinds of fruit, tree). In grades 4, 5, and 6, they could jump for footballs, baseballs, or whatever. We compared the first and second for the mid-term grade, taking into account other things they did in art, and drawings 1, 2, and 3 for the end of the year grade. The classroom teacher and I made the grades out together. Before the last art lesson for the last report card, we passed out all three drawings to each child, asked them to compare them, and spent the class time talking about what they had learned and how their ideas developed. (This process is now called "reflective thinking;" John Dewey called it, "articulating the experience" it turned the activity into a learning experience.) The students were quite surprised to see that they had improved. Also importantly, some of the teachers expressed surprise that their children learned something in art. That way, their report card grades were based on how well they improved individually, not on how they compared with others in the classroom. I saved the drawings from the first year, and repeated the sequence during the second. The children were even more surprised at their growth with six drawings to compare. I wanted this to be a longitudinal study but at the end of the second year, 1966, I left Commack to be Art Consultant for the Connecticut State Department of Education (1966-1992). There I taught workshops in school districts around the state for classroom and art teachers teaching Lowenfeld's motivations, and techniques, and on the creative mental processes which were discovered at Penn State during doctoral studies on differences between art students and non-art students (Lowenfeld, 1959).

GUIDEPOSTS FOR THE FUTURE

In the almost 40 years since Lowenfeld's death, the subsequent four revised editions of *Creative and Mental Growth* kept his philosophy and methods alive in teacher training programs. A variety of additional textbooks on art education have added substantially to the field. They tended to be studio oriented (art making). Some gave passing references or content about art history and appreciation. They varied between being child centered, product centered, or combinations of both. With the introduction of Discipline Based Art Education (DBAE) through the Getty Center for Arts Education about 1984/1986, a major shift toward the product and curriculum-centered art program was initiated. The laissez-faire let the children paint what they want philosophies came under considerable criticism, as did Lowenfeld's philosophy which has been mistakenly associated as such a philosophy. The above discussions of his methods and techniques should put that association to rest. With DBAE the structures suggested for art education programming were in areas of content, with a balance between Art Production (Studio Art), Art History, Aesthetics and Art Criticism. By this time Research and Development (R & D) teams during the late 1960s (Ecker, 1966), on Art History and Appreciation, found that Art Appreciation really had two components: Aesthetics and Art Criticism. Lessons were given a grade level structure, rather than a developmental structure. DBAE prepared the way for the current (1990 -2000) trend towards National Standards in Art, and National Assessment in Art Education. The standards are directed as much to test the accountability of the art teacher as to provide performance objectives for the children taking art. They have been fostered through the efforts of the National Art Education Association, the Getty Center for Art Education, and a wide selection of art teachers, college art educators, school district art directors, and state art and music consultants. Although planned for grade level achievements, they are not actually child-

> Unfortunately, contemporary art educators have perseverated [sic] on Lowenfeld's 'don'ts' and neglected his more constructive recommendations. Because of this narrow focus, we have schooled generations of educators who teach virtually nothing in art to young children for fear of damaging their creative self-expression. Clearly, this was not Lowenfeld's intention. Thus, what has filtered down to us as the contemporary legacy of Lowenfeld's great work is his rather romantic view of the child's psychological and mental abilities.

centered, but the teaching of them can be however. The developments, since Lowenfeld's death, in understanding the stages of growth, such as the multiple intelligences theory of how people learn, recognition of the left-right sides of the brain (which were foreshadowed by the visual-haptic continuum of Lowenfeld) provide a basis for balancing between the child-centered and the curriculum-centered program.

One of the differences between the Lowenfeld and the DBAE conducted art program is the type of motivation used for the child's art production. The Lowenfeld motivation focused on developing the child's own self-image, and activating their knowledge and concepts about themselves, and producing them in drawings, paintings, or Plasticine and clay. In many of the DBAE examples, the primary motivation for the child's art production is the famous work of art, to make a variation of it in a different or school art media. Although these projects were based on fine art references and qualities that may result in fine examples of school art, they did not lend themselves to studying the weaknesses of the children's production from one lesson to the next. During the Saturday morning laboratory classes at Penn State, we were taught to analyze the drawings and paintings of the children for weaknesses for which they needed additional art opportunities to strengthen, such as certain drawing characteristics, or details of self-image, facial features, body parts, arms and legs bending, next stage spatial concepts (base line, double base line, x-ray, fold-over, conceptualizations, overlapping, etc.) which are at the heart of the child-centered art program.

The Contextual Art Program: Balancing Child-centered and Discipline Based Art Activities

These two approaches need not create an either-or dichotomy in art education philosophy and programming, but a continuum, where one feeds the other as the children grow and pass to higher grade levels. A balance between the child/student-centered curriculum, and the discipline-based curriculum is possible within the context of the art program and the activities being taught. Within the structures/strictures set up by the National Standards, it is possible to still provide child/student-centered art activities by the type of subject matter selected for the art activities. For instance, during those ages/grade levels when students are more ego-centrically oriented than at others (i.e., kindergarten and first grade, fourth and seventh grades), art subject matter and motivations might be more child/student-centered than in the discipline-based context. The gradual shift to discipline-based art activities can be introduced in the third grade with some preparation for any assessment conducted in the fourth grade. The seventh grade, an ego-sensitive transition period into adolescence, development might have activities that relate to the student's tastes, home, self, dress, growth, and so forth; while the eighth grade has more social, community, and professional orientations to art and the art world. Seventh and eighth grades are also levels when students want more professionalism in their teachers, they want to know that the art teacher knows/ does what he or she is teaching about. In high school, there is again a shift from the student-centered program in the ninth grade to the professional and portfolio-based art program, for those who wish to make careers in art. The point here, is that it should not be an either-or child-centered versus discipline-based program, but a plan in which the developmental and class level orientations are merged on a graduated continuum, rather than considered dichotomous in a one over the other conflict. Within the context of the kindergarten-grade twelve art curriculum such a merger can take place to the advantage of both approaches. Within the kindergarten-grade twelve art curriculum, there is something self-denigrating in having an "Introduction to Art" course at the secondary level, when children have been taking art since kindergarten. Elementary art (kindergarten-grade 5/6) should be considered and called the "Introduction to Art" while middle school art might be called "Applied" and/or "Everyday Art" and high school art, called, "Advanced Art" or whatever is appropriate within the district art philosophy.

The radical alternative to predesigned, standardized curricula that Lowenfeld offered is this. *First* get to know the child and *then* make the educational plan. Please note he doesn't mean to merely know children, their normative and atypical development. Lowenfeld does require the prepared teacher to know the developmental stages in seven categories of growth, but also to know *that* child, their (sic) particular learning style and intellectual-emotional agendas, the trajectory of their (sic) schematic development over time, *then* customize one's interventions accordingly. In other words, work to establish a relationship with each student that moves in the direction of an I-Thou relationship. Hard? So what? Teaching well is hard. But so is teaching poorly, even harder because there is scant reward for either the student or the teacher. (Italics in text.)

Peter London, 1997, pp. 10-11.

References

Beittel, K. (1982, November). Lowenfeld and art for a new age. *Art Education,* 35(6). 18-21.

Buber, M. (1970). *I and thou.* (Walter Kaufmann, Trans., 1923). NY: Touchstone.

Cohen, S. B. (Ed.) (1998). *The Columbia gazetteer of the world.* Vol. 3, P to Z. NY: Columbia University Press.

D'Amico, V. (1953). *Creative teaching in art.* Scranton, PA: International Textbook Company.

Ecker, D.W. (Project Dir.) (1966). *Improving the teaching of art appreciation.* Research and Development Team for the Improvement of Teaching Art Appreciation in the Secondary Schools. USOE Cooperative Research Project No. V-006. Final Report RF 2006. Columbus, OH: The Ohio State University Research Foundation.

Edwards, D. (1982, November). Lowenfeld as mentor. *Art Education,* 35(6), 38-40.

Efland, A. D. (1990). *A history of art education: intellectual and social currents in teaching the visual arts.* NY: Teachers College Press. Columbia University.

Emerson. S. (1953). *Design: A creative approach.* Scranton, PA: International Textbook Company.

Faulkner, R., Ziegfeld, E. & Hill, G. (1941). *Art today.* NY: Henry Holt and Co.

Fletcher, S. S. & Welton, J. (Trans.) (1912). *Froebel's chief educational writings.* London: Edward Arnold & Co.

Hoffa, H. (1998). Remembering 'The Doc': Lowenfeldian lore, legend, and legacy. Unpublished manuscript, lent by the author.

Logan, F. M. (1955). *The Growth of art in American schools.* NY: Harper Bros.

London, P. (1997). *The Lowenfeld lecture.* Unpublished draft for lecture, lent by author.

Lowenfeld, V. (1947). *Creative and mental growth: A textbook on art education.* NY: Macmillan Company.

Lowenfeld, V. (1939/1952). *The nature of creative activity.* Translated by O. A. Oeser. London: Routledge & Kegan Paul, Ltd. (Also published in New York: Harcourt, Brace, and Co., 1939)

Lowenfeld, V. (1957). The adolescence of art education. *Art Education.* 10(7), 5-12.

Lowenfeld, V. (1958). *Viktor Lowenfeld: An autobiography.* Unpublished manuscript, taped by Ellen Abel during presentation by Dr. Lowenfeld, transcribed by Miami University Center for the Study of the History of Art Education, edited by John A. Michael, with verifications by Mrs. Viktor Lowenfeld.

Madenfort. D. (November 1982). Lowenfeld, myself, and the tragic dream. *Art Education.* 35(6), 22-24.

Mattil, E. L. (1959). *Meaning in crafts.* Englewood Cliffs, NJ: Prentice-Hall, Inc.

Mattil, E. L. (November 1982). Yes, I remember Viktor. *Art Education.* 35(6), 8-11.

Michael, J. A. (November 1982). Lowenfeld as humanitarian and teacher. *Art Education.* 35(6), 12-14.

Michael. J. A. (Ed.) (1982). The *Lowenfeld Lectures.* University Park, PA: The Pennsylvania State University.

Saunders, R. J. (1954). *The parallel development of art Education in Canada and the United States, with Emphasis on the history of art Education in Canada.* Unpublished Thesis for Master of Science Degree, Pennsylvania State University.

Saunders, R. J. (fall 1960). Contributions of Viktor Lowenfeld to art education: Part I. Early influences in his thought. *Studies in Art Education,* 2(1), 3-5.

Saunders, R. J. (winter 1961). Contributions of Viktor Lowenfeld to art education Part II: Creative and Mental Growth. *Studies in Art Education,* 2(2), 7-13.

Saunders, R. J. (1961). *The Contributions of Horace Mann, Mary Peabody Mann, and Elizabeth Peabody to art education in the United States.* Unpublished dissertation for Doctor of Education Degree, Pennsylvania State University. (University Microfilms, Ann Arbor, Mic. 61 2397.)

Saunders, R. J. (1971). *Art Education: History. The Encyclopedia of Education.* Vol. I. Acad-Canna. (282 289). NY: The Free Press, Macmillan Co.

Saunders, R. J. (November 1982). The Lowenfeld motivation. *Art Education.* 35(6), 28-31.

Slettehaugh, T. C. (1955). The Coloring Contest Controversy. Photocopies of collection of Letters to the Editor, *The Centre Daily Times,* State College and Bellefonte, November 29-December 14, 1955, with subsequent articles in the *Pittsburgh Press,* December 18, 1955, and *Newsweek,* January, 2, 1956. Unpublished collection, photocopies supplied to the author by Thomas C. Slettehaugh.

Smith, P. (1996). *The history of American art education: Learning about art in American schools.* Westport, CT: Greenwood Press.

Smith, P. (1983). *An analysis of the writings and teachings of Viktor Lowenfeld in art education in America.* Unpublished doctoral dissertation. Arizona State University, Tempe, AZ.

Tharp, L. H. (1950). *The Peabody Sisters of Salem.* Boston: Little, Brown & Co.

Theisen, O. J. (1996). *The murals of John Thomas Biggers: American muralist, African American artist.* Hampton, VA: Hampton University Museum.

Viola, W. (1944). *Child art.* Peoria, IL: Charles A. Bennett, Pub.

Youngblood, M. S. (1983, November). Lowenfeld's unremitting legacy. *Art Education,* 35(6), 32-36.

ART EDUCATION AND HUMANISTIC VALUES
EDWIN ZIEGFELD (1905-1986)

I suspect that no civilization can be a great one without a basic interest in Art. Edwin Ziegfeld

Judith M. Burton

Unlike other authors in this volume, I did not have the privilege of knowing Edwin Ziegfeld in person. Although, in several curious ways, I felt I knew him even before embarking upon this tribute. I first encountered his name and reputation when as a teacher in England I came to know Eleanor Hipwell, then president of InSEA, who told me intriguing stories about the early years of the organization, all of which involved Edwin! Later, when I came to the United States to teach, I read the text *Art Today* which Ziegfeld had authored with Ray Faulkner in 1944, and was impressed by his commitment to the role of art in shaping the visual environment. It was not until I followed in his footsteps as Chair of Art and Art Education at Teachers College Columbia University and began to know some of those who had worked and studied with him that I began to understand the depth of his greatness as a teacher and thinker. At this point, having read many of the documents pertaining to his life and work, I sense that his legacy is so over-shadowed by his work in the Owatonna Project that the subtlety of his later thinking and commitment to art education in the public schools has been obscured. This chapter represents a personal point of view on Ziegfeld, the definitive text remains yet to be authored. In selecting the threads from the tapestry of an eventful life I have attempted to call him back to attention, and in doing so I have tried to let him speak for himself.

BEGINNING: ART IN LIFE

The Centrality of Art

In the years following the end of World War II, men and women released from the services were imbued with the need to build a new community of nations whose informed political commitments and social caring would prevent another global conflagration. For this group,

education was to become the salvation. While politicians struggled to unite nations in common cause, art educators in the United States and Europe, felt keenly the need for both national and global kinship dedicated to making a more kindly and aesthetically harmonious world; what they lacked, however, was a leader. By the 1950s, as fate would have it, they found one in Edwin Ziegfeld. Following his pre-war experiences in directing the Owatonna project and his Navy service during the war, Ziegfeld had come to believe that art educators could and

Edwin Ziegfeld in 1947 at the time he came to Teachers College. (Special Collections, Milbank Memorial Library, Teachers College, Columbia University.)

should serve the functional and aesthetic needs of community. This democratic vision for art education held that the arts, as common languages, transcended geographic boundaries and, as such, could become powerful harbingers of peace. In parallel with his post war appointment as head of Fine and Industrial Arts[1] at Teachers College Columbia University, Ziegfeld became enmeshed with the founding of both the National Art Education Association and the International Society for Art Education, becoming the first president of each organization.

As an educator and teacher of teachers, Ziegfeld came to prominence at a time when mainstream education in the United States fluctuated from concern with subject matter to concern with the child. As Efland points out in his introduction to this volume, in art education this pendulum swing took the forms of scientific rationalism and romantic expressionism. Eschewing both positions, Ziegfeld located his work in an interactive stance, exhorting art educators to interpret subject matter as outgrowth of the socio-cultural and personal forces operating in individual lives. His notion of community, as Efland notes, was pragmatic, but his commitment to art was to the central power of the aesthetic and creative experience in individual lives; his vision of education was deeply humanistic.

At almost every phase of his long life one sees both preparation for the role he was ultimately to play on the global stage and, in his writings, a growing alarm at what he saw to be the progressive dehumanization of the individual by "making him over in the image of the machine" and a passive acceptance of the willingness to be machine-fed in culture, sports and entertainment. In a real sense, and in his personal life, Edwin Ziegfeld was something of a Renaissance man; he was a collector of antiques, a knowledgeable musician, a gourmet cook and, overall, a kindly and thoughtful man.

At the time we were growing up the concept of a poverty level had not yet been developed, but if there had been such a standard the Ziegfeld family would have been hovering right around that level.	From childhood, Edwin pursued excellence: he strove to excel, and his unwillingness to accept less than the best from himself was one of his striking characteristics.
Ernest Ziegfeld	*Ernest Ziegfeld*

His original intention was to become a landscape architect and he prepared himself with degrees in this field, bolstered by others in education and psychology. His commitment to the centrality of art in humanizing life, however, which was to remain at the root of his entire professional career, emerged early in life.

Family: The Importance of Community

Edwin Ziegfeld, was born on August 15, 1905 in Cleveland, Ohio, the third youngest in a family of nine children. According to his younger brother Ernest:
> The family was of limited financial means wherein the need to share was less of an obligation than a necessity. Out of these experiences Edwin developed a strong sense of family which shaped him throughout his life.[2]

In those years, art education in the public schools of Ohio was minimum, yet Ziegfeld developed an early interest in art which he was able to pursue throughout his schooling. Explaining the origins of his interest in an interview given to Anne Gregory in 1983[3] Ziegfeld recalled:
> I am not sure when I became interested in art, but my sister was a teacher and subscribed to magazines which included art activities. In high school I took art whenever I could, and the teacher when I was a junior got me a Saturday morning scholarship at the Columbus Art School.[4]

When describing his experiences in these after school classes in later life he remembered:
> Each week I drew plaster casts of ears, noses and mouths, and later, busts of Brutus and the Medici and figures of winged victory and the Farnese Hercules. While these were often frustrating encounters they were never meaningless ones.[5]

For the most part, however, Ziegfeld's school art experience, like those of many youngsters of the time, was confined to picture study which, even at this young age, he found to be too formalized to his taste. In light of his later belief that involvement in the arts could improve community life, it is engaging to see that his first artistic experiences were, in fact, based on a conception of art and culture for the masses designed to instill a deep respect for moral and aesthetic values.

As he recounted to Anne Gregory (1987):

> Each student has his own little picture and you were told what to look for, what was there and how it was composed. There was nothing done to draw out the students' reactions to what they saw (p. 2).

When he was not engaging with his artistic pursuits, Ziegfeld was to be found digging in his garden, something that was to become a lifetime passion akin to his love of the arts. In later life he would take refuge in gardening. According to his younger brother Ernest:

> Every time Edwin got near his garden there was a near-miraculous surge of energy as he dug and planted and pruned.

The Landscape Architect: A Place For Community

The Ziegfeld parents were highly invested in the education of their children. According to Edmund Burke Feldman, who studied with Edwin at Teachers College in later years, the Ziegfeld father was a master carpenter, and something of a free thinker, who entertained the writer James Thurber to "long and intricate conversations." Perhaps stemming from his insights into the dubious life and trials of an artist, his father had taken him at a young age to a local phrenologist who confidently predicted the boy was an excellent candidate for the legal profession! Thus, when Edwin was in high school and planned to become an art major he felt guilty about choosing a field of which he knew his father would disapprove. He admitted to Anne Gregory that:

> I hid it from my parents because for my father it was the one thing he did not want. He was looking forward to us being upwardly mobile (p. 2).

However, all was not lost and a compromise was quickly arranged; an older sister who was already enrolled at Ohio State University and knowing his interest in the arts and plants, saved the day by suggesting he try for landscape architecture. Ziegfeld proved to be an excellent student and by 1927 was awarded his B.S. Coming to the end of his studies in Ohio, the head of his department suggested he move on to Harvard School of Landscape Architecture for his M.A. degree. Coming from a large family and needing to work to support himself, the prospects of Harvard were dim until friends found a wealthy patron

who supported him with $75 a month allowance through the two years of study needed for the degree. This largess did not quite stretch to life at Harvard in the late 1920s and Ziegfeld was obliged to work for the Fletcher Steel Company which at that time was the best in the country in landscape architecture.

Ziegfeld graduated from Harvard during a time of unprecedented economic depression, four months before the stock market crash of October 1929. Again he had distinguished himself as an excellent student and was awarded the prestigious Charles Elliot Traveling Fellowship receiving the then princely sum of $1,500 for a journey to Europe. This year was, according to his brother Ernest, "one of great wonder and discovery." One can imagine this young American, primed with his newly minted Harvard degree, progressing in the manner of The Grand Tour of a previous generation. Here, among the ancient splendors of Europe–churches, wall murals and formal sculptures, Ziegfeld must have glimpsed for the first time an art of daily and spiritual life that was to mark his artistic consciousness henceforth. This first opportunity also gave him a great thirst for travel and later, when teaching at Columbia University Teachers College, he conducted a number of tours to Europe and, according to his students of the time, he took delight in sharing his enthusiasms.

THE SEARCH FOR BEAUTY AND ORDER

Owatonna: The Social Functions of Art Take Shape

By 1930 Ziegfeld was back in the United States and looking for work. The stock market crash he thought would "blow over" had bitten hard and disastrously, and work was hard to come by. Landscape architecture seemed to him to be a dead-end and breaking into it at that time with hundreds of landscape architects out of work an impossibility. A friend told him about an art project funded by the Carnegie Corporation which had been set up in Minnesota and asked if he would be interested. He was interested, yet, decided to return to Ohio State to fill a temporary teaching vacancy in Landscape Architecture. With an eye on the future, perhaps, and in the knowledge that there was a great shortage of teachers in the post depression years, while at the University he completed a B.A. degree in education. In the interview with Anne Gregory in

1983, Ziegfeld admitted that he had never actually wanted to be a teacher and while he had received several offers to teach when he graduated from Harvard "I said to myself that I would rather starve than teach. I found myself starving!"

In 1932 with three degrees under his belt and with no regrets about his newly minted decision to teach, Ziegfeld moved to Minnesota where he was to remain for 5 years. Minnesota in the 1930s, by all accounts, was one of the most creative centers in the country in the field of education thanks in no small measure to the University Dean of Education, Melvin E. Haggerty. Haggerty was, at the time, widely regarded as one of the countries most brilliant scholars and educators who had already made an outstanding contribution to the field of measurement in achievement and intelligence. While Haggerty made no bones about his own lack of artistic education and ability, he none the less believed that the arts could and should enrich the common life of ordinary people. In a talk to artists and teachers of art, Haggerty (1938) recalled:

> ...the bleakness of the school room I had known as boy, my own childhood home with its shiny, machine made furniture; the ugliness of frontier towns and cities; the dreariness and monotony of life deprived of color and the rhythm that abound in nature (p. 23).

He concluded his talk by asking what the teachers of fine arts could do to protect young people from such boredom and monotony? Specifically, he asked:

> Is the program of art instruction in the school geared to elevate community taste in all those matters that make up the visual aspects of American life? Is the major task of art instruction in the schools to be the specialized training of the few or the cultivation of taste in all? (p. 23).

The answer to these questions came, over time, to inform what was to become the Owatonna Project, the conceptualization and activities for which took shape during the years 1931-33. Conceived by Haggerty who argued vehemently that art could not, and should not, be detached from life as it had so demonstrably become in schooling:

> Art is a way of life. That is, the life of every person will be richer and more satisfying if he can learn to make his environment as pleasing to the

senses as nature originally made it for her children. The impulses which lead to art lie deep in human nature...Men strive for art experiences just as they reach out after knowledge or moral integrity.

> It follows from this view that all the evidences are to be found widely distributed in the practices and institutions of a community in the homes people maintain, in the stores they patronize, in the clothes they wear, in the fields they lay out, in the trees they plant, in the animals they breed, in the cultivation of the religious, in the manner in which they find their amusement...

> The problem for education in this matter is to discover how the art interests of people create art needs, and to formulate a plan of teaching that is related to these needs in a thoroughly realistic way (p. 24).

Haggerty's combination of clear-headed argument and passion persuaded the Carnegie Corporation to give $11,000 to fund a one year field experiment to focus on the artistic needs and problems of young people in ways that would directly enrich their lives. Haggerty brought Edwin Ziegfeld to Minnesota to head up the school component of the experiment and later to become the resident director of the Project. Thus began a creative partnership between the two men which, in the short run, was to have great impact on one small midwestern town and, in the long term, was to shape a strand of thinking and practice in art education in the United States which continues to reverberate over half a century later.

Haggerty's own arts education experiences were in no way unusual. Reflected in the schools of the early 1930s art was mostly confined to the development of technical skills for the few and the encouragement of dilettantism for the many and had little to do with children's everyday lives. Moreover, the 1930s was a time when voices were raised to call American Schools into the service of social reconstruction following the deprivations of the Depression. In an uncanny echo to the background of the last years of the 20th century, schools were being asked to change in response to the larger social transformations wrought by the industrial era. As Ziegfeld (1944)[7] later pointed out, and not surprisingly, new educational thinking of the time was not sympathetic to the arts:

> In the uncertain thirties such critical analysis brought many people to the conclusion that art was one subject which could well be spared from the public school curriculum. All over the country, art teachers were dismissed because art seemed to be one of education's frills, a pallid luxury-subject without sufficient vitality to be considered essential to the training of children (p. 1).

On the other hand, Ziegfeld pointed out, there was a group of practical and down-to-earth people: businessmen and industrialists who were increasingly becoming aware that art was important. They realized, for example, that if their products were to be competitive in times of economic constraint they needed an added "luster" to make people want to buy them. Artists were increasingly hired in the capacity of graphic designers to give products visual appeal; this was found to be enormously profitable not with standing the depleted economic climate. Thus, Ziegfeld stressed, while art was being withdrawn from the schools, it was at the same time playing an increasingly important role in business and industry. He was quick to point out, too, that while many artists of the time were making profitable livings as commercial designers they were not undermining their integrity as artists.

> Far from selling their Muse in the slave market of commerce, far from "prostituting" their art, they were following a long and honored tradition. They could well be compared with the Leonardo's, and the Cellini's of Renaissance Italy–all the hundreds of artists who regarded themselves as craftsmen trained in trade...who did their work on commission, and who lived and flourished and made money like other business people by fashioning objects that could be used and would bring satisfaction to the users (p. 3).

The solution to the dilemma was clear, to put art and its practices back into the community life of people from which it had originally come and this was to be the purpose of the Owatonna Project. On a much smaller scale, but none the less influential, had been John Dewey's lab experience at the University of Chicago in the early years of the century dedicated to discovering how a school could function as both an educative and cooperative community. Haggerty's vision took this to new heights.

Owatonna: In Practice

The first task of the Project team was to select a 'typical' American community in which to carry out its grand experiment. After much careful scrutiny, and according to the final report, Owatonna was chosen for various reasons: it was a small agricultural community (population 7,600) with a balance of inhabitants, straightforward domestic architecture, varied industries and total lack of art education in the lives of its 1,500 children who attended the four elementary and combined junior and senior high schools! The town had an additional advantage in that it was located some 75 miles south of Minneapolis, far enough to be removed from the cultural influences of an urban metropolis yet, near enough to the University for the project team to travel back and forth. According to Ziegfeld and Smith (1944):

Owatonna during the Ziegfeld years

The team itself was interesting and eclectic for the period and the selection of it's members was no less critical than that of the town itself: One had experience in interior design and museum work; one had specialized in industrial and commercial design, one in architecture and painting; one in modeling and sculpture; one in textile and dress design, one in journalism, one in art history, one in art education and one in landscape architecture. All were recent college graduates...all had broad cultural backgrounds...three had studied in Europe (p. 11).

In its refined form the intention of the Project, or the experiment as it was properly called, was to find out to what degree art entered into the lives and daily activities of the community and to arouse in them an interest in the further use of art in their daily lives, The final and, perhaps, most critical purpose of the project was to develop a school program based on community needs and requirements. In their report, Ziegfeld and Smith go to some length to stress that this 'experiment' was not a 'scientific study' in which needs were atomized and analyzed in splendid isolation. The experiment was, in contrast, 'unorthodox' yet 'realistic' and set out to create a context within which to understand community needs and create an educational experience in the arts in relation to those needs. Today we would probably envision such a study in terms of a combination of ethnographic and case study methodologies–but the 1930s was an age invested in scientism wherein researchers doubted the truth of naturalistic forms of experimentation. Taking their scholarly courage in both hands, and within this more naturalistic framework, the project team began its community study with a series of daily visits to homemakers, traders, and industrialists. Over time, and as people got used to their presence, the team gave advice about the arrangement of furniture, the treatments and displays in shop windows, the drapery in a dentist's waiting room, and painting of the boiler room in the municipal power plant. They studied gardens, plantings and lawns and, throughout their conversations and activities, took notes on interviews learning about the communities activities and attitudes towards the arts. Gradually, as they got to know the team better and understand their purposes, the community became active in framing its own needs requesting evening classes in the creative arts and art history, and a summer school for both children and adults. At the end of the first year, Royal Baily Farnham, president of the Rhode Island School of Design (RISD), was dispatched to Owatonna to review the project. On the strength of his enthusiasm the Carnegie Corporation gave additional funding of $25,000.[8]

The various reports of the project from inception to conclusion reveal how deeply Ziegfeld's ideas about art and art education contributed to and were shaped by this experience. While his own role within the project was to design and make possible art education activities for children and adolescents, he appears to have been deeply enmeshed in every facet of the community inquiry. Interestingly enough, however, the art program in the schools began simultaneously with the community study and did not arise from its

findings, although as the project progressed its finding came more and more to shape the in-school art experiences. The rationale Ziegfeld offered for this simultaneous beginning was largely based on the assumption that while the community of Owatonna used art in many and diverse ways in their daily activities the team did not want the art program to reinforce in the children some of the uninformed artistic sensibilities and poor practices of their parents. The aim of the art program was, in contrast, to extend children's abilities and interests into new avenues. Based on his own growing interest in the more psychological aspects of artistic learning, Ziegfeld also envisioned that an art program which recognized the social and cultural needs of children must also be responsive to their individual and inner needs. In their 1944 Report, Ziegfeld and Smith recognized that the team could not:

> ...impose a ready made curriculum upon them and make it work...We must scrutinize their behavior all the way through childhood and adolescence. We must supplement what psychologists have told us about them with our own observations of their varying abilities and interests...Any successful program of activities, educational or political, must grow out of the natural desire and natural habits of living and thinking of the human being it serves. This is true of children as it is for adults, and if for no other reason than this the staff in Owatonna was fortunate in being able to develop a tentative art program in the schools before the results of the community study became crystallized and usable (p. 61).

As it emerged, the art program was taught in relation to what the team envisioned as "fundamental areas of living." For example:

> To everyone, young or old, one's own self and one's personal problems constitute the most important areas of experience. Next comes one's home, as the results of the community study so unexceptionally revealed. Next, for children comes the school, and after that the community as a whole (p. 62).

The subject matter of art for the schools was organized in relation to these areas of daily experience in order that it should have "inherent vitality." However, the team's view was not limited to aligning arts education to the practical experiences of daily living and included in its thinking the need to offer young people creative and expressive experiences of making through exploring the materials of the fine arts of painting and sculpture and acquiring knowledge of art history. Moreover, they recognized that children encountered the problems of daily living and personal expression at different levels according to their ages and past experiences:

> One's attitude towards himself and his home change constantly as one grows older, learns more about himself and his environment, discovers new and more challenging problems in these areas, and finds within himself fresh and unsuspecting resources with which to solve them. The art program must keep pace with the child's increasing maturity and the steady flow of new experiences that broaden his horizons; each area must be presented from the point of view of the child's expanding perceptions and interests... Based on this assumption, the Owatonna art program began to take on the pattern of a spiral, ever-swelling, ever-increasing in breadth and scope (p. 63).

The staff of art and classroom teachers under Ziegfeld's direction offered young children 5 half-hour periods of art a week; in the junior high section where art was elective it was offered for 6 one-hour periods a week and at senior high, 5 one-hour periods a week. The curriculum combined individual and group activities, design projects and expressive experiences, and teachers were urged to relate art to the other subject matter disciplines of the curriculum. The young people were taken on field trips, encouraged to read widely in relation to each project, collect illustrative materials and discussed informally the arts of Owatonna and their relation to the arts of other times and place. Looking back on the project Ziegfeld saw that the art experiences they had offered to the young people of the town reached beyond the walls of the schools. Young people had, among other activities, painted murals in the town, design in-school bulletin boards, produced journals and magazines, designed settings and costumes for plays, helped with the redecoration of the high school building and grounds and assisted with the garden club. Above all:

> ...the art program developed from two sources–the needs, interests, abilities and attitudes of children of all ages and the role that art played in their own environment, a typical community. Each child

was led to develop his unique characteristics to the extent that they harmonized with those of his social group. The ideal was neither rugged individualism nor complete conformity but a realistic acceptance of the place of man in his society. The concept of art as part of the total culture rather than as a series of special skills is related to this ideal and determined the teaching philosophy of the Owatonna art program (p. 68).

Owatonna: In Retrospect

The funding for the Owatonna project ran out in 1939 and Ziegfeld returned to the University of Minnesota as a part-time instructor in art education. In later years he described to Anne Gregory (1987) how he felt his background in landscape architecture had helped him make a unique contribution to the project:

> I think I had a broader point of view than the average person in art education who was trained for classroom teaching. The people who worked on the Owatonna project had a considerably broader view than other teachers in the field. These experiences also rubbed off on my later teaching (p. 8).

It is also important to note that Ziegfeld had a considerably broader perspective on the role of arts education in community and individual experience than did Melvin Haggerty. Looking back on this experience Ziegfeld also recalled that Haggerty had in mind a much more functional and narrower interpretation of art then he did, although he had no quarrel with art being an important part of the functional aspects of life. Speaking of Haggerty's rather narrow view of art:

> He died the year before the project was completed, and I know if he had lived, there would have been a confrontation between himself and me on the interpretation I was going to put on art, and what he would have done with it (p. 6).

While he did not elaborate on this statement, looking at the evolution of his thinking about the central creative, individualizing and humanizing purposes of art over the ensuing years, one can see how the more deeply pragmatic and instrumental views of Haggerty's might have constrained him.

It is difficult, perhaps, for today's art educator to understand the importance of the Owatonna project

Ed Ziegfeld's contribution to the social uses of art education are recognized whenever writers attempt to set our profession in a historical context.

Al Hurwitz, former student, Professor Emeritus, Maryland Institute College of Art

We all know that the Navy Department is a very large and complex bureaucracy: and that those who had to deal with it sometimes wondered whether there might be a difference between human intelligence and military intelligence. But Edwin had this happy ability to describe the annoyances and frustrations with amazement and amusement, and never with anger.

C. Robert Pace, longtime friend

and the degree to which is was successful in highlighting the social dimensions of artistic need and behavior. To many later art educators and scholars, what occurred in this out of the way Minnesota community offered dramatic evidence of the ways in which a community could not only be served but altered through art education when the larger curriculum stressed public service as well as personal expression. Ziegfeld's belief that art as a medium of expression should be taught in relation to enhancing social life, projected into the 20th century an older belief systems formulated by 19th century craftspersons such as William Morris and captured in the much quoted dictum of John Ruskin that "industry without art is brutality."

While Ziegfeld himself might have taken issue with Melvin Haggerty, had he lived, over his narrow 'functional' view of art, he nonetheless agreed with the principles which informed the Project. In their 1944 report, Ziegfeld and Smith argued that:

> ...everyone uses art in many of the experiences of his life; that art problems arise in practical and meaningful situations; that although most people feel a deep satisfaction when they solve their art problems successfully they still do not have sufficient ability or knowledge to do this often; they are frequently aware of the beauty in their own surroundings; and that their tastes and interests in the various fields of art are usually inconsistent–all these discoveries owe little, if anything, to whatever is peculiar or unique in the soil, the climate, the social and economic life of Owatonna. They owe much more to the deep lying desires and the struggles of man, whose search for beauty and order and delights that please the eye has been hardly less a driving force than his search for food and shelter, for love, and for God (p. 95).

Like Haggerty, Ziegfeld believed that it was critical for children to study and use art as a language in the common course of their work and play. He also believed that if art could be made part of daily living it

would be supported by other educators and, most critically, by local school boards–a view about which, in later life and in light of experience, Ziegfeld was less sanguine.

Interestingly, apart from the first year appraisal by Royal Baily Farnham of RISD, the Project was never fully evaluated, thus, the point of view it espoused was never fully tested for its broader validity even at the time. While history does not relate how far the example of Owatonna radiated and took hold in other communities, that it must have done so comes from an intriguing source. In his seminal 1943 text, *Education Through Art*, Sir Herbert Read offers a lengthy account of a study carried out at the University of Minnesota in 1936 of a one-room school house in Hennepin County, Minnesota. Quoting Florence Tilton, author of the report:

> The minute I entered the doorway I knew I had entered a school where art was part of daily living...Children were taught to be conscious of beauty in all things...they accept appraisal of school work for its artistic merit as naturally as they accept appraisals of speech (p. 238).

Tilton's account is fulsome and focuses on how children in this one-room schoolhouse in a midwest farming community were able to make associations with beauty in their immediate surroundings, in nature, man-made articles, their own efforts in arranging their classroom, choosing their manner of dress, and their personal explorations with the materials of art. Art was related to all other subjects and the teaching was balanced between work designed to foster self-expression and make artistic choices in every day life. Imagination was prized and took priority over copying.

In light of their later close association in the inaugural years of InSEA, Read's comments on this report are interesting. In the chapter entitled "The Natural Form of Education" he states:

Such, it seems to me, is the realizable pattern of education, in London or New York as well as in Hennepin County, Minnesota. That single-handed rural teacher, working in a one room school, is the model for all teachers, elementary or secondary, even university. I will add nothing to the force and Platonic truth of this one example (p. 239).

Indeed, speaking half a century later, Al Hurwitz, a student of Ziegfeld's at Teachers College in the 1960s, later Chair of Art Education at the Maryland Institute College of Art in Baltimore, and also Past President of InSEA, stressed:

Ed Ziegfeld's contribution to the social uses of art education are recognized whenever writers attempt to set our profession in an historical context... Ziegfeld and his associates envisioned art as a force that could permeate an entire community. The art teachers required for such a socially active program would not only be able to teach the usual array of studio subjects...but be prepared to serve as consultants for public needs.[9]

When funding for the project ceased, Ziegfeld returned to the University of Minnesota as an instructor in art education and while teaching began to work towards his Doctoral Degree in educational psychology which he completed in 1947.[10] According to C. Robert Pace, who was a graduate student at the time, and who was later to become a close friend:

This apparent shifting of fields, from landscape architecture to art education to educational psychology, was not really a shifting; rather it was a progressive accumulation of knowledge, and it illustrates Edwin's awareness and insight and about the importance of an expanding scholarship in the pursuit of a career.[11]

While teaching at the University of Minnesota, Ziegfeld met Ray Faulkner who had taught in the summer program at Owatonna in the years 1935-38 and had been on the faculty of the General College at the University of Minnesota. Faulkner had developed a non-traditional course at the University called "Art Today" which, in spirit, was at one with the mission of the Owatonna project. This fortuitous meeting of minds and interests led in 1941 to the first publication of the textbook *Art Today*. The book, co-authored by both men along with

Gerald Hill, explored the importance of art in the home, the community, industry, and commerce. It dealt with design and the materials and processes involved with the production of art. The book was popular with a broad readership and by 1969 was in its 5th edition; a 6th edition appeared in 1986 just before Ziegfeld died.[12] Asked by Anne Gregory (1987) what he considered his main contribution to art education, Ziegfeld claimed his book, *Art Today*, because it:

...changed direction of the course for the general education student in the country. The books I had known before had all dealt with painting and sculpture. They had to have a historical cast, but *Art Today* looked upon all of the visual environment as worth of study and included it. It also emphasized the "contemporary" rather then the "historical" background (p. 15).

While Ziegfeld's stay as a teacher at the University of Minnesota was relatively short, he must have made a considerable impact over the ensuing years because the University honored him in 1956 with an Outstanding Achievement Award.

NATIONAL AND INTERNATIONAL CULTURAL LIFE

Interlude: World War II

In the academic year of 1941-42, Ziegfeld was appointed Assistant Professor of Fine and Industrial Arts at Teachers College Columbia University, a position he was not able to take up until 1946. In 1942 the United States entered World War II and the same year Ziegfeld left for Washington where he worked for the War Department; in 1943 he joined the Personnel Research Section, which had charge of the army testing program. By the latter part of 1943 he had joined the Navy as a commissioned officer and returned to Washington to join the Educational Services section. As head of the program he was, at one point, in charge of about 550 officers throughout the world whose responsibility was to organize continuing educational opportunities for enlisted men. In this capacity he met and worked with Ralph Tyler who was the acknowledged authority on educational measurement at the time, and who devised a series of general education tests for the military which eventually became the GED.

An occurrence towards the end of Ziegfeld's time in government service was to herald another new direction in his life. Asked by an Amy recruiter "why is it that art people do not know the leaders in their own fields? We get in touch with an art educator and he knows people only in his own area. With music it's very different. Music educators know the leaders in all parts of the country. Why don't the art educators know the leaders in their field?" Ziegfeld was stung by these remarks but on reflection his hunch was that music educators had a large national organization which brought them together in community, whereas in art there were only regional associations.[13]

NAEA: The Maker of a Professional Community

Returning to civilian life in 1946 "all fired up with the idea that we should have a national association," Ziegfeld was promoted to Chairman of the Department of Fine and Industrial Arts at Teachers College Columbia University, then, like now, the pre-eminent institution in the United States in teacher education. Before joining Teachers College, however, Ziegfeld had been program chair for the Western Arts Association when in Owatonna, and once in New York joined the Eastern Arts Association where from 1946 onward he went to every summer and winter meeting. While at the time there was a National Art Association—in existence since the early 1930s—which held twice yearly conventions, its membership was very small and it had no relationship to the four regional associations to which most art teachers gave their allegiance. Moreover, the regionals were very protective of their membership and there was little interchange among them.[14]

Teachers College supported Ziegfeld's growing interest in the development of a single professional art organization. He traveled widely round the country attending regional meetings and arguing for a single unified community of arts educators and was "buoyed up by the many art educators who supported the idea." By 1949 his dream of a national organization had become a reality and he its inaugural president. The first meeting of the fledgling NAEA was in the spring of 1950 in Chicago; the first meeting to draw a genuinely national audience was the following year in New York which attracted over 1,500 delegates. Ziegfeld was given the responsibility for drawing up

the first Constitution of the Association and, looking back, remembered the establishment of a Policy and Research Committee which he saw as one of the major arms of the new association:

> Manuel Barkan was appointed the first chairman....That committee later was responsible for the journal *Research in Art Education*, but it did not appear until 1959. This was one of NAEA's major accomplishments.[15]

Notwithstanding its early successes, the new National Art Education Association faced formidable financial and membership problems. Intriguingly, one problem sat right on Ziegfeld's doorstep. Victor D'Amico, who was on the staff of the Museum of Modern Art as Education Director, had set up an organization called the Committee on Art Education. The Committee, located almost down the street from Teachers College, held annual meetings attracting well known names in the arts for "a contemporary artist could not refuse an invitation from the Museum of Modern Art."[16] Inevitably, young teachers were attracted to the annual programs of the Committee and, in a very real way, there developed an intense competition between the two organizations for members.

While recognizing that the Committee had helped to rebuild art education after the war, Ziegfeld nonetheless saw the limitations of tying an organization to one institution, even one with the prestige of MoMA. In contrast, the NAEA catered to members from across the country and held national conventions in different cities showcasing the accomplishments of the different regions and offering new possibilities for learning and practice. Moreover, the breadth of the NAEA made it possible to create close ties with other disciplines and administrative groups, something which the more parochial setting of MoMA precluded. Framing his comments from within the context of his commitment to developing a relationship between the arts and commerce, Ziegfeld offered his opinion on D'Amico and the National Committee:

> I knew D'Amico well, having first met him when I was in Owatonna in the 1930s. He was for many years the art teacher at a private school in the Bronx and had written a book on theater arts. Living in New York, I was able to attend the committee meetings every year and was on the program frequently. I also served two 3-year

terms on the Council of the Committee. Very frequently, Victor and I would discuss and argue about the NAEA. He maintained that because the NAEA had commercial exhibits at the same time as the conventions of conferences, it had literally sold its soul and all members were subject to irresistible pressures of commercial interests. I knew this was not so and suggested that if he were more familiar with public school programs he would realize the falsity of his criticism. D'Amico, I suspect, had aspirations of national leadership.[17]

Looking back over 30 years later, Ziegfeld expressed a sadness that over time the national meetings of the NAEA had tended to crowd out regional meetings, thus limiting the participation to people at the college level who were more able to get financial support for attending than could public school teachers. His deep commitment to public schools and to art education in the life of the community and the individual framed what he envisioned as the responsibility of the National organization. As he told Anne Gregory (1987):

> I think that the NAEA has fallen down in its appeal to all of the art teachers. One issue that has to be continually addressed is that the arts are an important part of basic education. I think that they have been neglecting to focus on this enough and it is the reason that people, such as deans of colleges of education, are having no compunction when they have to cut down, in removing or reducing the arts (p. 11).

InSEA: The Universal Language

By the early 1950s, peace was taking hold across Europe although normal cultural interchanges of artists had not been reestablished and it was felt that a constructive international effort along these lines was necessary. The mandate of the United Nations Education, Scientific and Cultural Organization (UNESCO) from its founding in the 1940s was to develop positive cooperation among all peoples of the world. The first Director General of UNESCO, Sir Julian Huxley, early on turned his attention to the establishment of a worldwide organization focused on the promotion of peace and international cooperation through the arts. At the first and second general conference sessions held in 1946 and 1947 resolutions were adopted to initiate

inquiries into art education:

> To make use of the comments received from member states upon the draft questionnaire already circulated on Music and the Visual Arts in General Education, and in consultation with three or four experts in these fields, to prepare a program of concrete proposals for submission in 1948 to member states for comment and subsequently to the Third General Session of the General Conference.[18]

Organizations around the world were invited to respond to this initiative and in a thank you letter to Ziegfeld, then President of NAEA, in August 1948, Huxley wrote:

> UNESCO welcomes and values the cooperation of your Association as its work depends very much on the national bodies in different countries. In particular, we hope in the future, to be able to expand and develop our program for the arts in general education and we shall appreciate if you will keep us in touch with the work of your Association.[19]

In 1950, at UNESCO's 5th General Conference the idea was proposed to organize a seminar for member states which would promote the exchange of information and children's artwork. A letter of invitation was sent out outlining the objectives of the seminar.

> To examine the theory and practice of visual art education at different age levels in various types of educational institutions with reference to the conditions prevailing in various countries; to consider the ways in which the teaching and appreciation of the visual arts can enrich national cultural life and contribute to international understanding; to provide a basis for future UNESCO activities which would serve to stimulate and facilitate art education in Member States and promote cooperation for this purpose.[20]

In 1951 in his capacity as President of the NAEA, Ziegfeld was invited to attend this international seminar on 'The Teaching of Art in General Education' held in Bristol, England. Twenty countries were represented at the seminar and they met for just under 3 weeks. Each delegate was invited to bring along a paper about art education in his/her own country along with an exhibition of young people's artwork. The first week of the seminar was given over to presentation of papers and the second and third weeks to discussion of general issues and directions for the future. Delegates attended sessions for 12 hours a day, 5 days a week. Reflecting on that first meeting Ziegfeld (1951) noted that "after a terrible war, to meet about something that all people were interested in was important." More generally he saw this as event of great significance for art education:

> ...for not only was it an expression of interest by UNESCO in this area but it also served to bring together specialists from all over the world to talk about and further the cause of art education. The effects of this seminar will leave an indelible mark on our future (p. 1).

Ziegfeld was struck by the variation among the children's work the delegates from the different countries had brought with them. He noted that this:

> ...depended upon such factors as economic conditions, traditions, or the impact of ideas and concepts by important and forceful educators. For example, in the Swiss schools, in addition to the freer and more creative work, considerable emphasis is placed on accurate object drawing which is felt to be important in the training of the many technicians which are important in a whole Swiss economy. In the work from Australia, the spirit and content of Cizek tradition could still be seen. The examples from Egypt were compelling in their emotional intensity and reflected an educational philosophy which placed great emphasis upon the intuitive and emotional basis of art (p. 8).

The Bristol meeting was organized in terms of seven major topics, ranging from the nature of art education to indigenous art education and folk art to art education and international understanding. On the nature of art education, participants held that it should allow for:

> ...creativeness, that skill should develop in relation to the needs of expression, that the child should have freedom in the choice of his subject, and of the technique he would use to carry it out. All agreed that art education should develop taste. Finally, it had been generally stated that the purpose of art education was to assist the learners to grow intellectually, emotionally and socially.[21]

A more substantive and fine grained interpretation was placed on the 'needs of expression' in the session which discussed education through art and in which Herbert Read (later to become Sir Herbert) was the main speaker. Read, then perhaps the most respected art critic, historian and philosopher in Great Britain had devoted much of the World War II years to the study of child art—an unlikely preoccupation for a man of his eminence. Read had also become a tireless champion for the promotion of peace and understanding across national borders through art which he had put forward in the early years of UNESCO. He found what he believed to be an astonishing consistency between the images created by children and modern artists and Jung's archetypes. He came to believe that all art sprang from human experience, and this had archaic and universal roots with significance for society and education; all children could and should learn both in and through the arts. As in his book, he argued that all human beings possess an inherent capacity to respond to and construct ideas about their worlds aesthetically. For Read, the educational implications of this position were clear in that art education needed to preserve the natural intensity of all modes of perception; that the different modes of perception needed to be coordinated in relation to each other and to the environment and that children needed to be taught how to communicate and express their ideas and thoughts in a variety of symbolic forms. He noted that:

> Our educational systems have tended to ignore the various types of symbolic communication. However, we are beginning to question the adequacy of our verbal modes. The movement which had led to this liberation is beginning to recognize the fact that human beings are dependent upon symbolic as well as conceptual means of thought.[22]

At the session on Art and International Understanding a working committee was formed to offer practical suggestions for the establishment of an international organization to further the work of the Bristol Seminar. Towards the end of their time together the delegates voted unanimously for such a new organization to be supported by UNESCO to perpetuate the kind of interchange that had taken place in Bristol. According to Ziegfeld (1978):

> The members felt strongly that art was a powerful force in the development of international

understanding and good will and recommended that steps be taken for an increased interchange of ideas, work, and materials on a world-wide basis. There are sound, basic recommendations, powerful in their validity and potentialities...The most obvious solution was to establish an international organization devoted to art education. This was done during the next three years, and the name and viewpoint the society are heavily influenced by the philosophy of Sir Herbert Read who, as a special guest, read a paper at the seminar (p. 24).

A 4-person committee was elected to carry forward this mandate, of which Ziegfeld was designated chair; he was to spend the next 9 years of his professional life on the task of originating a complex international organization.

InSEA: International Possibility

It was not surprising, however, that in the early 1950s Read's sentiments about the role of art in human experience should find an echo in the hearts and minds of his American visitor. The American philosopher John Dewey, in his seminal 1934 book *Art as Experience,* had argued for the critical importance of the arts in industrial society, and introduced the idea of developing individuality through initiation into a tradition. Such ideas cannot have gone unnoticed by Ziegfeld who was by then a professor at Columbia University where Dewey himself had taught. Indeed, Ziegfeld's own work in the Owatonna project in the 1930s had already given practical realization to Dewey's belief that art consciously undertaken is instrumental to the education of the individual, development of new modes of perception, aesthetic insight, and the betterment of society. The caveat was, of course, this occurred only where there was structure combined with freedom, without repressive constraints inhibiting the development of the child's experience. It was this last issue that was to fuel much of the thinking that shaped the formation of InSEA.

The early years of the 1950s appeared to be the high points of Ziegfeld's life. For 3 years he was busy drafting the constitution for the new international organization which, despite considerable problems of communication and limited financial support from UNESCO, gradually took shape. The committee of

Edwin Ziegfeld with an exhibition of international children's art.

four given the responsibility for drafting materials included: Ziegfeld, C. Dudley Gaitskell from Canada, A. Barclay Russell from the United Kingdom, and Mme. Henriette Noyer from France. A letter from

I was hooked, and never since that moment have I lost that flush of euphoria. It was then that I understood what Ed was trying to tell me. In discussing this with him at a later date, he commented, "You were slower to come around than I thought, but I knew eventually you'd understand what I've been trying to say."

Al Hurwitz, on his first brush with InSEA

Edwin was a living example of the vitality and relevance of art in human experience; and a living example of what a college professor at the highest level of merit ought to be.

C. Robert Pace, friend

Instead of being caught up in the idea of an international community of art educators, I remained an outsider without that feeling of solidarity that usually accompanies one's first experience with colleagues from other countries. It wasn't until a few years later, when I received an invitation from InSEA President to make a presentation at the meeting in Coventry, that I knew what lay behind Ed's passion...and his understanding of what it means to have a universal rather territorial sense of community.

Al Hurwitz, former President of InSEA

Trevor Thomas, Program Specialist for Art Education, sent from the UNESCO House in Paris offers a glimpse of the work and early accomplishments of the group: He reports:

> A recommendation is being submitted to the next general Conference of UNESCO for a grant-in-aid for an international association for education through art. From participants we have received word that they have appeared before many groups, telling of the Bristol meetings, of what was undertaken and planned there, and of hopes and recommendations. In a number of countries, new and active groups of art educators have been brought into being to further the cause of art education. Some of these groups have already pledged their support for the international association.[23]

Two provisional meetings of InSEA were held in the years 1952 and 1953 in which some 75% of the Bristol participants acted as founder members of the new society. At the second provisional meeting, Ziegfeld was elected interim chairman and empowered to conduct the affairs of the society until its constitution was approved.

Through the good offices of UNESCO, the first formal meeting–or General Assembly–of what was to become the International Society for Education through Art was held in Paris in 1954. The meeting had twin purposes: to discuss and ratify the new constitution and to continue the work of the Bristol conference. Herbert Read addressed the opening session and the delegates ratified the constitution confirming Ziegfeld as the first President of InSEA, a capacity he served in until 1960. The final session of this first meeting was held at the International Center for the Study of Education at Sevres, where the Director spoke rather forcefully on the 'Role of Artistic Activities in General Education.' Thinking back, perhaps, to the days of Melvin Haggerty and pre-Owatonna, Ziegfeld (1954) commented:

> It seemed clear that the problems which art educators face in securing a place for art in general education were general rather than local, and it was heartening to know that these are general educators who see clearly and are convinced of our destined role in the education of young people (p. 4).

Drawing on his past experience in establishing the NAEA as both a regional and national body, one sees Ziegfeld's hand reflected in much of the new constitution. The fledgling society committed itself to annual regional meetings to be held in various parts of the world, and a General Assembly to be held every 2 years. The international exchange of materials, publications, children's art work was encouraged, along with ongoing discussion of the humanizing aims and purposes of art education in the various member countries. A second General Assembly of InSEA was held in the Hague, the Netherlands, and in spite of grave financial concerns and unsettling political events in Hungary and the Near East, the meeting attracted a great many attendees. The meeting was devoted to Art Education for Adolescents, a theme that had been seriously neglected among member nations and one that was especially dear to Ziegfeld's heart. While art education for the primary or elementary pupil had been the topic of much research and discussion, the needs of adolescents who would carry adult responsibility for fashioning the state of the world in the coming decades, had been ignored. For this meeting

> He taught classes in art and community at a time when art education was little interested in this kind of idea, this was focused not on houses but on public places—he gave me a vocabulary for discussing public places. This is still not part of general art education teaching.
>
> *Edmund Burke Feldman, former student, Professor Emeritus, University of Georgia*
>
> In art education, the Ziegfeld years were good years, growth years, free of the divisiveness, the retreat from professionalism and the influence of big bucks that characterize the present era. Today, his kind of unselfish and inspired leadership, his ability to attract support for the right minded goals and his quiet but skillful diplomacy is sorely missed as the idea of art education as a discipline is slowly but surely being diminished.
>
> *John Lidstone, former student and studio assistant, late Dean of Education, Queens College, NY*
>
> There really was no one else quite like him at the time; he was personally shy and gentle, but held me to high standards. He always did his homework, if you took a chapter to him he actually read it, unlike many other professors!
>
> *Edmund Burke Feldman*

I am fortunate to have
known Edwin Ziegfeld;
to have had the help
and friendship of a
gentle, tough-minded
man, who always keep
the world in perspec-
tive and his values in
sharp focus.

*Phyllis Gold Gluck,
former student,
Professor of Art
Education,
Brooklyn College*

Ziegfeld arranged an international exhibition of children's drawings and paintings (The Art of the Adolescent) which "was a real smash."[24] Some 500 works were selected from thousands of submissions representing 40 countries including Africa, Asia, Russia, Europe and North America. Among the committee selecting the work were Johannes Itten and Sir Herbert Read.

Looking back on this event during his interview with Anne Gregory (1987), Ziegfeld recalled:

I had written to ask the Russians to come and the second to last day they wrote that some would arrive. This caused quite a commotion because this was the first time they had taken part. They brought along a lot of highly proficient work which was viewed with some suspicion as to how it was selected (p. 14).

Ziegfeld's third, and last, General Assembly as President of InSEA was held in Manila in the Philippines and the theme was based on "Man and Art in East and West." This theme was in keeping with a major project of UNESCO based on 'The Mutual Apprecia-

tion of the Cultural Values of Orient and Occident' and reflected a shift away from a primary concern with Western affairs and influence towards the underserved eastern part of the globe. In her dissertation, written at Ohio State University "A History of the Origins and Development of the International Society for Education through Art: The Edwin Ziegfeld Years," Jane Rhoades (1987) offers a snapshot of his legacy to that organization:

Ziegfeld was an avid communicator. I have read through hundreds and hundreds of letters of correspondence. His brilliant leadership ability made the organization work. He effectively delegated the responsibilities and delicately had led sensitive international miscommunication issues...he is thought of as a dynamic, diplomatic, hard working, innovative leader (p. 139).

The early days of InSEA and Ziegfeld's Presidency were largely those of the Cold War and it was not until much later and the General Assembly meeting in Prague in 1966 that Eastern European delegates could attend in any numbers. Commenting to Anne Gregory (1987) Ziegfeld remembered that this meeting was:

...filled with East Germans, Czechs, and a lot of Yugoslavs. Since the Hague meeting, the Russians have been to practically every meeting. I know that the meeting we had in Yugoslavia had some very articulate and interesting Russians who were familiar with the writings of a large number of American art educators. They were an impressive group (p. 15).

Ziegfeld was responsible for broadening the membership of InSEA during the time he was President and for many years after that, as its senior apostle he canvassed for members among his students and on his many travels. He pushed for the inclusion of members from second and third world countries, but became troubled by what he saw as the effects of emerging tensions among nations upon arts educators. Years later, in a conversation with Phyllis Gold Gluck, a former graduate student and subsequently Professor of Art Education at Brooklyn College, Ziegfeld expressed disquiet about the way in which he believed different political and cultural ideologies were distorting the original goals and vision of InSEA.

Edwin Ziegfeld Collection: The Art of the Adolescent. Secondary school student painting from Germany.

Edwin Ziegfeld Collection: The Art of the Adolescent. Secondary school student linoleum print from South Africa.

QUICKENING AESTHETIC SENSIBILITIES

At TC: A Professor of Exigency and Kindness

Edwin Ziegfeld took up his professorial duties at Teachers College (TC) Columbia University in the academic year 1945-46 where he was to remain until he retired in 1970. In those early years, under the Presidency of Nicholas Murray Butler, TC boasted a faculty of formidable scholars including Harold Rugg, George Counts, Hollis Caswell, all of whom were Professors of Education; Margaret Meade was Adjunct Professor of Anthropology. On the list of active Emeriti were James Earl Russell, William Heard Kilpatrick, and Edward Lee Thorndike. Although TC's most famous scholar, John Dewey, had retired in the academic year of 1927-28, his formidable reputation lingered to shape many of the intellectual preoccupations of the ensuing years.[25] By the time he retired, Ziegfeld was Chairperson of the newly named Department of Art and Education[26] and had worked with another generation of influential teacher scholars including Lawrence Cremin, Maxine Greene, Philip Phenix, and Harry Passow.

The Ziegfeld years at Teachers College were marked by a curriculum of teacher education which then, as now, intermingled and integrated studio work with courses concerned with theories of child development, curriculum and method. Ziegfeld's commitment to the importance of design in the education of artists and teachers is seen reflected in an array of studio courses: color and design, design analysis, design structure in space, environmental design, textile design, and publicity design. In the early 1960s, the faculty of Teachers College voted for a new type of Doctoral Degree in the College Teaching of an Academic Subject. By all accounts, Ziegfeld pressed for, and was active in shaping, the requirements for this degree which, in the arts, gave priority to high level studio work bestowing on the 'exhibition' equal status with the written dissertation. This new degree afforded public recognition of his abiding concern to "dig deep" into the center of artistry in order to give substance and vitality to its core and practices.[27]

> Through his commitment to design in art he opened up art education to a wider set of issues than the subjective and touchy-feelie.
>
> *Edmund Burke Feldman*

By all accounts, Edwin Ziegfeld was low key, shy, and modest about his accomplishments but exuded extraordinary powers as an innovative leader and teacher. Those who worked and studied with him at Teachers College in those years saw him as the most convincing spokesperson for art education in the country, a key figure in shaping art education both nationally and globally. According to his younger brother Ernest, from childhood Edwin pursued excellence and his unwillingness to accept less than the best from himself was one of his most striking characteristics. Years later, as an advisor to doctoral students he:

> ...sometimes caused anguish by his impatience with fuzzy thinking and faulty syntax. But when this happened it was because he felt he would be failing in his job if he did not elicit the best possible work from his students.[28]

Yet, his exigencies were balanced by extreme kindness. According to Phyllis Gold Gluck he:

> was very kind and supportive of my need to balance family, studies, parenting and teaching. He protected me and yet propelled me forward to do many things. 1968 was an uneasy and dangerously turbulent time at Columbia...Ed encouraged me to participate in the College governance structure...and spoke of my duty to help change.[29]

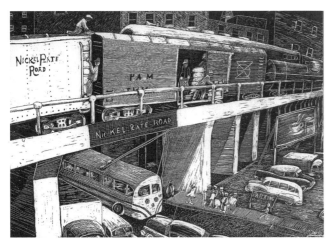

Edwin Ziegfeld Collection: The Art of the Adolescent. Secondary school student scratch board from the USA.

Talks To Teachers: The Necessary Role Of Design

Given what must have been a crushing work schedule shaped first by his involvement with establishing the NAEA and then InSEA, redrafting *Art Today,* editing the journal *Art Education Today*, and authoring articles, it is a wonder that Ziegfeld had time and energy left over for his work at Teachers College. However, this man of enormous energy and efficient organization began to set his stamp on art education at the College equally as he challenged some of the cherished icons of the general field.

John Lidstone, a doctoral student in the 1950s and later Dean of Education at Queens College in New York, also remembered his kindness. John remembered a time when he almost burnt the College to the ground by leaving on a faulty kiln over an entire weekend. Ziegfeld offered nothing close to a rebuke, but instead

> ...he pointed out what a crummy room I had been assigned, how he had endeavored over and over without result to get the College to fix it up and how I had succeeded where he had failed... He, with his sensitivity to the problems of the other guy, had turned a negative into a positive one.[30]

His interest and continuing participation in InSEA caught fire with his students at Teachers College many of whom became members under his urging. Al Hurwitz recalled how when he spoke of matters concerning international art education, or his historical collection of child art, or of the many personalities such as Sir Herbert Read and Henry Moore whom he had met through InSEA "his eyes shone with the fervor of a true believer."

> There were really three Ed Ziegfeld's I came to know—the formal exceedingly considerate person one met at professional and social events, the warmer personality that emerged in his interaction with students, and an intense, persuasive side that was revealed when discussing any matter that related to international art education in general, or InSEA in particular.[31]

While Ziegfeld seems to have written and spoken very little that was directly focused on teacher education per se, we see his thinking during his tenure at Teachers College etched most clearly in his commitment to the critical importance of the arts in public school education and to the responsibilities he though central to good teaching. According to Professor Maxine Greene, who knew him as a colleague at Teachers College, he was "not a conservative thinker." Indeed, his belief that art was an instrument for interpreting and changing the social order led him to challenge major figures in education for their neglect and

> The Ziegfeld Legacy is a powerful guiding force for the challenges facing art education as we move into the 21st century...the insights of Edwin Ziegfeld... provide us with important perspectives for contemporary times.
>
> *Elaine Foster, former student, Professor of Art Education, Jersey City State College, NJ*

Edwin Ziegfeld Collection: The Art of the Adolescent. Secondary school student painting, USSR.

lack of informed support for the subject in general education. In a speech delivered to the Maryland Conference on Secondary Education (1961a) he noted:

> We have intelligent and generally well-meaning critics of our schools who are exerting tremendous influence. James B. Conant, for example, states that the arts are fine but we have no time for them. A naval admiral, and self appointed critic of education whose influence is considerable, probably does not even know that the arts exist or, if he does, he would not, I suspect, care. All public school programs are being subjected to enormous pressure to increase offerings in science and mathematics and foreign languages. This is not to suggest here that these areas are not vitally important. The point is being made that if we bow only to the pressures from limited subject areas, we are laying the groundwork for an impoverished culture, one without vitality or valid meaning (p. 44).

Edwin Ziegfeld Collection: The Art of the Adolescent. Secondary school student print, Japan

This challenge to established thinking was delivered during the immediate aftermath of Sputnik and the renewed call for a central focus on mathematics and science education to restore U.S. technical and military prominence in the world. Ziegfeld's claim that the visual arts should also be seen as areas that affect all people were based on his long-term commitment to the belief that:

> Everyone sees art, makes judgments and selections of art products, and is affected by what he sees and the judgments and selections he makes. We cannot avoid these pervasive influences any more than we can live without breathing (p. 15).

Ziegfeld's real passion focused on art education during the secondary school years, for it was from this level of schooling that he foresaw future leaders in the arts and culture would come. His view of why art is important as a curriculum subject developed in *Art for*

the Academically Talented Student in the Secondary School (1961b) sounds unbelievably modern in its commitments:

> As a humanistic subject, the visual arts have unique and essential contribution to make to education. Their locus is in the realm of values and feelings; they extend, deepen and mature the emotions. They introduce students to new means of communication; they complement the highly intellectual approach to learning which characterizes most of their schooling; they intensify visual and sensory experience, encourage inventiveness and a creative approach to problems. They aid in evolving criteria for judging the many forms of art products from which all must make choices, and bring to all an increased awareness and a realization of the obligation to improve the environment. By making one visually aware they give color to the most common of everyday experiences and make possible the enjoyment of some of the greatest of human expressions (p. 64).

The kind of language used by Ziegfeld and the sentiments expressed in his writings of the 1950s onward are much evolved from his earlier thinking in Owatonna. A clue to the stimulus for much of this new thinking can be found in some of his writings of the pre-sputnik era when, shortly after his arrival at Teachers College, and with the accomplishments of NAEA and InSEA, he envisioned a time of hope for art education. Engaging in some historical reflection, he invited teachers to learn from the "really remarkable progress" of the past 50 years in order to orient themselves for future developments in the field. He praised Arthur Dow, his predecessor at Teachers College during the first decades of the century, for shifting the field away from what he saw as the restrictions of "representative drawing" in favor of a focus on the principles of composition and design within which all areas of the graphic and plastic arts could be contained. For Ziegfeld, writing in the journal *Art Education Today* (1941), design:

> ...may be defined as the giving of orderly form to materials to meet a variety of human needs; a goal-directed activity concerned with human problems and aspirations, with expressing and communicating ideas, ideals, and experiences, and with providing useful objects that help man adjust to his environment (p. 92).

Ziegfeld praised the work of Dow in the area of design in education as "Quite clearly, one of the most startling developments in art education of this century has been the broadening of the conception of what it embraced" (Ziegfeld, 1951-52). In later writing, he chided teachers saying that they had never made clear to students that design is something more than a set of theoretical and formulaic ideas but has a fundamental and organic origin in human experience:

> The constant beating of our hearts, the regularity of our breathing, the alternation of our periods of tension opposed by periods of relaxation are recognized in our interest in rhythm, continuity, repetition, progression and alternation. Such human experiences are the basis of our understanding of design...An organic basis of interpretation of design, even if difficult to prove, appears logical. Although there is nothing new to this point of view, it is seldom understood to a meaningful degree (p. 96).

Turning his attention to an equally striking development he continued:

> After the first World War, great teachers like Franz Cizek made the discovery that creativity is a common and not occasional attribute of mankind. This development paralleled Dow's, for just as his principles of design made clear the extent of art education in the visual world, so the realization that all men are creative pointed out that art education must deal with all people. These two concepts have more than any other, revolutionized art education. Both are excitingly democratic in nature and their validity and vigor have, in large part, accounted for the steady strengthening of the role of art in education (p. 97).

Ziegfeld also noted the emergence of research in child development which had called attention to the importance of emotional development in children along with the relationship between creativity and mental and physical growth. In keeping with his commitment to the organic base of design in art education, he argued that while design principals per se constitute abstract and mature concepts that need to be explored consciously, they actually have their artistic origins in the expressive work of young children where they arise spontaneously and are explored intuitively:

> Intelligent use of design principles requires a detachment from the work being produced that is normal only to persons of some maturity. For immature workers of a young age, such detachment is a break in the creative experience that leaves its mark on the product. A child painting a picture of a windy day, absorbed in his subject, will probably use rhythmic lines and forms as a natural means of expressing the spirit of his painting. In doing so he draws on his personal experience, on what he feels to be the movement caused by the wind, and this direct relation of experience to expression gives a spontaneous directness that is often the envy of professional artists (p. 97).

In stressing the intuitive organizational proclivities of childhood art, Ziegfeld urged teachers to be thoughtful and sensitive in how they guided children towards an understanding of more mature and abstract principles.

> Older children can be guided...but such guidance is far more than handing out rules of design. The transition from art production in which color and form are felt and expressed intuitively to that stage at which this experience can be guided and charged intellectually is both delicate and difficult. Attempted too early, the change destroys more than it adds, and causes the production of labored, spiritless art. If introduced when the child is ready, however, an intellectual consideration of design can promote work in which intuition is clarified and fortified by rational analysis (p. 98).

> Of those human capacities to which Edwin refers, feeling and emotion have been particularly vulnerable to omission in our unbalanced educational orientation towards job and skill development for life.
>
> *Elaine Foster*

The Dow Awards given annually at Teachers College.

Talks To Teachers: Promoting Uniqueness And Developing Autonomy

In his later writings, Ziegfeld became increasingly concerned with the growing fragmentation and mechanization of his time. The hope and possibility he saw for art education offered by Owatonna, a small midwest town, was replaced by a larger and darker vision of the world in which the inventions of science and technology had outstripped the human benefits they were invented to serve. Concern about the drift of the world towards increasing mechanization, underlined what he perceived as an urgent necessity for providing educational experiences of an individualizing and integrating nature. In looking forward Ziegfeld urged teachers to take advantage of the broad sweep of possibility within art education to provide experiences in support of such human needs. However, writing in (1961b) teachers were to proceed with some exigency and caution. They were to remember that creativity and intuitive reasoning could not be reduced to right answers or predictable outcomes and that:

> There is no right way to draw a tree. There is no right way to draw a figure. Artists over a period of many thousands of years have drawn figures and trees and animals in many different ways and artistically they are all "right" (p. 22).

Similarly teachers were to explore the potential in the arts for carrying out activities which promote uniqueness and which develop autonomy.

We live in a time when the pressure against individualism is tremendous. We are subjected to massive pressures for conformity. They appear on television and radio, in magazines and advertising, in mass production and large scale marketing (p. 46).

Ziegfeld notes that paradoxically, the conformism that society had accepted had not led to the security it sought, rather human beings had become increasingly alienated one from another. He urged art teachers to offer experiences which placed a premium on uniqueness and individuality and which allowed the creative explorations of the tensions and feelings associated with self and world to be explored and, where possible, resolved. Part of the way a teacher could promote such experiences was by emphasizing sensory and humanizing values of design–design used in the pursuit of shaping personal 'feeling' content and not as a formal end of art education. Foreseeing a future computerized age, a time when the machine could be made to think and make judgments, Ziegfeld asked:

> If all knowledge is something that can be put on a small piece of glass and machines can do the work of the world, then what is left? The human brain becomes cumbersome and fallible, the human body frail and undependable. We are in great danger of forgetting that a work in which human beings are not at the center of all our concerns would be senseless and empty. It must be education's central concern to keep man central in education. The recent pressures on education to increase instruction in mathematics, science, and foreign languages have not increased the humanizing value of education, but rather, lessened them (p. 51).

To maintain the individual at the center of his humanity the art teacher should play a profound and constructive role. The experiences teachers were to offer had to be in depth and intense and not superficial. The pupil should be offered experiences that:

> Compel him to explore possibilities which are not superficially obvious but must be "dug" for which require concentration and sustained effort (p. 52).

Inveighing against the common practice of working with materials that amounted to nothing more than mindless play he notes:

> Learning the quality of things–their texture, their forms, their feel, their smell and their taste–is

basic and this is best discovered by working with materials and things. But in too many of our art classes working with materials has degenerated into a series of manipulative exercises in which, frankly, it is often impossible to distinguish between the work of the fourth graders and tenth graders. Nothing is demanded past handling of materials. There is no seeking out of special characteristics, no searching for relationships. No growth takes place because no demands are made (p. 52).

Edwin was a man of many talents and many interests, a man with humor and compassion, a generous man and, above all, a modest man, probably the description that would most have pleased him is to say that he was in all respects, a man of excellence.

Ernest Ziegfeld

Above all, for Ziegfeld, this kind of mindless manipulation of materials denied to the art process the thoughtful guiding of individual expression and weakened the stimulus to deal with meaningful problems. Unless, teachers understood deep within themselves the nature of the artistry which they encouraged in others they could not couple inventiveness, imagination and creativity to the kind of selecting, ordering and integrating essential to a successful and unique art experience for their pupils. No only this, but to neglect the exploratory and unique was to perpetuate one of the great problems in art education, namely, to sensitize people to forms which are new to them. Noting that almost without exception great artists of the contemporary era had been rejected out of hand:

The effect of rejection by the general public of contemporary art works is that people are never able to enjoy art of the period of history in which they are living, and those are the works of art which should speak to them most forcefully (p. 24).

Noting that art in American culture was becoming increasingly non objective, and that by throwing off the shackles of subject matter and post-renaissance traditions in painting, the artists was freeing himself to seek:

...truths, universal truths, and for him the universal truth resides in the particular...because this is a time when our culture needs emphasis on the individual, the painter, more often than not looks within himself for subject matter (p. 35).

He thought it important that teachers of adolescents should engage them with contemporary art, not as a hold-over from the renaissance, but as contributing to all areas of life, such as to: industry, the theater, television, journalism, advertising, city planning and transportation. However, it was unfortunate that:

...it is easier for the average twentieth century man to accept and enjoy revolutionary ideas in contemporary functional design such as airplanes and automobiles than new forms in painting and sculpture (p. 36).

Noting that a common characteristic of an artistically naive and insecure people is the rejection of the contemporary world as being "aesthetically useless" he continues:

One of the most important outcomes of art instruction at any level is the realization that the twentieth century has its own unique problems to solve and that these problems can be expressed in art just as well as those of any other period. And this outcome is best reached by involving students with today's world and making a study of the efforts of contemporary artists to bring aesthetic order into modern life (p. 36).

Writing near to the end of his professional life, Ziegfeld's view of art education and art educators becomes increasingly bleak. He chastises art teachers for succumbing to pressures from outside the field, from an uninformed society, from educators unsympathetic or ignorant about the essential human values of education:

In taking a somewhat dim view of current developments, the outlook is not necessarily hopeless. The current situation is one of our own doing and by the same token as the fact that it is we who have created it, we should be able–if we wish–to change it (p. 44).

His concerns, however, were many and echo those expressed at the turn of the 20th century equally as they were to foreshadow those of its closing. He saw the growing dominance of science and technology to be both triumphant and dangerous for "efficiency and productivity tend to make us ignore or suspect the subjective and spiritual sides of life" (Ziegfeld, 1961b). Science and technology which gave promise of freedom, actually functioned to contract the world and made possible annihilation. Equally, the material and functional gains which were the envy of the world also reduced the worker to the status of automata who could only follow simple and repetitive tasks. This he saw as bringing loss of pride in accomplishment and promoted strong trends towards conformism.

Ziegfeld saw these cultural crises in the context of an educational crisis, as an imbalance between scientific and humanistic concerns. Like Dewey, in his writings he saw the importance of art, science and technology not, as usually interpreted in education in terms of rigidly fixed ends, but as thought and action liberated and made available to experimentation, where anything might happen. The banishing of the concept of the fixed end-product which seemed to him and others like spiritual impoverishment working against change, was replaced in his thinking by an emphasis on process which made possible the importance of human purposes and freed the mind to reshape existence (Burton, 1999). The role of art in human experience, he envisioned as one of quickening aesthetic sensitivities such that an individual would be propelled to take control over change in his or her own surroundings. Writing in (1961b), he states:

> Certain values in the visual arts derive clearly from process, from the activity itself. Inasmuch as the visual arts draw upon one's experiences, the individual is required to confront himself—to choose, to reorganize, to integrate. At the very least he deals with things which interest and have meaning for him; he may also, through this confrontation, make discoveries about himself...Inventiveness, imagination, creativity–all are essentials of the successful art experience. These are particularly apparent in the art process because the range of acceptable and 'right' solutions is infinite (p. 22).

ENDINGS AND THE LEGACY

Retirement

Following his retirement from Teachers College, Ziegfeld stayed in New York for 8 years entertaining friends in his beautiful Greenwich Village house and home in Connecticut. Here in his homes, by all accounts, he engaged in his passions for gardening and for making fudge! According to his brother Ernest, growing up in a strict German Lutheran family meant that many Sunday afternoon pastimes usually allowed

Ziegfeld, just before retirement. (Special Collections, Milbank Memorial Library, Teachers College, Columbia University.)

to children were denied the Ziegfeld youngsters, except for making fudge. Edwin developed a talent at this culinary art and a taste for Mamie Eisenhower's fudge recipe! Over the years, this youthful skill would be joined by others as Ziegfeld developed a great love for cooking at which he became a notorious master–to the great satisfaction of his friends. According to all of those who enjoyed his warm hospitality, and many parties, Ziegfeld's 150 year old house in the Village was a collector's paradise, for over the many years of his travels he had amassed a collection that was remarkable for its diversity as well as for the taste that inspired it. Here, he loved to listen to music and, by all accounts, had created an astonishing collection of records. He thought he would never leave this house. One can only imagine how wrenching it must have been for him to leave this home for Claremont, California, where he was to live in very quiet retirement for the next 9 years. Asked by Anne Gregory in her 1987 interview if he was still actively involved in art education, Ziegfeld replied "Not in any major way. I worked so hard for 40 years that I find it very difficult to make myself work anymore. Now, living in California, I have more things to do than there is time for."

Art Today, A Humanistic Legacy: Guideposts To The Future

Ziegfeld's life spanned three cataclysmic world events: the stock market crash and Great Depression, World War II, and the Cold War. Each event provoked the asking of questions about the role and purpose of education in the life of communities and the individual, and repeatedly placed in contention the existence of art education. As we look at his professional life as it spans these world shaking events, we see that Ziegfeld's career was, in some measure, shaped by the checks and balances of each. We still have much to learn from the accomplishments of his life for many of his concerns remain with us still:

- that the idea of community-in-culture, interwoven with a belief in the fundamental need for art as a humanistic language, is as critical now as it was 50 years ago;
- that the unifying power of professional organizations such as the NAEA and InSEA resides in a commitment to art as a language of peace, within which the aesthetic and creative sensibilities of individuals interplay dynamically with those of the group;
- that the fundamental importance of art education in the life of all children and adolescents requires that public schools are morally responsible for including the arts as part of a comprehensive education;
- that the experiences individuals bring with them to the practice of art making involves imagination, creativity, a respect for materials and an ability to 'dig deep' into ideas and problems;
- that art-as-subject rests in a conception of design, as an organizing principle, originating in the organic experience of the individual rather than in theoretical formulas;
- that perception and knowledge gained through careful attention to the phenomena of the world engages sensory and emotional responses as central ingredients shaping individual artistic experience; and
- that the sociocultural context that stimulates individual artistic endeavor must be the beneficiary of the fruits of that endeavor.

Acknowledgments

Thanks are due to the following people who assisted in the preparation of this chapter. To the late Anne Gregory, whose interview with Edwin Ziegfeld offered an important context in which to set his life; her all too early passing is a great loss to us all. To Ernest Ziegfeld, whom I have been privileged to meet and whose words brought his brother to life for me; to my graduate assistant at Teachers College, Barbara Salander, whose help in so many ways moved forward the work. Many of the quotes and some of the information included in the chapter are drawn from papers presented at 'A Tribute to Edwin Ziegfeld' the 4th session in Exploring the Legends series, held at Teachers College Columbia University on Friday, February 19, 1993. Other sources of information come from personal conversations with those who knew Ziegfeld, and my own reading of his writings, and writings about him and his work. Of particular help was a dissertation written in 1987 at Ohio State University, by Jane Ellen Rhoades, which focused on Ziegfeld's role in the founding of InSEA. All sources are attributed in the text and endnotes.

Endnotes

[1] Ziegfeld is first mentioned as a faculty member at Teachers College in the Bulletin of 1941-42. He is listed as Assistant Professor on a faculty that included: Ray Faulkner, Henry Tannerhill, Charles Martin, Arthur Young, Elise Ruffini, Belle Boas, and Belle Northrup.

[2] Ernest Ziegfeld, 'A Brother's Memories.' A tribute written in September 1987. Ernest is also an art educator, craftsperson and author of distinction who, for many years, was a professor at Jersey City State College, NJ.

[3] Anne Gregory's Interview with Dr. Edwin Ziegfeld was included in the *Journal of Multicultural and Cross-Cultural Art Education,* Fall 1987, an edition dedicated to Edwin Ziegfeld. She also gave a spoken version of this interview as her tribute at the Legends Symposium, held at Teachers College, February, 19 1993.

[4] Now called the Columbus College of Art and Design.

[5] Ernest Ziegfeld, 'A Brother's Memories.'

[6] Ibid.

[7] Edwin Ziegfeld and Mary Elinore Smith co-authored volume 4 in a series of 10 publications arising out of the work of the Owatonna Project.

[8] The final cost of the 5-year Owatonna Project was $65,000.

[9] Al Hurwitz, 'A Tribute to Edwin Ziegfeld,' delivered at the Legend's Symposium, Teachers College, February 19, 1993.

[10] The title of Ziegfeld's dissertation: *An experimental investigation to determine the effects of different methods of instruction in painting on the ability to make discriminatory judgments in the field of painting and in other fields of art.* University of Minnesota, 1947.

[11] C. Robert Pace, 'A Tribute to Edwin Ziegfeld,' written September 1987. Pace was a longtime friend of Ziegfeld's, they had known each other since Owatonna days.

[12] The second edition of *Art Today* appeared in 1947, the third edition in 1956, the forth edition in 1963 and the fifth edition in 1968.

[13] Taken from the NAEA 39th Annual Convention Catalogue (1999) which ran a five-page account of 'A Conversation With Edwin Ziegfeld on the Founding of the National Art Education Association', written by long time friend, Larry Kantner, University of Missouri-Columbia.

[14] Ibid.

[15] Ibid.

[16] Ibid.

[17] Ibid.

[18] Quoted in Rhoades, Jane (1987) *A history of the origin and development of the International Society for Education through Art: The Edwin Ziegfeld Legacy. Unpublished dissertation,* The Ohio State University, p. 113). Much of this section on the founding and early years of InSEA owes to this source.

[19] Ibid., p. 48).

[20] Ibid., p. 95).

[21] Ibid., p. 102).

[22] Ibid., p. 104).

[23] Ibid., p. 108).

[24] The collection of art made for the Hague Assembly, now called The Edwin Ziegfeld: Art of the Adolescent Collection, is housed in Special Collections at Teachers College Milbank Library where, as a historic document, it is available for study purposes.

[25] Taken from the *Teachers College Bulletins,* 1941-42 through 1969-70.

[26] So called in the *Teachers College Bulletin* of 1969-70. The program, now called Art and Art Education, is part of the larger Arts and Humanities Department.

[27] The Ed.D.C.T. continues to exist at Teachers College and attracts students whose aim is to become studio teachers.

[28] Ernest Ziegfeld "A Brother's Tribute."

[29] Phyllis Gold Gluck "Tribute to Edwin Ziegfeld" delivered at the Legends Symposium, Teachers College, February 19, 1993.

[30] John Lidstone, "Tribute to Edwin Ziegfeld." John also remembered the hesitation of speech that sometimes left students hanging for seconds at a time and that it was typical of the man to refer to this problem at his retirement banquet. John remembered him saying: I know many of you have been disconcerted from time to time with a hesitation in my speech which I know left you hanging while, it would appear, I was gathering my thoughts. In actuality, those pauses were and are the result of a speech dysfunction I have had all my life and I want to apologize to those for who it may have caused some anxiety.

[31] Al Hurwitz, "Tribute to Edwin Ziegfeld."

References

Burton, J. M. (1999). *The Ziegfeld collection: International art of adolescents from the 1950s.* NY: Teachers College Columbia University, Department of the Arts and Humanities.

Gregory, A. (1987). Interview with Dr. Edwin Ziegfeld. *Journal of multicultural and cross-cultural art education,* 5 (1).

Haggerty, M. (1938). *Enrichment of the common life.* Minneapolis: Colwell Press, Inc.

Rhoades, J. (1987). *A History of the origin and development of the International Society for Education through Art: The Edwin Ziegfeld legacy.* Unpublished dissertation, The Ohio State University.

Read, H. (1943). *Education through art.* London: Faber and Faber.

Saunders, R. J. (1985). Owatonna: The American Camelot. In *The history of art education: Proceedings from the Penn State conference,* (pp. 152-157). Reston, VA: NAEA.

Ziegfeld, E. (1941). The teaching of design. *Art education today,* Bureau of Publications, Teachers College Columbia University, NY.

Ziegfeld, E. & Smith, M. E. (1944). *Art for daily living.* Minnesota: University of Minnesota Press.

Ziegfeld, E. & Faulkner, R. (1944). *Art today.* New York: Holt, Reinhart, and Winston.

Ziegfeld, E. (1951). A report to American art education: The UNESCO Seminar in Art Education, Bristol, England, July 7-29, 1951. In *Art Education: Journal of the National Society for Education through Art* 4 (4).

Ziegfeld, E. (1951-52). Art and the secondary program. *Art Education Today.* Bureau of Publications, Teachers College Columbia University, NY.

Ziegfeld, E. (1952). *The visual arts in general education: Report on the Bristol Seminar,* UK, 1951. UNESCO/CUA/36.

Ziegfeld E. (1953). *Creative teaching in the visual arts: A symposium on education through art.* UNESCO.

Ziegfeld, E. (Ed.). (1954). *Education and art.* UNESCO.

Ziegfeld, E. (1957). The story of InSEA. *Arts and Activities,* May.

Ziegfeld, E. (1961a). Emerging frontiers in the fine arts. *Maryland State Department of Education, Conference on Secondary Education,* March, pp. 23-24.

Ziegfeld, E. (Ed.). (1961b). *Art for the academically talented student in the secondary school.* Washington, DC: National Art Education Association.

Ziegfeld, E. (1978, February). InSEA: Notes on its history. *Art Education: Journal of the National Society for Education Through Art,* pp. 24-26.

EPILOGUE: LEGENDS IN CONTEXT

Elizabeth J. Saccá
Photographic Research by Julia A. Lindsey

Through a friend I arranged a visit for us on a Monday when the museum was closed, and we were bussed in. The students were excited and fascinated by the paintings. They ran from room to room exclaiming, calling to one another, uninhibitedly enjoying these 'strange paintings with such glowing color[1]!' No one was bored. No one had ever been in an art museum before (Catlett, 1989, p. 244).

I suggested that one of the women run (for President of the Ohio Art Education Association). To my surprise, they said they wanted a 'man' to be President because they said the organization would have greater influence and gain more respect if a man was in charge. I had never heard that argument before but all the women seemed to agree (personal communication, J. A. Michael, April 13, 1999).

As educators, most of us find our satisfaction in the achievements of others….Women of my generation in particular have been programmed...not to claim credit for what we do (Laura Chapman, 1979, as cited in Stankiewicz and Zimmerman, 1984).

The first of these accounts is told by Elizabeth Catlett, who had been a Durham, North Carolina high school art teacher and supervisor of art programs beginning in 1936 (personal communication, Rikki Asher, March 3, 1999). The art class she took to the museum in 1941 was from Dillard University. The reason the students had never been to an art museum was, as she explained, "because the museum was closed to us because it was in City Park, where Blacks were not permitted" (Catlett, 1989, p. 244).

The second story takes place in 1963. John Michael explains that he declined the nomination for President because the previous president had been from his university. He suggested that instead of him, a woman should run. He continues, "So they searched and searched for a man who was somewhat well-known in the state….From 1963 to 1989, there was only one

Black Woman Speaks by Elizabeth Catlett, 1960, lithograph. Courtesy Sragow Gallery, New York City. © Elizabeth Catlett/ Licensed by VAGA, New York, NY. Photo credit: Sara Wells 1997.

woman [Ohio] OAEA President!" He notes that this is the case even though "there were many, many more female teachers/art teachers than men" (personal communication, J. A. Michael, April 13, 1999).

Why do we hear or read less about Elizabeth Catlett or for that matter Samella Lewis (personal communication, Ellen Sragow, May 24, 1999) than we do of others in the field? Both of these women taught at Hampton University with widely-discussed Viktor Lowenfeld whose work is studied in this volume. Her art and teaching address issues central to U.S. society, and she challenged race and gender segregation years before the Civil Rights and Feminist Movements. The second story which is told by John Michael raises the question, "Is it possible that people were still expecting women to defer to men as recently as 1963?" The third quotation, by Laura Chapman raises the question of the conditioning that underpins many situations, especially the recognition of women's achievements and promotion of women to visible positions such as association president. Do these accounts represent isolated incidents or are they symptomatic of larger social expectations? If they are symptomatic, these three accounts challenge our assumptions that our society in general, and our field in particular are fair and balanced.

If these questions are symptomatic of social expectations, these social expectations are important aspects of the context in which we view the works of Rudolf Arnheim, Victor D'Amico, Viktor Lowenfeld, and Edwin Ziegfeld. Many of us developed our views of art education reading their books. While we admire their achievements, these questions make us pause. As we look back from today's perspective, we are jolted by the absence of women among their ranks. We ask "Why?" and "What social context and attitudes support the absence of women?"

Considering Women

When we look back to the 1950s, we see several examples of work that incorporated the achievements of women. In 1954, J. Biggers completed a dissertation entitled *The Negro Woman in American Life and Education: A Mural Presentation* (as cited in Michael, 1982), and in his 1955 history of art in public schools, Fred Logan discussed women's achievements.

Twenty years later, colleagues began to address the under-representation of women in art education history and research (Collins, 1977; Lovano-Kerr, Semler and Zimmerman, 1977; Michael, 1977; Packard, 1977; White and White, 1973). A decade later, this author reviewed U.S. and Canadian art education journals and found that the activity of the 1970s addressing women had subsided (Saccá, 1989).

In 1982, *Women Art Educators* (edited by Enid Zimmerman and Mary Ann Stankiewicz) was begun to address the gender gap in the historical record. This series continued to report on women's achievements with Volume II (1985) edited by Mary Ann Stankiewicz and Enid Zimmerman, Volume III (1993) edited by Kristin Congdon and Enid Zimmerman, and most recently *Women Art Educators IV: Herstories, Ourstories, Future Stories* (1998) edited by Elizabeth J. Saccá and Enid Zimmerman. Also, in their chapter of Renee Sandell and Georgia Collins' book *Women, Art, and Education* (1984), Mary Ann Stankiewicz and Enid Zimmerman reviewed the historical research on women art educators, including work by Laura Chapman, Mary Erickson, Anne Gregory, Sally Hagaman, Jerome Hausman, Sandra Packard, Gordon Plummer, and Robert Saunders. They also highlighted achievements of women after 1800 that warrant further research. In histories published in 1983 and afterward, Foster Wygant (1983), Arthur Efland (1990), Peter Smith (1996), and several essays in Donald Soucy and Mary Ann Stankiewicz's anthology (1990) discussed women's contributions. A number of women art educators have been the subject of more detailed dissertation research, for example, Ella Victoria Dobbs (Eyestone, 1989; see also Eyestone, 1992), Maude Kerns (Maude Kerns Art Center, 1996; Yates, 1993), Verna Wulfekammer (McNeill, 1995; see also McNeill, in press).

Through firsthand experience, professional lore, and works such as those mentioned above, we know that women have developed and promulgated visions of art education. They have done this through their teaching, supervision, leadership in professional organizations, and writing. Researchers, including some of those above, remind us that, regardless of their achievements, women disappear from art education's long term memory. They demonstrate that balanced historical research is needed.

Why Do Women Disappear from Our Memory?

One of the arguments one hears regarding why women disappear from the historical record is the following: "Women are concentrated in positions where they are less likely to write books and articles which become part of the written record. Therefore women are less likely to become part of the historical record." Firstly, it is true that women were, and are, concentrated in positions such as public school teaching and local and regional leadership. John Michael (1977) discusses leadership positions of women and men in art education. He shows the concentration of women in the positions of state art supervisors/directors, art supervisors/directors of large cities, and presidents of state art education associations; with a higher percentage of men in positions which receive more recognition such as chairpersons/heads of college/university art education programs, officers and council/board of regional associations and the National Art Education Association. In his *History of NAEA 1947-1997*, one sees a continuation of under-representation of women in national posts (Michael, 1997).

Regarding the second part of the argument that women do not as often write books, so are typically lost from the historical record, we can review some of the writings of women in relation to the writings of men featured in this volume. The following chart lists some women art educators whose books were published before, and concurrently with, the books of Arnheim, D'Amico, Lowenfeld, and Ziegfeld. The chart is based on Mary Ann Stankiewicz and Enid Zimmerman's 1984 chapter, with additions. The additions include books by women suggested by art education colleagues[2] and books by Arnheim, D'Amico, Lowenfeld, and Ziegfeld in bold.

Early (1924-1957) Books by Arnheim, D'Amico, Lowenfeld and Ziegfeld, and Contemporaneous Women, with Selected Later Volumes

1924 Belle Boas, *Art in The Schools*

1924 Margaret E. Mathias, *The Beginnings of Art in the Public Schools*

1924 Ella Victoria Dobbs, *Our Playhouse*; in 1936 *First Steps in Art and Handwork*

1925 Harriet and Vetta Goldstein, *Art in Everyday Life*

1926 Florence Goodenough, *Measurement of Intelligence by Drawings*

1928 Margaret Naumburg, *The Child and the World; Dialogues in Modern Education*; in 1947 *Studies of the "Free" Art Expression of Behavior Problem Children and Adolescents as a Means of Diagnosis and Therapy*

1931 M. Rose Collins and Olive L. Riley *Art Appreciation For Junior And Senior High Schools*

1931 Victor D'Amico, *Theater Arts*[3]; in 1942 *Creative Teaching in Art*

1932 Rudolf Arnheim, *Film als Kunst*

1932 Ann Shumaker with Gertrude Hartman (Eds), *Creative Expression: The Development of Children in Art, Music, Literature and Dramatics*

1932 Sallie Tannahill, *Fine Arts For Public School Administrators*

1940 Natalie R. Cole, *The Arts in the Classroom*; in 1966 *Children's Arts from Deep Down Inside*

1941 Edwin Ziegfeld with Ray Faulkner, *Art Today: An Introduction to the Visual Arts*; in 1944 with Mary Elinore Smith, *Art for Daily Living: The Story of the Owatonna Art Education Project*

1942 Olive Riley, *Your Art Heritage*

1947 Rose H. Alschuler, *Painting and Personality: A Study of Young Children*

1947 Anna Berry, *Art for Children*

1947 Louise Kainz and Olive Riley, *Exploring Art*

1947 Viktor Lowenfeld, *Creative and Mental Growth: A Textbook on Art Education*

1948 Marion Elaine Richardson, *Art & the Child*

1950 Maude Ellsworth with Michael F. Andrews, *Growing with Art*; in 1954 Maude Ellsworth, *Art for the High School*

1951 Florence Cane, *The Artist in Each of Us*

1951 Elizabeth Harrison, *Self-Expression Through Art; An Introduction to Teaching and Appreciation*

1951 Mildred Landis, *Meaningful Art Education*

1951 Rosabelle MacDonald (Mann), *Art as Education*

1954 Margaret Erdt, *Teaching Art In The Elementary School; Child Growth Through Art Experiences*

1954 Rudolf Arnheim, *Art and Visual Perception: A psychology of the creative eye*

1957 Jane C. Bland, *Art of the Young Child:3 to 5 Years*

1957 Miriam Lindstrom, *Children's Art: A Study of Normal Development in Children's Modes of Visualization*

Natalie Robinson Cole[4],
1976.

Olive Riley[6], prior to 1960.

Sallie B. Tannahill[5],
c. 1940-1950.

We can see that women, even with the limited resources of art teachers and art supervisors, did write books on art education. A number of these books were very well received and widely read. Harriet and Vetta Goldstein, for example, wrote *Art in Everyday Life* in 1924, and other editions were published in 1932, 1935, 1940, and 1954. (Stankiewicz and Zimmerman, 1984) Margaret Mathias' well known *The Beginnings of Art in the Public Schools* was published in 1924. Mary Elinore Smith was the coauthor of what is widely referred to as Edwin Ziegfeld's book, *Art for Daily Living: The Story of the Owatonna Art Education Project*. This reinforces the point that even when women enter the written historical record in consistent and important ways, they are lost from art education's long term memory, invalidating the second part of the argument as to why women disappear from the historical record.

This juxtaposition of women's and men's achievements leads us to ask, "What was the interaction among these women's ideas and the ideas of the legends whose achievements were discussed at the University Council for Art Education series of seminars?" "Why are the achievements of these women not recognized?" Today we do not ask, "Why have there been no great women art educators?" but instead, "Why don't we recognize the great women art educators?"

As mentioned earlier, written work is a small fraction of women's contributions to the field. Betty Tisinger documents the leadership of supervisors such as Sara Joyner and Mary Godfrey in improving instruction. (personal communication, Pearl Quick, May 1999). Many women working as supervisors were responsible

for writing curriculum which is rarely part of the historical record. How much can be attributed to women's being conditioned not to claim credit for their own achievements, as discussed by Laura Chapman (1979) and how much can be attributed to women and men's conditioned reluctance to recognize women?

Intertwining of Women's and Men's Ideas: Whose Achievements Are They?

The achievements of Rudolf Arnheim, Victor D'Amico, Viktor Lowenfeld, and Edwin Ziegfeld are intertwined with the achievements of women who remain unheard. Many women enhanced the recognition of these men—a fact that we would never see if we limited our view to the official record. Arthur Efland provides the example of June King McFee applying and extending the ideas of Rudolf Arnheim:

> Arnheim's *Art And Visual Perception* was an important piece of writing that was influential on June King McFee, for example. Her perception delineation theory probably had a greater impact upon art education than Arnheim's work, for example. Belle Boas certainly extended and elaborated Dow's work. (personal communication, Arthur Efland, May 1999).

He provides another example, that shows the important role women art teachers played in D'Amico's work:

> And D'Amico certainly relied upon groups of artist teachers who were mainly women to exemplify his ideas about how arts should be taught. These include Jane Bland and Lois

Lord. Each wrote textbooks. There are wonderful letters in the D'Amico Archive at (Teachers College) when Lord and Bland were staff members of D'Amico's at the Children's Art Carnival in Brussels in 1958. These exemplify a high degree of collaboration between them (personal communication, Arthur Efland, May 1999).

Turning to the organizational side of art education, two authors discuss the context for Edwin Ziegfeld's being credited for the founding of NAEA. In these stories we see the complex interdependence of men's and women's roles: Edwin Ziegfeld arrived toward the end of an all-day meeting called to discuss unifying four regional arts associations and a state association. Marion Quin, who was working to unite the regional art education associations, had invited him to attend. Both were members of the Eastern Arts Association, but Ziegfeld was considered the appropriate chair for the committee that was subsequently formed to hear alternatives and propose possible consolidation into a national organization.

Although Ziegfeld was a member of EAA, he was considered free of regional commitments, probably because of his work with the Owatonna Project in Minnesota (1944), his work on the *40th NSSE Yearbook* (1941) (the first comprehensive statement on art education in America), his text, *Art Today* (1941), and his administrative work in the Navy (Michael, 1997, p. 17).

Edwin Ziegfeld was the Head of the Art Education Department of Teachers College, Columbia University, while Marion Quin Dix was an art teacher and art supervisor. When the National Art Education Association was formed, Edwin Ziegfeld was elected Interim President, and Sara Joyner, Director of Art Education, State Department of Education, Richmond, Virginia, served as Interim Vice President (de Francesco, 1949).

When Ziegfeld's term was to end, Marion Quin Dix was asked to run for the presidency. She refused so that all regions could be involved. She later recalled that when she had been asked to run, she had said, "No, that would ruin things before they got off the ground." She continued saying,

By this I meant that we needed to go as far away from the East as we could in our selection of the next President and I suggested Dale Goss of the Pacific Region. He was elected in 1951 and I was Vice President during this time [1951-53]. I became the third President in 1953 (Gregory, 1982, p. 67).

Going even further back in this story, we see the possibility that a woman "started the ball rolling" on the formation of the NAEA.

Idella Church, President of National Education Association Department of Art Education in 1945 through 1947, brought about the meeting of Presidents of the four art education regionals and should be somewhat credited with bringing about the founding of the National Art Education

Belle Boas[7], c. 1920-1930.

Marion Quin[8] (later Marion Quin Dix), c. 1946-1947, year NAEA was founded.

Sara Joyner[9], c. 1949.

Association. It was her idea to do this when she was Vice President of the NEA Department of Art Education in 1944, but she was not in charge then. However, when she did become President, she finally did schedule a meeting at the NEA Convention on March 4, 1947 ...when all the Presidents of the Regional Art Education Associations went for a breakfast meeting which lasted all day. I think this shows great leadership. We tend to look to only Ed Ziegfeld as instrumental in bringing about the NAEA and he did play a great role at the breakfast meeting and thereafter, but it was Miss Church who started the ball rolling which captured the imagination of those present (personal communication, J. A. Michael, April 13, 1999).

These common occurrences reflect the deference most people expected. The men, who had greater access to university teaching positions, had more mobility and could easily involve themselves in national publications and projects far from their places of employment. They received recognition, while women often played facilitating and supporting roles.

University teaching was generally considered an activity for men. This was even more so early in the century (Roby, 1973). Abilities valued in the universities were those that were generally considered men's strengths (Addelson, 1983). When women did teach at the university level, they were usually responsible for teaching and service while men were viewed as scholars (personal communication, Enid Zimmerman, 30 November 1998).

Women's Lack of Visibility and 'Upward' Mobility

Women's lack of visibility was largely due to the restricted gender roles that limited their access to the university circuit and corresponding visibility. The

Idella Church[10], c. 1947.

Mary A. McKibbin[11], c. 1949-1950.

women focused their energy on improving elementary and secondary art teaching, leading professional organizations, and publishing books and curriculum.

The 'glass ceiling' limiting women's upward mobility (Morrison, 1987) was lower than it is today. Few women had the option of moving into the university circuit to share the podium with distinguished professors. The result of this restriction is that the work of these women, aside from their books, has remained largely undocumented, and many of the historical traces are disappearing, underlining the need to include these women's contributions in the oral and written histories of the field.

A recent request for names of women deserving legendary status in art education brought forth an abundance of suggestions, some of which are included in the references mentioned above and some of which are more contemporary than the time period covered in this book. Women not already cited are Ruth Freyberger, Mary Adeline McKibbin, and Helen Rose, and Alice Schwartz. Senior women in the field who are well known through their teaching and publications who have not already been cited include Mary Rouse, Elizabeth Adams Hurwitz, Corita Kent, Mary Lou Kuhn, Helen Merritt, Bonnie Snow, and Marilyn Zurmuehlen.

Another factor in the issue of recognition is that women are concentrated in certain areas which are under-recognized in art education and less frequently represented in our written history. These areas include media with which women are associated, local and regional administration, and neighboring countries with whom there has been an ongoing exchange of ideas. For example, one area where women work, is the cottage industries of craft work in which women "organized, taught and provided income for the poor whites in Appalachia" (personal communication, Billie R. S. Rothove, April 17, 1999). A few examples are Mary Francis Davidson, Marion Heard (Turner,

1993), Sister Remy Revor (Casey, 1982), Persis Grayson (*Shuttle, Spindle and Dyepot*, 1994).

As mentioned by John Michael (1977) women occupied many of the posts in local and regional art education (and less frequently national and university art education). In terms of art education administration, two examples from one region include Alice Robinson who was in charge of art education at Ohio State University from 1911 until 1947 and Amy Swisher who was Head of Drawing at Miami Teacher College in 1918-1919 and Chair of the new Art Education Department from 1927 to 1949 (personal communication, J. A. Michael, April 13, 1999, see also 1977). Many regions could contribute to this list. If we expand our view to include neighboring countries with whom there has been an exchange of ideas, we can cite Marion Richardson and Seonaid Robertson (England), Ann Savage and Irène Sénécal (Canada), and Edna Manley (Jamaica), to name a few.

Balancing the Picture

Art education continues to build and record its history, including this volume dedicated to four distinguished males. We sense the wealth awaiting rediscovery as we recognize females who, while not *in* the spotlight, were just *outside* the spotlight developing ideas, teaching and making things work. Future researchers have a great tangle to sort out to trace the creation of ideas and construction of recognition, not just among men, but among men and the invisible women.

In addition to the stories contained in this volume, we anticipate the work of future researchers bringing us more of the untold stories of women. As we celebrate the achievements of Rudolf Arnheim, Victor D'Amico, Viktor Lowenfeld, and Edwin Ziegfeld whom we recognize as legends, we can see the picture is incomplete. As the excitement over ideas and commitment to art education moves forward, this volume invites us to work to complete the picture and to assure that our historical record of art education is a balanced portrayal.

Endnotes

[1]The author thanks Rikki Asher for suggesting Elizabeth Catlett and locating the gallery exhibiting her artwork.

[2]The author thanks the individuals who made suggestions of women art educators to be included as legends in art education. Those who made suggestions include Elizabeth Ament, Rikki Asher, Angela Baker, Dolores Cederberg, Georgia Collins, Nadine Gordon-Taylor, Al Hurwitz, Karen Keifer-Boyd, June Jilian, Mary Beth Koos, Paula McNeill, Robert Parker, Pearl Quick, Billie Rothove, Robert Saunders, Peter Smith, Debbie Smith-Shank, Mary Ann Stankiewicz, and Betty Tisinger. The author thanks John Michael, Enid Zimmerman, Sylvia Corwin, Larry Kantner, and Arthur Efland for their detailed suggestions.

[3]Personal communication, Robert Saunders, May 9, 1999.

[4]Figure 2 Natalie Cole Robinson photograph reproduced with permission of The John A. and Betty J. Michael Autobiographical Lecture Series in Art Education, Center for the Study of the History of Art Education, Miami University, Oxford, OH. The author thanks Julia Lindsey for locating, researching, and reproducing this photograph.

[6]The sources of photos for Natalie Robinson Cole, Olive Riley, Belle Boas, Marion Quin [Dix], Sara Joyner, Idella Church, and Mary A. McKibbin are from the Center for the Study of the History of Art Education, Miami University, Oxford, OH. The author thanks Julia Lindsey for locating, researching, and reproducing these photographs.

[5-11]The sources for Figures 3 through 7 are from the Center for the Study of the History of Art Education, Miami University, Oxford, OH. The author thanks Julia Lindsey for locating, researching, and reproducing thee photographs. Figure 3 Sallie B. Tannahill source: Ebken, Ruth M. (Ed.). *1910-1960: Prospect and Retrospect.* Kutztown, PA: Kutztown Publishing, p. 21. Figure 4 Olive Riley source: Ebken, Ruth M. Photo of Sallie B. Tannahill source: Ebken, Ruth M. (Ed.). *1910-1960: Prospect and Retrospect.* Kutztown, PA: Kutztown Publishing, p. 39. Figure 5 Belle Boas source: Ebken, Ruth M. (Ed.). *1910-1960: Prospect and Retrospect.* Kutztown, PA: Kutztown Publishing, p. 17. Figure 6 Marion Quin source: Vaughan. Dana P. (Ed.). (1946). The Council 1946-1947. *Art Education for One World: 1946 Yearbook of The Eastern Arts Association,* Vol. 3, No. 1, 96. Kutztown, PA: State Teachers College. Figure 7 Sara Joyner source: de Francesco, I.L. (Ed.). (1949). The National Art Education Association…A Department of N.E.A. Officers and Council 1947-1949. *Art education Organizes: N.A.E.A. Yearbook 1947-1949.* Kutztown, PA: Kutztown Publishing, p. 9. Figure 8 Idella Church source: de Francesco, I.L. (Ed.). (1949). The National Art Education Association…A Department of N.E.A. Officers and Council 1947-1949. *Art Education Organizes: N.A.E.A. Yearbook 1947-1949.* Kutztown, PA: Kutztown Publishing, p. 10. Figure 9. Mary A. McKibbin source: Reynolds, Gordon I. (Ed.). (1949). Officers 1949-1950. *Art in General Education: 1949 Yearbook, Eastern Arts Association,* p. 7.

References

Addelson, K. P. (1983). The man of professional wisdom: cognitive authority and the growth of knowledge. in S. Harding & M. B. Hintikka (Eds.), *Discovering reality: Feminist perspectives on epistemology, metaphysics, methodology, and philosophy of science.* Boston: S. Reidel.

Casey, P. (1982). Sister Remy Revor. In A. Bletzinger & A. Short (Eds.), *Wisconsin women: A gifted heritage.* (1st ed., pp. 312-215). Amherst, WI: Palmer.

Chapman, L. (fall 1979). Leadership and the question of professional identity in art education: Some personal reservations. NAEA Women's Caucus *The Report 13,* 8.

Collins, G. (1977). Considering an androgynous model for art education. *Studies in Art Education, 18*(2), 54-62.

Congdon, K. & Zimmerman, E. (Eds.). (1993). *Women Art Educators III.* Bloomington, IN: Indiana University.

de Francesco, I.L. (Ed.). (1949). The National Art Education Association, A Department of N.E.A. Officers and Council 1947-1949. *Art education organizes: NAEA yearbook 1947-1949.* Kutztown, PA: Kutztown Publishing.

Eyestone, J. E. (1989). *The influence of Swedish sloyd and its interpreters on American art education.* Unpublished Doctoral Dissertation. University Of Missouri, Columbia.

Eyestone, J. E. (1992). The influence of Swedish sloyd and its interpreters on American art education. *Studies in Art Education, 34*(1), 28-38.

Efland, A. D. (1990). *A history of art education: intellectual and social currents in teaching the visual arts.* New York: Teachers College, Columbia University.

Gregory, A. (1982). Marion Quin Dix: A "People Picker" and an Innovator in American Education. In E. Zimmerman & M.A. Stankiewicz (Eds.), *Women Art Educators.* Bloomington, IN: Indiana University.

Lovano-Kerr, J., Semler, V. & Zimmerman, E. (1977). A profile of art educators in higher education: Male/female comparative data. *Studies in Art Education, 18*(2), 21-37.

Logan, F. M. (1955). *Growth of art in American schools.* New York: Harper.

Maude Kerns Art Center (1996). *Ms. Maude: Who was Maude I. Kerns?* [On-line].

McNeill, P. (1995). *Verna Mary Wulfekammer at the University of Missouri: Factors affecting her career development in art education 1928-1968.* Unpublished Doctoral Dissertation. University of Missouri, Columbia.

McNeill, P. (in press). Verna Wulfekammer's Story. In P. Bolin, K. Congdon, and D. Blandy (Eds.) *Histories of Community-Based Art Education.* Reston, VA: NAEA.

Michael, J. A. (1982). *The Lowenfeld lectures.* University Park, PA: Pennsylvania State University Press.

Michael, J. A. (1997). (Ed.). *The National Art Education Association: Our History—Celebrating 50 Years, [1947-1997].* Reston, VA: NAEA.

Michael, J. A. (1977). Women/men in leadership positions in art education. *Studies in Art Education, 18*(2), 7-20.

Morrison, A. M. (1987). *Breaking the glass ceiling: Can women reach the top of America's largest corporations?* Reading, MA: Addison-Wesley.

Packard, S. (1976). Tottering on the brink: The future of women art faculty in higher education. In F. V. Mills, C. McCulley & D. Maddox (Eds.), *The status of the visual arts in higher education.* Pretoria, IL: National Council of Art Administrators.

Packard, S. (1977). An analysis of current statistics and trends as they influence the status and future for women in the art academe. *Studies in Art Education, 18*(2), 38-48.

Roby, P. (1973). Institutional barriers to omen students in higher education. In A. Rossi & A. Calderwood (Eds.), *Academic women on the move.* NY: Russell Sage Foundation.

Saccá, E. J. (1989). Invisible women: Questioning recognition and status in art education. *Studies in Art Education, 30*(2), 122-127.

Saccá, E. J. & Zimmerman, E. (Eds.). (1998). *Women Art Educators IV: Herstories, Ourstories, Future Stories.* Boucherville, Quebec: Canadian Society for Education through Art.

Smith, P. (1996). *The history of American art education.* Westport, CT: Greenwood Press.

Smith, P. (1999). The unexplored: Art education historian's failure to consider the South West. *Studies in Art Education, 40*(2), 114-127.

Soucy, D. & Stankiewicz, M.A. (Eds.). (1990). *Framing the Past: Essays on Art Education.* Reston, VA: NAEA.

Stankiewicz, M.A. & Zimmerman, E. (Eds.). (1985). *Women Art Educators II.* Bloomington, IN: Indiana University.

Stankiewicz, M.A. & Zimmerman, E. (1984) Women's achievements in art education. In Collins & Sandell, *Women, Art, and Education,* pp. 113-140. Reston, VA: NAEA.

Sullivan, D. L. (fall 1994). The legacy continues, honoring Persis Grayson and Elizabeth Terlow, their enthusiasm and inspiration. *Shuttle, Spindle & Dyepot,* 38-40.

Turner, L. (November 10, 1993). Former Director of Arrowmont honored for craft contributions. Mountain Press.

White, B. E. & White, L. S. (1973) Survey of the status of women in college art departments. *Art Journal 32,* 420-422.

Wygant, F. (1983). *Art in American schools in the nineteenth century.* Cincinnati, OH: Interwood Press.

Yates, F. E. (1993). Remembering artist and educator Maude I. Kerns: An historical study using oral history techniques and a contextual approach. Unpublished doctoral dissertation. University of Oregon, Eugene.

Zimmerman, E. & Stankiewicz, M.A. (Eds.). (1982). *Women Art Educators.* Bloomington, IN: Indiana University.

About the Authors

JUDITH M. BURTON is Professor of Art and Art Education and former Chair of the Department of the Arts and Humanities at Teachers College Columbia University. She has taught courses in art and aesthetic development at the Massachusetts College of Art and Boston University. She is Chair of the NAEA Task Force on Student Learning and a member of the Council for Policy Studies in Art Education. Her writing includes: a widely acclaimed series of articles published under the general title of *Developing Minds; Trends and Issues in Visual Arts Curriculum; The Arts and School Reform: Other Conversations; Natural Allies: Children, Teachers and Artists*. She is currently working on a study of the transfer of learning from the arts to other domains of knowledge: *Learning in and Through the arts: a question of transfer*.

SYLVIA K. CORWIN supervised art student teachers at New York University, chaired the Art Department at John F. Kennedy High School in The Bronx where the NYSED validated program "Reading Improvement Through Art," was demonstrated. She is author of NYSED curriculum publications, the filmstrip series *America in Art, Meet the Artist and Pioneers of Modern Art,* and served as President of NYSATA and NYCATA/UFT. Currently, she edits *UCAE News* for University Council for Art Education and serves on the board of The Arts Education Group (AEG).

MICHAEL DeSIANO is Associate Professor of Art Education at Kean University in New Jersey. His areas of interest are visual creativity and thinking. He authored *The Principles and Elements of Design*. From 1998-2000, Dr. DeSiano was President of University Council for Art Education, co-sponsor of *Exploring the Legends: Guideposts to the Future*.

ARTHUR D. EFLAND is Professor Emeritus in the Art Education Department at the Ohio State University. He authored the elementary and secondary guidelines in art education for Ohio, winning an award of excellence from the National Art Education Association in 1982. He has published *A History of Art Education* and has written, with Kerry Freedman and Patricia Stuhr, *Postmodern Art Education: An Approach to Curriculum*. His articles appear in *The Journal of Aesthetic Education* and *Studies in Art Education*. Efland serves as International Scholar in Canada, Finland, Sweden, and Taiwan.

ELIZABETH J. SACCÁ is Professor of Art Education at Concordia University in Montreal where she has served as Department Chair and Graduate Programs Director. She was Principal of Simone de Beauvior Institute and taught at the former Philadelphia College of Art. Her recent publications address aboriginal art and human rights. She edited the *Canadian Review of Art Education Research*, and co-edited *Women Art Educators IV: Herstories, Ourstories, Future Stories*. She also co-authored *Visual Arts Reference and Research.*

PRABHA SAHASRABUDHE, having retired from full-time faculty, is Adjunct Professor of Art and Art Education, Teachers College Columbia University, New York City. Prior to this he taught and administered a large suburban visual arts program. Dr. Sahasrabudhe came to the United States on a Fulbright scholarship. He holds a B.Sc. in Physics, a B.A. in Philosophy from Agra University, a fine arts degree from Sir J. J. School of Art, Bombay, a M.A. and Ed.D. from New York University. He served as President of NYSATA, on the New York State Education Commissioner's Arts and Humanities Committee on Curriculum, and on two NAEA study commissions. His research interest in multicultural and cross-culture studies led to the Presidency of United States Society for Education through Art (USSEA) where he represented USSEA at InSEA's World Council.

ROBERT J. SAUNDERS is Art Consultant Emeritus, Connecticut State Department of Education, graduate student under Viktor Lowenfeld, Pennsylvania State University 1953-60. Widely published in NAEA art education periodicals, author of *Teaching Through Art*, Abrams Art Print Program Manuals Grades K-6, Series A, B, and C, *Relating Art and Humanities to the Classroom, Joseph Stella: Brooklyn Bridge* (with Ernest Goldstein), and *Understanding and Creating Art, Books 1 and 2* co-authored with E. Goldstein, J. Kowalchuk, and T. Katz); Editor, *Beyond the Traditional in Art: Facing a Pluralistic Society,* report on the USSEA symposium in 1991 (NAEA). Currently, docent, Wadsworth Atheneum, Hartford, and artist, Artworks Gallery, Hartford, CT.